BR 1806

BRITISH MARITIME DOCTRINE

Third Edition

By Command of the Defence Council

[signature]

London: TSO

Published by TSO (The Stationery Office) and available from:

Online
www.tso.co.uk/bookshop

Mail, Telephone, Fax & E-mail
TSO
PO Box 29, Norwich, NR3 1GN
Telephone orders/General enquiries: 0870 600 5522
Fax orders: 0870 600 5533
E-mail: book.orders@tso.co.uk
Textphone 0870 240 3701

TSO Shops
123 Kingsway, London, WC2B 6PQ
020 7242 6393 Fax 020 7242 6394
68-69 Bull Street, Birmingham B4 6AD
0121 236 9696 Fax 0121 236 9699
9-21 Princess Street, Manchester M60 8AS
0161 834 7201 Fax 0161 833 0634
16 Arthur Street, Belfast BT1 4GD
028 9023 8451 Fax 028 9023 5401
18-19 High Street, Cardiff CF10 1PT
029 2039 5548 Fax 029 2038 4347
71 Lothian Road, Edinburgh EH3 9AZ
0870 606 5566 Fax 0870 606 5588

TSO Accredited Agents
(see Yellow Pages)

and through good booksellers

BR 1806

BRITISH MARITIME DOCTRINE

Third Edition

FOREWORD BY

Admiral Sir Alan West GCB, DSC, ADC
First Sea Lord and Chief of the Naval Staff

Even a cursory review of this third edition of BR 1806 will reveal the significant progress that has been made in the formulation of British Maritime Doctrine since this publication replaced the 'old BR1806' – The Naval War Manual – in 1995. Having ready access to authoritative and comprehensive guidance on the employment of maritime power is vitally important for the professional development of our own people. Moreover, such guidance forms a vital element in the formulation of joint doctrine, informing the other Services of the maritime contribution in the joint environment; it also helps to inform and educate the public on the contribution that we make to Defence.

As my predecessors made very clear in their forewords to the first and second editions, the content of BR1806 is not to be regarded as dogma. In the British Approach to Military Operations, described in the latest edition of British Defence Doctrine, a flexible and pragmatic attitude is an essential part of our way of thinking. It is one of the reasons why the British Armed Forces are able to apply themselves to the broad range of operations demanded of them today – a range that has developed since the end of the Cold War and continues to evolve in the wake of the atrocities of 11 September 2001 and the war in Iraq in early 2003.

Just as Nelson expected his Captains to take the initiative, so our approach today must be based on all of our people doing likewise. Initiative is not born of a rigid adherence to rules, but of a willingness to take a calculated risk in the face of prevailing circumstances. On the day, that is more easily achieved if we all think through the fundamental principles that shape our profession and regularly challenge orthodox thinking. This book is intended to stimulate that process, not to suppress it, to ensure that we remain "a world class Navy, ready to fight and win".

Contents

Chapter   Editor's Introduction

1   Maritime Doctrine in Context   1

2   The Maritime Environment and the Nature of Maritime Power   17

3   Principles Governing the Use of Maritime Power   41

4   The Application of Maritime Power   57

5   Maritime Logistics and Support   93

6   Maritime Command and Control   105

7   Planning and Conducting a Campaign or Operation   131

8   Maritime Fighting Power and Operational Capability   167

9   Future Maritime Operations and Concepts   201

From Trafalgar to Today: A Bibliographical Essay on Doctrine   211
and the Development of British Naval Strategic Thought

Abbreviations   229

Glossary   234

Index   299

The Type 42 Destroyer HMS GLOUCESTER in the Indian Ocean

EDITOR'S INTRODUCTION

This new edition of *BR 1806* has been written against a rapidly changing strategic background that has included the New Chapter (2002) to the 1998 Strategic Defence Review (SDR) that followed the terrorist attacks of 11 September 2001, a subsequent reappraisal of the Military Tasks of the Armed Forces, and the aftermath of the war in Iraq in early 2003. However, this has not resulted in significant changes to maritime doctrine at the *military-strategic* level. The doctrinal principles contained in *BR 1806* are enduring and, although there is clearly a relationship between policy and doctrine at the strategic levels, changes in policy will not necessarily have an immediate effect on doctrine. Indeed, fundamental principles of military doctrine are influential in the sense that they contribute to defining the limits of policy by helping to inform political decision makers about the strengths, weaknesses, advantages and disadvantages of military options. It is only policy shifts over extended periods that ultimately shape grand-strategic doctrine that, in turn, has an influence on military-strategic doctrine. The SDR was an important process that set much of the current policy context for doctrinal development. Importantly, the SDR and its New Chapter confirmed the direction in which Britain's security policy has been going since the end of the Cold War. That direction is away from a substantial physical commitment on the continent of Europe, consisting of largely static, defensive forces, towards an expeditionary posture in which strategic mobility and flexibility are the principal features and in which the doctrinal principles discussed in this book assume an enhanced significance.

General Principles Applicable to Maritime Forces

The general principles that determine the ways in which all of the UK's maritime forces are applied in support of national interests are discussed in detail in *British Defence Doctrine (BDD)*. The strategic level effects supported by the use of military force, such as *deterrence*, *coercion*, *destruction* and *disruption* are endorsed and also defined in the Glossary at the back of this book. Also accepted are the notion of a spectrum of conflict, the principle of limitation and the methods by which it is achieved, and the notion of intensity. Types of conflict, ranging from general war to counter-terrorism, are acknowledged with the caveat that, while general war may be considered unlikely, it must still be included for doctrinal, as distinct from policy, reasons.

While **BR 1806** can be read on its own as a comprehensive statement of British maritime doctrine, all professional students of the subject should also study the latest **Statement on the Defence Estimates** and **BDD** to place maritime operations in the broader politico-strategic and doctrinal context.

The Joint Approach to BR 1806

During the editing of this book at the Maritime Warfare Centre, HMS DRYAD, I have been reminded of the maritime contribution to *joint* operations on a daily basis. The Normandy landings in 1944 were planned in Southwick House, latterly HMS DRYAD's Wardroom but then the headquarters of Admiral Sir Bertram Ramsay, Allied Naval Commander Expeditionary Force. In one of the ante-rooms the famous Wall Map, set for H-Hour on D-Day, is a lasting testament to the endeavours of the joint planning staffs under General Eisenhower who, with the historic (if rather brief) words "OK, we'll go", initiated the greatest joint venture in our history. It is perhaps fitting that this edition of **BR 1806** is published in its 60th anniversary year.

Recently, I had a more poignant reminder of the Royal Navy's historical role in joint operations when I visited the Boer War battlefields in Kwazulu-Natal, South Africa, and discovered a handful of Royal Naval Brigade graves in the military cemetery at Chieveley, in the heart of the battlefields on the approach to Ladysmith where Royal Navy 12 pounder guns played such a significant role. More recent operations, from the Falkland Islands to the Arabian Gulf, have underlined the inherently *joint* nature of maritime operations at the *operational* and *military-strategic levels*. Nevertheless, there are important differences between the ways in which land, air and maritime forces operate, and although the need for a clear articulation of maritime doctrine has to be met by those who have a deep professional understanding of the maritime environment, the assistance of Army and

The D-Day Wall Map in Southwick House

RAF representation on the Editorial Consultative Board has been regarded as essential during the revision of this book.

The increasingly joint "feel" of **BR 1806** reflects continuing doctrinal and institutional developments since the earlier editions were drafted. The publication of **BDD** and the development of a new hierarchy of joint doctrinal publications have moved joint thinking forward. The establishment of the Permanent Joint Headquarters (PJHQ) for the conduct of joint operations and the Joint Services Command and Staff College (JSCSC) for the command and staff training of officers from all three services have influenced joint thinking, as has the formation of the Joint Doctrine and Concepts Centre (JDCC). Importantly, the Maritime

Contribution to Joint Operations (MCJO) concept developed during SDR, more accurately entitled "Maritime Capabilities in Joint Operations and their Wider Utility", has been validated in a number of operations, for example in Sierra Leone, Afghanistan and Iraq. It can now be considered to be doctrine, and its principles have therefore been incorporated where appropriate in this edition, rather than standing alone in a separate, conceptual chapter. The Future Maritime Operational Concept (FMOC) has replaced MCJO and is now the major concept for the development of UK's future maritime capability. Its principal features are discussed in Chapter 9.

Applications of Maritime Power

When the first edition of *BDD* was being drafted, in the latter part of 1996, it became obvious that it would not be possible to use *BR 1806's* categorisation of the application of maritime forces (*Military, Constabulary and Benign*) for non-maritime purposes. There was, for example, reluctance to apply the word 'constabulary' to military operations conducted ashore. Nevertheless, navies have historically been employed in policing activities and continue to be so. Fishery protection, anti-piracy and drug interdiction operations are classic examples of 'constabulary' operations that are routine functions for navies around the world. It has also been suggested that the use of the word 'benign' for essentially philanthropic activities has the unfortunate effect of implying that all operations not categorised as benign might be regarded as malign. However, the use of a word like 'benign' to describe an activity does not necessarily imply that all other activities are, by definition and by default, 'malign'. Criticisms of the three categories have not, therefore, been persuasive and each continues to be discussed in the chapter on the Application of Maritime Power (Chapter 4). However, whilst earlier editions of *BR 1806* articulated the applications of maritime power under the headings of Military, Constabulary and Benign, this edition uses the framework of the new Military Tasks (2003). It is considered that this provides a more methodical explanation of how maritime power is applied within the extant policy framework in operations at home and overseas. The underlying principles, however, have not changed measurably.

The Structure of BR 1806

BR 1806 is designed to be read as a logical progression from chapter to chapter. However, a reader who is broadly familiar with the subject matter but is investigating a specific topic will find that individual chapters stand largely on their own, with some of the more important principles illustrated and stressed in more than one chapter - this is deliberate repetition and not poor editing!

Chapter 1 discusses the nature of *doctrine* and places maritime doctrine within a general context. Chapters 2 to 9 are arranged logically and, in effect, in three separate sections. Chapters 2 to 4 deal with the fundamental principles and represent the core doctrinal chapters of the book. Chapter 2 describes the maritime environment, the distinctive features of the sea and the attributes of maritime forces. Having set the scene, Chapter 3 examines specifically maritime doctrinal principles, in particular *sea control*, *maritime power projection* and *maritime manoeuvre* and considers styles of warfare in the maritime environment. Chapter 4 covers the application of maritime power and the range of tasks that can be conducted at sea and from the sea involving *military* use of forces, as well as those tasks involving *constabulary* and *benign* use of maritime forces that are also important, especially in peacetime.

Having dealt with the core of maritime doctrinal principles at the *military-strategic level*, the second part of the book describes maritime logistics and support (Chapter 5), how command and control is executed (Chapter 6) and, finally, the ways in which maritime *operations* and *campaigns* are planned and conducted (Chapter 7). These three chapters move the discussion from the *military-strategic level* towards the *operational level* and represent the essential link between what is contained in the main part of this book and what is contained in **The Fighting Instructions**, the RN's principal operational and tactical level doctrine publication, and other national and Allied publications.

The penultimate chapter of the book defines fighting power and operational capability and, in so doing, describes the UK's current maritime capabilities and how they are packaged to support joint operations (Chapter 8). Finally, Chapter 9 looks ahead to the nature of future maritime operations and new concepts that will shape doctrine development in the intervening years before the next edition of this publication.

Glossary

The extremely wide range of definitions contained in the Glossary has been improved and updated to reflect developments since 1999. Definitions that do not show a source, principally of either *JWP 0-01.1 (the United Kingdom Glossary of Joint and Multinational Terms and Definitions) or AAP-6 (the NATO Glossary of Terms and Definitions)*, are specific to this book, or are awaiting Joint or Allied agreement. As in the 1999 edition, terms included in the Glossary are printed in italics in the main body of the book. To further assist readers, the Index lists in bold print the numbers of those pages on which the principal reference to each entry is made. Other pages on which entries are mentioned are noted in standard type.

Further Reading

For those with a wish to develop further their understanding of the subject, a bibliographical essay is provided immediately after Chapter 9. It contains reference to the principal available works, both classic and contemporary, together with brief comments on them.

Feedback

It is important to acknowledge the role of feedback in the process of doctrinal development. This new edition of *BR 1806* has benefited from comments received from service personnel and the general public about the content, style and presentation of its predecessors. Such comment is greatly valued and encouraged. While the principal readership of this book will undoubtedly be serving officers within the UK's *Naval Service*, whose opinions are especially important, others with a view can be assured that their feedback will be most gratefully received. The address for feedback is:

SO1 Maritime Doctrine
Maritime Warfare Centre
PO Box 325
Cosham
Portsmouth
Hampshire
PO6 3SX

Acknowledgements

So many people have contributed to this edition that it would be impossible
to mention them all. However, the following deserve special mention: the
Editorial Consultative Board; the Joint Operational Doctrine Committee;
staff at the Joint Doctrine and Concepts Centre and the Joint Services
Command and Staff College; the Naval Historical Branch; the Naval Staff
Directorate (Strategy Division); the Fleet Regional Photographic Unit
Portsmouth; Admiral Sir John 'Sandy' Woodward; and Dr Andrew Gordon.

HMS OCEAN, with Support Helicopters from
the Joint Helicopter Command on deck

Maritime Doctrine in Context

In the Royal Navy, the existence of formal doctrine can be traced back to the original edition of *The Fighting Instructions*, issued to the Fleet in 1672, and to a code of tactical signals promulgated during the Commonwealth in 1653. The development of maritime tactical doctrine is thus a well-established process going back over 300 years. The Royal Navy's current *operational* and *tactical* doctrine is still promulgated in *The Fighting Instructions* and a wide range of supporting publications. These are also subjected to regular review as technology and equipment is developed and enters into service and as a consequence of both operational experience and the analysis of operational and exercise performance. By its nature, much of this doctrine is specialised, is essentially the domain of those involved in operational and tactical decision-making and is not very widely disseminated. Indeed, many aspects of operational and tactical doctrine are sensitive and are covered by appropriate security classifications.

However, once we move up the hierarchy, from the *tactical* and *operational* levels to the *military-* and *grand-strategic levels*, doctrine becomes less the exclusive business of the deep military specialists and more the legitimate interest of any with a professional, academic, political or social stake in the use of military power. There is also an especial need to recognise that, for reasons of motivation, morale, commitment and professional operational understanding, junior military ranks need to have access to an understanding and interpretation of the strategic context in which their profession is expected to operate.

The emergence of *military-strategic level* maritime doctrine can be traced back to the late nineteenth century and the early years of the twentieth century. Arguably, until the American Alfred Thayer Mahan applied his mind to the subject, there was little, if any, structured, academic thought given to the attributes of maritime power and how it might best be applied in support of national interest. If one accepts the dictionary definition of 'doctrine' as "that which is taught", then the conclusions of Mahan and those of a number of distinguished British maritime strategic thinkers could be credited with the doctrinal label. In the UK, perhaps none was so influential as Sir Julian Corbett, in particular the views he expressed in his profoundly important book *Some Principles of Maritime Strategy*. If, however, we restrict 'doctrine' to that which is officially promulgated, the only higher level maritime doctrine that has been acknowledged officially in the UK has been that contained in the various editions of *BR 1806*. This was originally called *The Naval War Manual*, its last appearance under that title being in 1969 (previous editions dating from 1948 and 1958).

In 1995, the new *BR 1806* was published under a different title: *The Fundamentals of British Maritime Doctrine* (this became *British Maritime Doctrine* in the Second Edition). The new *BR 1806* complemented similar publications published by the Army and the RAF to form a stable of documents dealing with *military-strategic level* doctrine. Eventually, in 1996, the individual Services' doctrinal books were joined by the military-strategic level joint doctrine publication, *British Defence Doctrine (BDD)*, the second edition of which was published in 2001. *BDD* provides the higher level framework from which *operational level* joint doctrine cascades.

A Joint Approach

Maritime doctrine as discussed in this book is not simply 'naval doctrine'. While this edition of *BR 1806* has been edited at the Maritime Warfare Centre under the auspices of the *Naval Staff* in the Ministry of Defence and is, in that sense, a single-Service statement of doctrine, it is not, nor could it be, concerned solely with matters of a naval nature. The maritime environment is inherently *joint*. Air power is as vital to operations at sea as it is to the conduct of military operations ashore. Naval forces themselves exist to influence events ashore; they have never operated strategically in an exclusively naval environment. This book is not, therefore, about 'sea power'. It is, rather, about the maritime dimension of *joint* operations. An air force fighter aircraft and an army infantry battalion may well be components of a maritime force because the word 'maritime' refers to the environment in which they are operating, not to that institutional part of the UK's armed forces that might be providing them.

Since the Cold War the focus of maritime attention has shifted towards *littoral* operations in support of operations ashore (arguably this constitutes a return to pre-Cold War circumstances). For this reason there is an increasing emphasis placed on joint operations and the concomitant need for each Service to understand the modus operandi of the other two. Joint operations in the littoral present a complex mix of opportunities and challenges that will at times be difficult to meet. However, the Royal Navy's traditional flexibility of approach and its instinctive reliance on initiative to achieve maximum effect sit very easily with the *manoeuvrist* culture that guides military operations today. Both the joint approach and *manoeuvrist* thinking are essential elements of the British Approach to Military Operations articulated in **BDD**.

Despite the shift of focus towards the *littoral*, it is important that the deep-water environment and the continuing need to be able to conduct open ocean sea control operations are not neglected. For example, the submarine threat may have changed but it has not disappeared. The UK's maritime forces must retain their ability to carry out effective anti-submarine warfare (ASW) operations, especially in support of ballistic missile carrying submarine (SSBN) deployments but also in the often (though not necessarily) shallower waters of the *littoral*. Maritime doctrine at all levels reflects operational imperatives in deep water as well as in the littoral.

The Purpose of Maritime Doctrine

Doctrine is a framework of principles, practices and procedures, the understanding of which provides a basis for action. Maritime doctrine fulfils this function for the use of military power at and from the sea. The doctrine contained in this book covers principally the strategic and, to a certain extent, the *operational levels* of military planning, both in conflict and in the peacetime applications of military power. In general terms, the main purpose of maritime doctrine, at all levels, is to derive the greatest benefit from current maritime forces in support of national policy. However, in achieving this aim it also serves a number of subsidiary purposes.

It has internal educational and training functions that contribute to the professionalism of the UK's maritime forces and the men and women who serve in them. There is a particular emphasis on the education of the officer corps and the *Navy Board* has instructed that all officers in the RN and RM should undergo formal study of the fundamental principles of maritime doctrine contained in **BR 1806**. This commences during New Entry courses at Britannia Royal Naval College (BRNC), Dartmouth and the Commando Training Centre, Royal Marines (CTCRM), Lympstone and continues during the Initial Command and Staff Course (Maritime) (ICSC(M)) and Advanced Command and Staff Course (ACSC) at the Joint Services Command and Staff College (JSCSC), Shrivenham. By the time officers reach subsequent mid-career staff appointments, on *Flag*, Ministry of Defence or *joint* staffs, they should be familiar with the principles underlying the use of maritime power. All officers receive a personal copy of the book and all warrant officers on promotion are also made aware of its contents.

In so far as it produces a way of thinking about the utility of maritime power and the conduct of *operations*, doctrine also has a professional motivational function through providing maritime forces with clear statements about their roles and objectives. At the *military-strategic level*, doctrine also informs the wider defence community (including politicians, industrialists, academics, etc), as well as interested members of the general public, about the roles and political utility of maritime forces.

The Equipment Capability Customer in the MoD uses a centrally endorsed terminology called the Equipment Capability Taxonomy to articulate a practical definition of military and equipment capability and the strategic, operational and tactical effects desired from new equipment. These differ from doctrinal concepts that are used for strategic or operational planning. However there is an important role for doctrine, particularly that at the *military-strategic level*, in informing the higher level definition of equipment capability and the particular operational effect required. In examining the overall utility of a joint asset (an aircraft carrier, for example) it is necessary to assess its characteristics and likely employment in relation to doctrinal principles applicable in all relevant operational environments.

The Nature of Doctrine

Within the UK's armed forces the general definition of military doctrine is very similar to that used in NATO. To quote **BDD**, it is: "fundamental principles by which military forces guide their actions in support of objectives. It is authoritative, but requires judgement in application". The second part of this definition is intended to convey the message that doctrine should not develop the rigid authority of dogma but should remain flexible.

Doctrine must be flexible in two senses, therefore. First, it must convey the importance of initiative and not discourage commanders from challenging received wisdom when appropriate. Second, it must be subject to regular formal review to ensure that the accumulated wisdom being promulgated in the form of doctrine is as robust and relevant as possible. However, in conducting regular review, care must be taken not to make change for change's sake. At the *military-strategic level*, the fundamental principles will probably change only very rarely. In contrast, at the *tactical level*, doctrine will clearly be directly affected by current challenges and capabilities; tactical doctrine is equipment, threat and environment driven.

The Hierarchy of Doctrine

Maritime doctrine does not exist in a vacuum. As has already been mentioned above, **BR 1806** is but one of a stable of higher level doctrine publications. For a thorough understanding of the ways in which military forces are utilised in support of national policy there is no substitute for studying the range of doctrinal publications now available. At the military-strategic level, UK doctrine is articulated principally in **British Defence Doctrine**. **BR 1806, ADP Land Ops**, and **AP 3000 (British Air Power Doctrine)** each provides an environmental perspective on doctrine at the higher levels (military-strategic and operational). The principal capstone operational level document is **JDP 01, Joint Operations**. As far as maritime doctrine is concerned, for those with access to it, there is also **The Fighting Instructions** at the operational and tactical levels, which sits immediately below **BR 1806**. There is a form of symbiosis existing between all such documents and the development of maritime doctrine through the publication of this book will have an influence on the development of the others.

Finally, the importance of NATO doctrine, while it exists in a separate hierarchy outside that for UK national doctrine, must be acknowledged. A great deal of the doctrine applied at the operational and tactical levels by the UK's maritime forces is agreed with Allies and promulgated in NATO publications. It is UK policy that its national doctrine should be consistent with NATO doctrine other than in those exceptional circumstances when the UK has elected not to ratify the relevant NATO doctrine. With the UK as the principal European maritime power, UK influence on the development of NATO maritime doctrine is profound; so much so, indeed, that a similar symbiosis exists between UK and NATO maritime doctrine to that which exists between UK maritime doctrine and other publications in the UK national doctrinal hierarchy. A similar linkage also exists between NATO and UK joint doctrine.

Levels of Military Operations

BDD recognises the different levels at which decisions are made and at which operations are conducted. They include the *grand-strategic*, *military-strategic*, *operational* and *tactical levels*. **BR 1806** promulgates maritime doctrine at the military-strategic level but in so doing also discusses relevant aspects of the operational level. As already stated, the RN's operational and tactical levels of maritime doctrine are promulgated in

The Type 23 frigate HMS NORTHUMBERLAND escorts a
TRAFALGAR Class nuclear powered submarine

The *Fighting Instructions* and other national publications, with much
additional tactical doctrine contained in NATO publications.

At each level, consideration has to be given to the types of operations that
are to be conducted and the extent to which force needs to be applied to
achieve political and military objectives. Ultimately, the UK's maritime
forces must be capable of operating within the extremes of violence typical
of those associated with general war. While general war is currently

considered to be an unlikely eventuality, the intensity of violence associated with it cannot be dismissed to the same extent. High intensity operations may be required to achieve success in conditions falling well short of general war. Maritime forces must be able to function in high intensity situations and survive them in order to ensure success. The tendency for lower intensity operations to escalate, and for original limited objectives to expand, means that reserves of combat capability will be necessary to provide higher level decision-makers with an adequate range of options. Maritime forces must, therefore, be equipped and trained to allow for escalation to a higher intensity of operations than those for which they may originally have been deployed, consistent with the central philosophy of the British approach to military operations in the round; namely that retention of a warfighting ethos is central, ready to be applied if the circumstances demand it.

The Influence of Law on Maritime Operations

Regardless of the level, intensity and type of maritime operations being conducted, including routine peacetime activities, they must be carried out within the limits imposed by international law and, where appropriate, within the limits imposed by either UK domestic law or that applying in other jurisdictions. Notwithstanding the inherent right of self defence, legal restraints on all maritime operations will be reflected in the *Rules of Engagement* (ROE). Royal Navy warships invariably operate with promulgated ROE, including during the conduct of routine peacetime activities.

1/1. The Principles of War

Essential to the art of military leadership and command is the ability to learn from one's own experience and that of others. The *Principles of War* are a distillation of experience and a simplification of complex and sometimes contradictory ideas. They are broad precepts for the conduct of armed conflict. They should be used to inform all military strategic and operational decisions rather than as a planning checklist. The ten Principles recognised by the armed forces of the UK are described in detail in *BDD*. They are illustrated below, in the context of the campaign to regain the Falkland Islands in 1982, by Admiral Sir John 'Sandy' Woodward GBE, KCB, the Commander of the Falklands Battle Group:

The Selection and Maintenance of the Aim

The initial aim was stated as "Prepare to land with a view to repossessing the Falklands" about one week after the Argentineans invaded. It was changed to "Repossess the Falklands" on May 12th. While the first aim could, at least in theory, have been met without getting up from one's armchair, it was 42 days before a simple, clear aim was given. Events up to that time reflected the excessive vagueness of the first aim and the consequences of that vagueness. Events subsequent to 12th May reflected the importance of having a clearly stated aim as early as possible. However, it was not easy, mainly on political grounds, to be more definite much earlier. The military plan, only developed and disseminated on April 17th, had repossession very much in mind and, for a range of reasons, assumed an end date to the campaign of June 14th. As far as 'maintenance of the aim' is concerned, the campaign would appear to have been a classic example since it was achieved on the precise date forecast!

Maintenance of Morale

Quite a problem, aggravated by 'war' never being declared or over. However, morale was maintained by all the usual means without making any special efforts. My own general theme was 'Don't concern yourselves too much about why we are going down, or even whether we will get away with it if it does come to war, just do the very best you each can, if nothing else that is your best chance of survival'. The extent to which this approach was successful is probably best judged by the remark of one Senior Rate from HMS COVENTRY who came up to me back in UK later and said "You always knew we were going to be sunk, didn't you?"

Offensive Action

The very nature of the operation had perforce to be offensive. The difficulty was to know what offensive, or defensive, activities would be successful in a largely untried-in-war force essentially trained for a completely different kind of war. Consequently, the early stages after entering the Exclusion Zone were frequently experimental in nature on the basis that depending on results, we would reinforce success and retire from failure. Wherever possible, the initiative was retained while we tried to find out what worked best.

Security

The main problem was the media, who with cameras on the spot were initially slow to understand the requirements. This was also a major problem in press releases at home. The pastoral need to advertise the sinking of a warship was seldom/never weighed against the free damage assessment handed to the enemy. For instance, the Argentineans had no way of knowing whether their first Exocet attack had worked until the information about HMS SHEFFIELD was released in London. As for Force Protection, it is clear that we had enough, just. The sinking of the BELGRANO, while it did in fact, defeat the Argentinean Navy, could never be assumed to have done so, even after June 14th. It is only in the light of subsequent events that the effect of BELGRANO became apparent. I personally do not feel that I ever felt I had adequate security from start to my own finish on about July 3rd. I was always very conscious that the Argentineans could come again with just four A4s and ruin our day if we got careless and they got lucky. HERMES, then INVINCIBLE stayed well out at sea at nearly all times including the months after the land battle finished. It should be remembered that not only was no war declared at the beginning, no peace was ever declared after the main fighting was over. That said, lack of security must not allow you to be 'frozen' in your plans and operations.

The Type 42 destroyer HMS SHEFFIELD, damaged by an Exocet missile during the Falkland Islands conflict, 4 May 1982

Surprise

Surprise, often an important part of effective offensive action, was impossible to achieve in strategic terms. The enemy knew exactly what we hoped to do. At the tactical level, a degree of surprise was achieved in almost every area, usually preceded by substantial deception. Deception was used during the approach to the area (18th-30th April) to convince the Argentineans that we were coming straight in to the Stanley area for landing on May 1st/2nd. This was successful, drawing out the Argentinean navy and, less successfully their air force for two days, to attack us. It did much to defeat the Argentinean navy and convince us that the Sea Harrier was an effective interceptor after all. After that and before the landing, deception was used in Choiseul Sound to make it look as if we might land there. Deception was also used in all air operations from the carriers to disguise the Battle Group's position. Surprise was achieved in the main landing itself in San Carlos Water, in the Pebble Island raid (where the airstrip was virtually undefended), and in most land force attacks.

Concentration of Force

This was kept constantly in mind but was extremely difficult to achieve during the passage South as units were detached for other operations throughout the approach phase (HMS BRILLIANT Group, Op PARAQUAT). Thereafter it was kept constantly in mind despite the clear need to split forces at the landing phase.

Economy of Effort

This was always a battle requiring the maximum economy of effort. The battle hung in the balance throughout, whatever it may have seemed at home. Assets were invariably in short supply. For example, we started with only some 24 fixed-wing interceptors, over half of which had only a day intercept capability. One only was lost to enemy action and five to accidents. Reinforcement by limited RAF GR3 assets was critical to take the ground attack load off the Sea Harrier force remaining. Time and weather were against us. Re-supply routes were long. We only had two aircraft carriers in fleet service - during war operations, both were required 'up front' with no reserve. As an indication of the 'economy of effort', on about 12th June, the Battle Group had only one of seven channels of Sea Dart fire serviceable, no ASW Sea Kings in the role (some were sent inshore to assist land forces, the rest were doing what little they could to act as surface search and AEW), and the following evening, of four DD/FF requested for night operations in support of land forces, only two could get in and one of those had a shaft locked. 'Paucity' was more the word than 'economy'.

Flexibility

Bearing in mind that the Royal Navy had been training and equipping itself solely for an anti-submarine battle against the Warsaw Pact forces in the North Atlantic for over a decade and that it had not envisaged a supported amphibious operation for 20 years at least, switching to an anti-air, anti-surface battle in support of an offensive amphibious operation the other side of the world does imply a substantial degree of flexibility. Other examples of flexibility were a straight-off-the-cuff command organization at Northwood; first use of DSSS secure communications in major operations; re-write against the clock of Rules of Engagement; Ships Taken up from Trade in general and ATLANTIC CONVEYOR in particular (until sunk on 25th May, she considered herself almost a third aircraft carrier); use of RFAs as missile decoys; use of SSNs for air raid warning; use of T22/T42 combination in attempt to optimise interdependence of Sea Dart and Sea Wolf; Lynx were used as Exocet decoys; frigates were used for anything and everything from their many accepted roles to AD pickets, decoys, and even mine hunters.

Co-operation

Commodore Amphibious Warfare (COMAW) would say that he got little co-operation from the Battle Group Commander. The Battle Group Commander would say that he gave COMAW absolutely everything he could possibly spare and then some (see comments on 'economy of effort' above). Viewed more objectively, co-operation was force-wide but not without occasional and natural angst. The important thing to hang on to is that co-operation was entirely adequate to get the job done in the face of considerable odds.

Sustainability

Sustainability was critically reviewed on 17th April. From that assessment, the operational plan was laid out for the next two months. It assumed that fleet sustainability for war operations should last adequately until mid-June, although there were several major unknowns eg Sea Harrier effectiveness and serviceability over an extended period. Thereafter, we expected to be on an uncomfortably sharp downward trend. Events proved the assumption correct, to the day, even with the loss of Atlantic Conveyor, which was a very major setback for the land forces (75% of their helicopter lift - not to mention much else - went down with her). Sustainability after the end of the land battle was much less of a problem and largely confined to the continued health of the remaining Sea Harrier force supported by one carrier offshore.

Victorious Royal Marines in Port Stanley, Falkland Islands, June 1982

The Type 23 frigate HMS MARLBOROUGH in the Arafura Sea on passage to Singapore

The Maritime Environment and the Nature of Maritime Power

2

The maritime environment is the principal factor influencing the nature and attributes of maritime power. How those attributes are applied in any given set of circumstances will, of course, depend on the understanding and skill of those commanding maritime forces. Maritime commanders need a thorough understanding of both the environment in which they are operating and the attributes of those forces under their command. This chapter exposes the nature of the maritime environment, in all its principal facets, and identifies the attributes of those forces that operate within it.

The Maritime Strategic Environment

The sea covers seventy percent of the earth's surface and over two-thirds of the world's population lives within 100 miles of it. Over 150 of the 190 member states of the UN are coastal states. Since the 1970s they have extended their jurisdiction out to sea, in many cases as far as 200 nautical miles or further. Most human maritime activity – shipping, fishing, oil exploration etc – is conducted within that 200-mile coastal zone. This means that a substantial proportion of the world's economic and political activity is being conducted in a narrow strip of land and sea on average no wider than 300 miles. This is often referred to as the 'littoral'; it is certainly that area within which *littoral* operations will be conducted.

Strictly speaking, therefore, the maritime environment consists of a combination of land and sea and, of course, the airspace and outer space above both. The environment has seven dimensions of *military-strategic* relevance: economic, political, legal, military, scientific and technological, physical and socio-cultural. These are not listed in any order of importance, nor should they be regarded as distinct from each other. In examining each dimension in turn, aspects of the other six will inevitably be seen.

The Economic Dimension

Economically, the traditional use of the sea is as a medium for transport. Ships still account for 99.5% of trans-oceanic trade, the volume of which has increased by a factor of eight since 1945; and it continues to increase. Maritime trade will certainly remain the principal means by which raw materials and manufactured goods are transported between supplier and customer nations. One third of that trade is in oil and petroleum products, about half of that originating in the Middle East, most going to either Western Europe or Japan. Other cargoes of note are iron ore (9% of seaborne trade), coal (8%) and grain (5%). The remainder can be classified as 'other dry cargoes' (fruit, meat and manufactured goods). As an island nation, the UK relies particularly heavily on seaborne trade, as does the European Union as a whole.

Maritime trade reflects the increasingly interdependent and complex nature of the modern world and the operation of an intense free-market environment. Ships belonging to a company registered in one nation may be registered under the flag of another; they may also have multinational crews with conflicting loyalties. Shipping companies themselves may be components of international conglomerates, as may the owners of the cargo being carried. As a consequence, the identification of beneficial ownership and appropriate state responsibility for protection of shipping, together with interest in its employment and safety, are often complex matters. These complexities are of concern to the UK in connection with its own trading activities. However, they are also relevant when it comes to applying economic sanctions, through *embargo* operations.

Fish provides about 25% of the world supply of animal protein. The bulk of the world catch is taken in the relatively shallow waters of the continental shelf, within 200 mile *exclusive economic zones* (EEZs). About 75% of the

The Fishery Protection Vessel HMS TYNE

total catch comes from the North Atlantic and Arctic, North Pacific and the west coasts of Africa and the Americas. Approximately 70% of the total annual European catch is taken from within the UK's Extended Fishery Zone (EFZ). The control of fishing and the management of fish stocks is problematic, with most fishing nations deploying fleets to grounds within other states' EEZs. For some states, fishing can represent a substantial proportion of their economic activity; in the case of the Falkland Islands the sale of fishery licences is the principal source of income. Over-fishing is today a major feature of almost all world fisheries, with stocks declining as technology makes fleets more efficient. Scarcity of fish and over-fishing produce potential for dispute. To prevent over-fishing, more rigid and better policed regimes are required.

Nothing has motivated coastal states to extend jurisdiction more than the prospect of hydrocarbon riches on the continental shelf. This has also created potential for dispute. While maritime boundary disputes are generally resolved peacefully, there are some whose political, legal and economic complexities defy negotiated resolution. The reason for tension in the South China Sea, for example, is related (though not exclusively) to the prospect of substantial oil or gas fields in the region. Oil is a diminishing resource and will continue to be a highly attractive commodity of which states will wish to take full advantage.

Also within the economic dimension are illicit activities that can undermine the security of coastal regions and also threaten UK interests, both at home and abroad. Trafficking in people and illegal narcotics are perhaps the greatest criminal threats to our security in the long term and piracy remains a threat in a number of regions around the world.

The Political Dimension

The modern political dimension of the maritime environment took shape largely during the 1970s. For a great many coastal states, especially those in the developing world, the waters adjacent to their coasts represented the only prospect for expansion. The extension of sovereignty was often a political act that happened to have some economic consequences, rather than something that was done for objective, calculated economic benefit. Many states, especially small island territories, having asserted their rights to claim sovereignty over offshore resources, now find themselves without the wherewithal to police their *maritime domains* and manage their maritime resources effectively. Disputes over boundaries may be motivated more by political symbolism than by pragmatic calculation of costs and benefits.

Some states are increasingly regarding their maritime domains as part of their territory when, legally, territorial sovereignty is both restricted to a maximum of 12 nautical miles from the coast and limited by the rights of other states to exercise innocent passage. This is especially important in the context of international straits and *archipelagic* waters that define strategic choke points in which the coastal states have no right to suspend innocent passage. The extension of territorial jurisdiction has increased the likelihood of disputes over freedom of passage and use of *littoral* seas, with traditional maritime powers, including the UK and the US, resisting further restrictions on *high seas* freedoms. The US reactions during the 1980s to Libyan claims in the Gulf of Sirte are good examples.

The Legal Dimension

In 1997 UK became a party to the **1982 UN Convention on the Law of the Sea (1982 UNCLOS)**. The UNCLOS process has transformed the maritime environment, which has become far more complex in the legal sense. Those conducting maritime operations need to understand its complexities and should be familiar with the contents of the RN's *Handbook on the Law of Maritime Operations (BR 3012)*. This provides guidance on both the rights and obligations of all states enshrined in **1982 UNCLOS**, including precisely what is and is not permitted in the various jurisdictional zones that coastal states may now claim as elements of their *maritime domains*. Commanders of maritime forces cannot function legally without an instinctive feel for the restrictions imposed on them in *internal waters*, *territorial seas*, *contiguous zones*, *exclusive economic zones* and on the *continental shelves* claimed by coastal states. They will not be able to take full advantage of maritime mobility without a similar understanding of the rights of *innocent passage*, *straits transit passage* and *archipelagic sea lanes passage*.

International law provides free and legal access for ships up to the territorial seas of states and rights of innocent passage for the purpose of either traversing territorial seas without entering internal waters, or proceeding in either direction between the high seas and internal waters. There is also the right of unimpeded transit passage through territorial seas that comprise an international strait.

Law has a tendency to breed more law and there is little doubt that the legal dimension will continue to develop. Pressure for more law is currently focused on environmental concerns, which may further restrict ship movements and undermine flag state rights. There is a need for more effective policing of the existing regime, in particular in relation to fisheries and drug interdiction, but this has to be balanced against the need to retain freedom of navigation.

The Military Dimension

The seas have had a military dimension to them for well over 2500 years. This is not changing and shows no sign of doing so, despite marginal attempts to demilitarise the oceans. There are over 150 navies world-wide, ranging from the one remaining superpower navy at one end of the spectrum, to tiny, heavily resource constrained coastal policing forces from the developing world and former Soviet states at the other. Between those two extremes there is a considerable variety of expertise and ability. Navies of medium capability continue to develop and increase in number, those of India and Japan being good examples of maritime forces being consolidated, while that of China, impressive though it is in numbers, has some way to go before it emerges as a powerful and competent force. It is important to realise that relatively minor maritime powers can pose threats of significance, especially in the context of lower intensity maritime operations. With the bulk of maritime military operations likely to be concentrated in the *littorals*, small, fast vessels armed with relatively unsophisticated surface to surface missiles can complicate *sea control* calculations. Once open hostilities break out, this type of threat can be dealt with reasonably effectively by a competent and well packaged maritime force; it is in those periods of rising tension, when states are flexing their muscles and the atmosphere is one of ambiguity and caution mixed with firm assertion of rights, that the presence of such vessels generates most concern. Add to them a conventional submarine threat and the maintenance of adequate sea control becomes considerably more complex.

The Scientific and Technological Dimension

The military dimension of the oceans has a technological perspective. Navies are equipment intensive armed forces and modern warships are sophisticated weapons platforms linked to one another in *task groups* by equally sophisticated *command and control systems*. But technology is no panacea. Relatively unsophisticated vessels can seriously threaten the mission of the most sophisticated task group.

At the other end of the scale is the problem associated with highly sophisticated navies trying to operate with the less well provided. This is highlighted by the increasing need for individual navies to operate together in multinational forces. Difficulties of interoperability have been encountered when attempting to put forces together under the auspices of well-established alliance arrangements within NATO and the EU. They are made even more complex when the multinational forces are coalitions of willing nations whose navies operate with different doctrine, procedures, equipment and capabilities. The future compatibility between the US Navy and other navies' systems is a particular concern. Multinational maritime operations require compatibility in both equipment and doctrinal terms.

The Physical Dimension

A comprehensive knowledge of the physical environment is essential, as geographic, oceanographic and meteorological conditions will affect the ability of maritime forces to conduct operations. Oceans provide access to all parts of the globe, with the exception of those regions at the core of the large continents (85% of states have a coastline).

The operating areas of maritime forces range from the deep waters of the open oceans (known colloquially as blue water) to the more confined and often – although not invariably – shallower waters of *littoral regions*, estuaries and rivers (frequently, though misleadingly, referred to as 'brown water'). Perhaps the most significant physical characteristic, however, is the disposition of land bordering the sea. Maritime choke points are one manifestation of this factor. The Straits of Gibraltar, of Bab-el-Mandeb, of Hormuz, of Malacca and Formosa, are but five of the seventeen or eighteen most strategically significant in the world. The greatest cluster is in and around Indonesia, the Philippines and the South China Sea. The closure of significant straits in that region could increase deployment distance and times by substantial amounts for a US Navy Carrier Strike Group, for example, needing to deploy from Japan into the Indian Ocean and on into the Gulf.

Weather can have a significant *tactical* or *operational* impact and can influence *military-strategic* decision-making. The campaign in the South

A Meteorology and Oceanography specialist on board
HMS INVINCIBLE

Atlantic in 1982 was weather dependent and a delay much beyond the dates during which the conflict was conducted might have turned the balance of advantage towards the Argentineans with decisive effect. Seasonal fluctuations in weather can have strategic significance. Flying operations, amphibious landings and sonar performance may be made more difficult by high sea states and extreme high and low temperatures. However, these conditions will also affect an enemy. Skilful seamanship and well-rehearsed tactics and procedures can reduce these effects as can the acquisition of equipment designed to operate in a demanding maritime environment. Adverse conditions can also be used to advantage; a submarine, for example, can use poor sonar conditions to avoid detection. The mobility of maritime forces may allow them to move to an operating area where conditions are more favourable. An aircraft carrier can, for instance, seek out and exploit a local window in poor visibility to continue flying operations. This may be a particularly significant capability when shore-based aircraft are weather-bound. The Royal Navy's Hydrographic, Meteorological and Oceanographic (HM) capability enables commanders to exploit the maritime environment fully and minimise its adverse effects. The Recognised Environmental Picture (REP) consists of the foundation and dynamic information required to support the full range of military missions. The ability to maintain and exploit the REP, supported where necessary by *Rapid Environmental Assessment (REA)*, is an essential part of a maritime force's range of combat capabilities.

The Socio-Cultural Dimension

The socio-cultural dimension is principally concerned with the major socio-cultural cleavages within the international system. It is, therefore, of grand strategic importance but it does have some relevance at the lower military strategic, operational and tactical levels. Some societies and cultures may apply significant central control (along the lines of the old Soviet system, for example) which will have an effect on their command and control down to the tactical level. This can have an impact on the way that operations are conducted to the lowest levels.

Socio-cultural differences are an important consideration in relation to our own traditional allies. Although NATO processes and tactical doctrine are developed to assist with interoperability, some differences remain. Furthermore, not all our NATO Allies will apply Mission Command in the same way that we do. It is important to tackle such differences in two ways. First we must influence allied and coalition doctrine to iron them out and, secondly, we must recognise those differences that are more fundamental and enduring and take appropriate measures to cope with them. We may never achieve full compatibility of approach with ROE, for example, but knowing and understanding those differences will enable interoperability.

The Multi-dimensional Maritime Battlespace

Maritime forces must be capable of influencing events above, on and below the surface of the sea. The oceans provide three-dimensional space in which maritime forces can manoeuvre at a time of political choosing. They are an international arena for the demonstration of capability and the will to use force or apply influence. A threat can be posed from any direction and a recognised maritime picture must be established through comprehensive surveillance. All systems, including space and air based area sensors, must be co-ordinated to maintain a continuous, reliable and timely flow of useful data. The sea is, however, largely opaque to many sensors. It can therefore be used as a hiding place, for example by ballistic and cruise missile-firing submarines.

Surface ships can be detected by a wide range of sensors including satellite or air surveillance, but it is often hard to locate and identify targets with sufficient certainty to engage them, especially if they are not radiating on distinctive electromagnetic and acoustic emitters. In open waters, attacking forces will usually have wide options for manoeuvre and may pose a diverse, unpredictable threat which places large demands on defending forces, particularly if the attacking force has a balance of offensive and defensive capabilities. This can favour the offensive, though defending forces can concentrate strength around units at risk, thus increasing the options for offensive manoeuvre. The possibility of drawing the attacker to his destruction can redress the balance in favour of the defensive. Indeed an engagement might provide an opportunity to inflict *attrition* on the enemy.

Operations in the Littoral

The UK's maritime forces have always operated in the *littoral* regions of the world. Predictions of the future strategic environment indicate that little will change and that our interests will continue to be around the periphery of land masses, where centres of population, resources, industrial production, political control and trade are concentrated, and where crises involving UK interests may occur. Effective operations in these littoral areas are potentially of crucial importance, either as the scene of an operation itself or as the focus for deploying and sustaining forces deeper inland.

The Oxford English Dictionary defines the 'littoral' as "of or on the shore; the region lying along the shore". However, the term has in recent years developed a broader meaning in the military-strategic context. This book employs the following definition of *littoral region*: "Coastal sea areas and that portion of the land which is susceptible to influence or support from the sea". By this definition, the littoral is a flexible concept, the geographical extent of which will depend very much on the particular circumstances to which the term is applied. In one sense the littoral region can be described as a product of a coastal operational state of mind: one instinctively knows when one is in it because of the range and nature of operational challenges and opportunities one has to confront. These are, understandably, most readily apparent to those who operate routinely in the maritime environment. For those whose joint awareness is limited, the complexities of operations in the littoral and the opportunities for applying military force across environmental boundaries are not always so easily appreciated.

The proximity of land places certain limitations on freedom of movement, avenues of approach and on both offensive and defensive options. There may be no alternative to passing through geographic choke points or waters in which surveillance and defence options are difficult and the possibility of surprise, and possibly *asymmetric*, attack enhanced. The littoral environment will generally favour forces that can exploit limited warning time to their advantage, particularly when *sea denial* units are linked by sophisticated computerised counter surveillance systems. Thus, surveillance and weapon systems must be capable of dealing with the more complex littoral regions and confronting the particular problems encountered when crossing environmental boundaries. One such problem arises from the preponderance of population centres in the littoral regions of the world, which means that it is likely that many operations on the land will involve urban terrain, with its very particular complexities. Movement is constrained, communications can become disrupted and fire support can be rendered difficult by the proximity of civilians or sensitive infrastructure such as hospitals or centres of worship. The urban environment is also likely to be the battlespace of choice for terrorists, resulting in a continuing requirement for effective force protection.

Fighting Power

Fighting power defines armed forces' ability to fight and achieve success in operations. It is made up of an essential mix of three inter-related components: conceptual, moral and physical, with doctrine sitting at the heart of the moral component. None is invariably more important than the others, although, as Napoleon supposedly once remarked "the moral is to the material as three is to one". It matters not how advanced one's platforms, weapons and sensors are if the people manning them lack motivation, training or adequate leadership. A fuller exposition of this can be found in *British Defence Doctrine* and the UK's maritime fighting power is discussed further in Chapter 8.

Attributes of Maritime Forces

Success in a major operation will usually require the *joint* integration of maritime, land, air and special forces. Individual military units need to co-operate and complement each other to achieve the common aim. Commanders of *joint* forces must recognise the distinctive attributes of each of the components, in order to play each to its strengths, especially important in the conduct of a *manoeuvrist* campaign. Maritime forces have distinctive operational attributes.

Access

Over two-thirds of the world is covered by the sea and this allows maritime forces to exploit the oceans as a strategic medium for their relatively unhindered deployment to the most significant *areas of interest* and threat. Not only does this access allow intervention at a time and place of political choosing, but maritime forces may often be close to crises as they are developing. 85% of all states have a coastline and even many of those that are landlocked will be accessible from the sea with the co-operation of neighbouring coastal states.

Mobility

Maritime forces can move hundreds of miles per day. Mobility enables maritime forces to respond from over the horizon, becoming selectively visible and threatening to potential adversaries. It also adds a critical dimension to all *joint operations*.

Versatility

Warships can easily change their military posture, undertake several tasks concurrently and be available for rapid re-tasking. They can present a range of flexible and well-calibrated political signals. Furthermore, maritime command, control and information systems at the *strategic*, *operational* and *tactical* levels offer uniquely sensitive, flexible opportunities to co-ordinate maritime activity with diplomacy. The UK's maritime forces routinely operate with other nations' maritime forces, providing a flexibility of force packaging that transcends the limits of our own capabilities. There is, of course, a corollary to versatility in support of diplomacy. Those states being signalled may misunderstand the level of threat being posed, and concurrent diplomatic activity may be required to resolve unintended ambiguity. The elements of versatility can be summarised as:

Flexibility in Response Ships at high *readiness* are always manned and provisioned for hostilities and their systems and crews can respond rapidly to contingencies by progressing quickly from peacetime cruising, through enhanced readiness, to a more combative posture. This is important as periods of high intensity can occur in scenarios considered to be low intensity.

Adaptability in Roles An individual warship of frigate size and above will have defensive and offensive capabilities in all dimensions (air, surface, sub-surface and the electromagnetic spectrum). It can, therefore, operate in a variety of operational settings. Warships can be formed into *task forces* and *task groups* in which their individual characteristics combine to provide a mutually supportive, powerful and versatile combination of offensive and defensive capabilities. This, in turn, allows the group to operate at higher threat levels where conditions might be beyond the capability of a single ship.

Joint and Multinational Attributes Maritime forces have traditionally taken part in operations involving other services and the crossing of environmental boundaries. By providing an amphibious capability for a multi-threat environment, the UK's maritime forces regularly practise *joint operations*. Maritime forces are joint by definition, typified by balanced naval forces comprising air, land (in the form of amphibious elements) and integrated naval power under a composite command structure. *Joint Sea Basing* can provide afloat headquarters, logistics, area surveillance and denial platforms and facilities for joint forces offering advantages in flexibility, sustainability and access. Indeed, forces delivered into theatre by sea as part of an amphibious *task force* are configured tactically and deployed ready for use; they are not merely transported. They are available for a joint *task force* commander to be afloat or ashore - depending on the nature of an operation. Their integral combat power can be decisive in the shaping and sustaining of most modern operations. British maritime forces comprise discrete units well practised in operating in multinational groups, either within NATO or in ad hoc coalitions. Inherent mobility allows maritime forces to assemble easily and the use of NATO and multinational doctrine and procedures allows multinational groups to co-operate and combine with the minimum of planning and preparation. Multinational maritime forces benefit from frequent periods in company to exercise and develop their full operational effectiveness.

Sustained Reach

Maritime forces have integral *logistic* support, including repair and medical facilities. The range and *endurance* that these provide give individual

RFA FORT VICTORIA (centre) refuels the Type 42 destroyer HMS EDINBURGH and HMS OCEAN during operations in the Arabian Gulf

maritime units and task forces autonomy and sustained *reach*, which is the ability to operate for extended periods at considerable distance from shore support. *Reach* is enhanced by the provision of *organic* and *consolidation* tankers, supply and repair vessels. Only a maritime force so equipped can exploit the full potential of maritime power. If reach is to be sustained for an extended period, a *roulement* of replacement forces may be required. Seaborne logistic support provided by *sea basing* is an important element in sustaining forces employed in *joint* operations, particularly those engaged in *manoeuvre warfare*.

Resilience

Warships are designed to absorb substantial damage before they become non-operational. While a loss of capability through damage will degrade operational performance, a ship's company is trained to restore systems to use as quickly as possible. Warships are also designed to operate within areas contaminated through the use of *weapons of mass destruction* (WMD) with minimum degradation to their operational capability.

Lift Capacity

An important duty for maritime forces is protecting the unhindered passage of *sealift*. *Sealift* permits land and amphibious forces to transit and poise in theatre, and then enables joint power to be brought to bear ashore. Furthermore, it may often be the only practicable means of deploying mass (significant land and air forces, their battle winning equipment and logistic support) into a theatre of operations quickly and cheaply. For the UK, all major operations necessitate some maritime support to deploy, re-supply, withdraw, or re-deploy forces that have mass or have to deploy for extended periods (85% - 95% of lift in recent operations has been by sea). Although the *Royal Fleet Auxiliary* provides some sealift, a major operation relies for *lift* on chartered shipping, which may not necessarily be British registered or indeed readily available, and Joint Rapid Reaction Force (JRRF) *Ro-Ros*.

Poise

Once in theatre, maritime forces can remain on station for prolonged periods, either covertly or overtly. They can retain or seize the initiative or signal political resolve, and act as a force for *deterrence* or active *coercion*. The ability of maritime forces to poise in international waters allows the 'footprint' ashore to be optimised; that is to say the political complications and military risks of deploying forces and their logistic support for extended periods on land can be reduced. This unique capability to match the pace and reflect the tone of diplomatic activity is particularly useful in the dynamic and uncertain situations of the modern world. Poise exploits mobility, versatility, sustained reach, and lift capacity.

Leverage

Through suitable positioning and force packaging, maritime forces can provide leverage to exploit access and to influence events ashore disproportionately greater than the scale of force applied. Leverage is both a strategic and an operational concept, whose effects can be directly political or primarily military. Political leverage involves the coercion of governments which, in advance of *hostilities*, is an aspect of *naval diplomacy*. At the strategic level, a maritime nation or coalition can use maritime and other expeditionary forces to shape and exploit the battlespace and expose an enemy's flank and rear. At the operational level, joint forces on a seaward front or flank can provide *manoeuvre from the sea* to attack, *distract* and *fix* much larger forces ashore, *envelop* or otherwise achieve the *disruption* of an enemy.

2/1. Examples of Attributes

These are all drawn from the landings in Normandy in June 1944 and the events of the succeeding months.

Access

A statement of the blindingly obvious, perhaps, but it was the sea that provided the medium through which the invasion force was able to gain access to the French coast. Very obviously, access, as an attribute, was linked very closely with mobility.

Mobility

The inherent movement flexibility of a seaborne military force allowed the greatest possible choice of potential landing areas. In particular the force's great capability meant that the choice of landing area was not merely restricted to the shortest possible sea crossing.

Versatility

During the landings some of the inshore fire support was obtained by innovative and improvisatory conversions of landing craft to produce a support squadron armed with guns, of up to medium calibre, and powerful bombardment rockets. These were later used to defend the beachhead from German naval attack and were later to play an even more important role in the taking of Walcheren in the autumn.

Sustained Reach

The sustenance of the ever-growing Allied land and air forces for several months until a deep-water high capacity port could be operated in late autumn 1944 was a considerable achievement.

Resilience

The planning for Operation NEPTUNE had to take into account a number of adverse factors including weather and enemy measures from the air, on land and at sea; mines in shallow water and beach obstructions were particular hazards. The plans had not only to try and obviate these problems but allow for their effects.

Lift Capacity

On D-Day itself, some 130,000 troops, their equipment and initial logistic support were landed. By the end of the month over 860,000 men, nearly 160,000 vehicles and over half a million tons of stores had been put ashore.

Poise

Poise is generally associated with forces at sea, but not always; in this case, it was exercised with much of the force still in harbour. In any event the potential to have gone to any one of several destinations at a time of Allied choosing demonstrated a very useful degree of poise.

Leverage

In concert with poise, the ability to land in a number of locations and at almost any time, as perceived by the enemy, was very useful. It tied up a much greater land force of limited land mobility than the five divisions actually delivered by Operation NEPTUNE. A high degree of leverage was exerted.

Concluding Comments

Maritime power, in the broadest of senses, is military, political and economic power or influence exerted through an ability to use the sea. Maritime power has traditionally been employed to control sea communications for the general economic welfare or survival of sea dependent states. Military maritime power has an established ability to influence events on land through amphibious and ship launched land attack operations and as a component of joint operations. Maritime forces can shape and exploit a battlespace to enable the introduction or integration of land and special forces and the staging of major air operations. This force projection capability has greatly expanded with the combined effect of modern sea-based and maritime aircraft, evolving amphibious techniques and the introduction of land attack missiles. Thus, while maritime power has demonstrated an integral air, sea and land impact, the unifying factor is use of the sea.

A study of the use of maritime power throughout history (see Box 2/2) shows us firstly that a continental power can win a war if it is able to secure military command at sea, achieve *sea denial*, or even just dispute command of the sea vigorously. Second, for a sea power or a maritime-dependent coalition, command of the sea provides the strategic conditions indispensable for success in war. These propositions explain the strategic dependence of both the UK and NATO on maritime power, particularly in the modern, interdependent world.

The maritime power that a maritime nation and alliance requires for security in the event of major attack can be used to protect national interests in situations of lesser intensity and impact. Thus, the forces and systems available for deployment around Europe can be seamlessly transferred to any area of national or alliance interest accessible from the sea. It can also provide opportunities to contribute to wider security and stability through conflict prevention and conflict control. Maritime forces can maintain presence without occupation; coercion without *embroilment*.

The utility of maritime forces in *joint operations* is most evident in the execution of a strategy designed to achieve objectives ashore by using access from the sea as a principal factor. Land forces may only be able to obtain access if they are landed by *naval forces*, creating the conditions for success through shaping and amphibious operations. Even when this is not the case, ground forces may be prevented from achieving their objectives unless maritime forces can safeguard their *lines of communications*. Future operations will benefit from the ability of maritime platforms to support land operations by *joint sea-basing*. Movement of naval forces on the *high seas* can take place without prior diplomatic agreement. Furthermore, combat in open waters does not violate territorial integrity nor entail much risk of *collateral damage* to innocent parties. Maritime operations may therefore be conducted within a more flexible framework of political choice and risk than land operations. On the other hand a maritime force may include valuable units and there may be important political, psychological, and operational consequences if these are exposed to the possibility of *catastrophic* damage. The management of military risk is clearly an important element of any operation. The relatively unconstrained use of the seas allows the commander to manage risk to his force through choice of route and environment, and ease of extrication, conforming to the needs of political choice of time and space. In littoral waters, however, these options are likely to be more restricted, but are likely to be balanced by broader factors.

2/2. The Impact of Maritime Power

In his book *The Leverage of Seapower* Colin Gray points to the ability of maritime power to "control the geo-strategic terms of engagement in war". While it is important to appreciate that this will not invariably be the case, as Gray goes on to say:

"Depending on who controls the sea, water is a highway or a barrier. The continuity of the world's seas and oceans translates into a global mobility and agility for maritime forces which can have no continental parallel. That mobility and agility has been used time and again, in all historical periods to achieve surprise and the full strategic advantage of surprise effect. Finally, and notwithstanding the several revolutions in transportation technologies for all environments over the centuries, superior seapower has enabled its owners to knit together coalitions with a total strategic weight greatly superior to those secured by dominant continental strength".

It is also worth recalling the words of the Duke of Wellington during the Peninsular War:

"If anyone wishes to know the history of this war, I will tell them it is our maritime superiority which gives me the power of maintaining my Army while the enemy are unable to do the same"

And to demonstrate that 'littoral warfare' is by no means an entirely new concept, the words of Thomas More Molyneux from his 1759 work on *Conjunct Operations* (conjunct meaning joint):

"A military, naval and littoral war, when widely prepared and discretely conducted, is a terrible sort of war. Happy for that people who are Sovereigns enough of the sea to put it into execution. For it comes like thunder and lightning to some unprepared part of the world."

However, a balanced treatment will also accept the limitations of maritime power and who better to quote than Sir Julian Corbett, from his classic expression of British Maritime Doctrine, *Some Principles of Maritime Strategy* (1911). He argued that it was:

"almost impossible that a war can be decided by naval action alone. Unaided, naval pressure can only work by a process of exhaustion. Its effects must always be slow, and so galling both to our own commercial community and to neutrals, that the tendency is always to accept terms of peace that are far from conclusive. For a firm decision a quicker and more drastic form of pressure is required. Since men live upon the land, and not upon the sea, great issues between nations at war have always been decided - except in the rarest of cases - either by what your army can do against your enemy's territory or else by the fear of what the fleet makes it possible for your army to do."

A Royal Air Force Chinook helicopter prepares to lift a Royal Marine BV 206 all-terrain vehicle from the flight deck of HMS OCEAN

A Tomahawk Land Attack Missile (TLAM) launches from a nuclear powered submarine

Principles Governing the Use of Maritime Power

3

As an island nation, the United Kingdom must use the sea to deploy and support her armed forces wherever their capabilities are needed across the globe in support of national policy. This ability to conduct *Power Projection* relies on our maritime forces being able to exploit the sea for our own advantage while denying its use to a potential rival or enemy. Historical theorists of maritime strategy such as Rear Admiral Alfred Thayer Mahan USN and Sir Julian Corbett described this as *command of the sea*. However, modern strategists have generally acknowledged that achieving total command of the sea is most unlikely and that it may be limited in both time and space to what is actually necessary for a given operation. This limited form of command of the sea is known as *sea control*.

Sea Control

Sea Control is the condition in which one has freedom of action to use the sea for one's own purposes in specified areas and for specified periods of time and, where necessary, to deny or limit its use to the enemy. There is likely to be a requirement for sea control across the spectrum of conflict. At the lower end of the spectrum, maritime forces may be used to ensure freedom of navigation by a *deterrent* presence in areas where illegal acts or constraints are being threatened or applied to merchant shipping. At the highest end it may be necessary to use a huge array of maritime power to eliminate an enemy's ability to challenge sea control over large areas of ocean. The need for *sea control* is not dependent upon the existence of a substantial threat. If there is any risk to freedom of action, sea control is necessary. If the risk is small, the capabilities that will be needed can be correspondingly modest.

Early achievement and retention of the necessary level of sea control will be a component of any major maritime operation or *expeditionary* campaign. However, there can be no absolute guarantee of protection from attack at sea unless command of the sea has been achieved. Sea control must be related to acceptable risk. For operations to take place, a working level of sea control must be achieved to provide sufficient freedom of action within an acceptable level of risk. If sea control remains in dispute in a certain area, each side will be forced to operate in the face of considerable risk. However, sea control is most unlikely to be an end in itself; it is essentially a necessary condition to allow use of the sea for further purposes.

Sea control comprises *control* of the surface and sub-surface environments and of the airspace above the area of control. The control of airspace is also one of degree, and likely to require consideration of time and space aspects.   The minimum requirement for a successful operation is a *favourable air situation* although, to avoid an unacceptable threat to one's own forces, *air superiority* is highly desirable and often a necessity. *Air supremacy* is a necessary precondition of command of the sea.

The geographical extent of sea control may vary from local control around a single unit to domination of very large sea areas. In many cases, such as the protection of ports and anchorages, amphibious operations and providing support to the land battle, it must be achieved and maintained up to the shoreline. Air superiority may then be required across the shoreline and some distance inshore. Because of confinement and congestion, attaining sea control is a more complex task in littoral regions than it is in open ocean.

Sea Denial

Sea Denial is exercised when one party denies another the ability to control a maritime area without either wishing or being able to control that area himself. Classic means of achieving it are to lay a minefield or to deploy submarines to threaten enemy surface forces; a more recent method, particularly appropriate in littoral operations, is to mount surface to surface missile batteries along the coast to pose an unacceptable level of risk to enemy surface units.

Sea denial and *sea control* operations are not mutually exclusive. The denial of the enemy's freedom of action is a consequence of effective sea control operations. Sea denial operations in one element or area of the maritime *battlespace* may be necessary to achieve sea control elsewhere. However, the concept is only applicable when full sea control is not exercised by choice or out of necessity. At the *operational* and *tactical levels*, a zone of sea denial may be used as part of the outer defence of a force or area, or as a way of *containing* enemy forces. At the strategic level, sea denial can be used in a *guerre de course* or sustained attack upon a nation's shipping to prevent reinforcement and to sap national morale and the ability to wage *war*.

Battlespace Dominance

Battlespace dominance embraces control over the environments of the entire *battlespace*; the surface, subsurface, air, land and information environments, and the electromagnetic spectrum. Achievement of battlespace dominance in an area will necessarily entail *sea control* of the sea portions of that area. The concept of battlespace dominance is useful in *joint* operations, especially in the littoral, where there is a need to maintain freedom of action ashore as well as at sea.

Fleet in being

A nation deprived of *maritime superiority* might choose, or be forced, to adopt a strategy of *fleet in being*. By avoiding confrontation with a superior enemy, a nation can preserve its own maritime forces while continuing to threaten those of the enemy. The risk of attack complicates the enemy's choice of options. In the twentieth century the most obvious example of the conduct of a fleet in being strategy was that adopted by Germany through most of the First World War when, by keeping their major surface combatants away from decisive battle, they kept the British fleet tied down. The threat from a fleet in being can prevent superior opposing forces from establishing their desired levels of sea control by diverting forces to other tasks, such as *blockade* or *containment*, and as such is a method of *sea denial*. A fleet in being can *compel* the enemy to concentrate his forces in a valuable area, or around valuable units, cause him to route his passage to his disadvantage or to amend his operational plans.

Cover

An important function for the major elements of a maritime force to provide is 'cover'. This is the provision of support, if required, to less powerful units or detached elements of the force that are engaged in operations of their own, taking advantage of the wider *sea control* that the main force has achieved. An example of cover would be air defence provided to mine countermeasures units operating independently in an area of high air threat, but needing to do so in order to prepare a route into a landing for an *amphibious task force*. It is vital for the commander of a maritime force to recognise his responsibilities to provide cover for detached units.

The Type 42 destroyer HMS EDINBURGH fires a Sea Dart Medium Range Surface to Air Missile

3/1. Covering Force

During the Falklands Campaign of 1982, nuclear powered fleet submarines provided cover for the carrier and amphibious task groups engaged in the re-occupation of the islands. After the Argentine cruiser GENERAL BELGRANO had been sunk by HMS CONQUEROR, the rest of the surface forces of the Argentine Navy, previously of major concern to the British carrier task group commander, remained in their home waters. Thus other forces could maintain *sea control* against a reduced threat, and by so doing allowed for force to be projected successfully against Argentine forces on the islands.

Maritime Power Projection

Maritime Power Projection is the threat or use of maritime combat capabilities at global range to achieve effects in support of national policy objectives; usually to influence events on land directly. It exploits *sea control* to achieve access to littoral waters from where force can be threatened or projected ashore using amphibious forces, *organic* aircraft, land attack weapons and special forces.

Maritime power projection has broad application both during hostilities and for *crisis management*. In a crisis, power projection capability is an important contributor to *naval diplomacy*, providing the principal seaborne instruments for *deterrence*, *coercion* and reassurance. To be effective, the force employed needs to have a credible *operational capability* with the clear political will to use it, so as to back up concurrent diplomatic and economic activities. The sailing of maritime power projection forces demonstrates political resolve without a specific statement of commitment. They can poise at sea for long periods providing clear evidence of intent and purpose. A maritime power projection force can provide the main or the lead elements for an *intervention* operation and provide a mobile base for humanitarian assistance, peace support or *non-combatant evacuation* operations. Maritime power projection forces are a part of the maritime component of a national *expeditionary* capability.

During hostilities, they can use the sea to provide access to territory that is less accessible by land and air and to apply *manoeuvre from the sea*.

Manoeuvre Warfare and Maritime Doctrine

This brings us neatly on to the relationship between concepts of maritime warfare and those applied to campaigns ashore, a relationship of some importance given the extent to which the dominance of the littoral battlespace involves operations across environmental boundaries.

In achieving and maintaining *sea control*, maritime forces operate at the *tactical* level in a multidimensional environment. Sea control is normally a temporary condition and there is no direct parallel to the control of territory and the progressive advance across it. Concepts used in war on the land such as *lines of communications* and *the forward line of own troops*, have no direct analogies in warfare at sea at the *tactical level*. A commander of a tactical formation is likely to have *organic logistics* in the form of tankers and stores ships and he is unlikely to be as constrained as a land commander by the movement of his logistic *consolidation*. This is not to imply that lines of communications have no relevance at the tactical level. In maritime parlance, they are more generally known as *sea lines of communications* (SLOCs) and a tactical commander may have protection of shipping as his mission. But in such a context, the SLOCs concerned are likely to be strategic and his own organic logistics will obviate the need for him invariably and continuously to consider the protection of his own lines of communications.

However, in a *joint campaign* and, specifically, during *force projection* operations, concepts of war on land become relevant. At the *operational* and *strategic levels*, maritime warfare acquires some of the geographic characteristics of land warfare. The geographic relationship of events at sea to those ashore will usually be important to the operational commander. The apportionment, sustainment and protection of maritime *logistics* at the operational level are of a similar concern to a maritime commander as those of ground forces to a land commander. The operational commander will have the problem of consolidating his logistic shipping and, perhaps, of setting up a separate tactical operation to protect consolidation shipping and reinforcements. It would be wrong to underestimate the distinctive nature of the maritime environment, in particular its vastness, featurelessness, absence of impediments to movement, and the difficulties of achieving and avoiding encounter. However, at the *operational* and *strategic level*, joint doctrinal concepts are likely to prevail. These demand careful study by maritime commanders and staffs and will include campaign planning concepts such as *end-state*, *centre of gravity*, *decisive points* and *lines of operation* (see Chapter 7). Maritime commanders also need to be fully conversant with the overarching concept of *manoeuvre* warfare.

Manoeuvre Warfare

The UK armed forces have adopted the *manoeuvrist approach* to operations. *Manoeuvre* is the employment of forces through movement in combination with fire, or fire potential, to achieve a position of advantage with respect to the enemy in order to accomplish the mission. *Manoeuvre warfare* is a warfighting philosophy that seeks to defeat an enemy by shattering his moral and physical cohesion – his ability to fight as an effective, co-ordinated whole – rather than destroying him through incremental attrition.

Thus manoeuvre is a concept of particular importance having two distinct but related meanings. Firstly it describes one of the combat functions used in *joint operations*, in which context it is a phrase closely approximating in meaning to 'mobility'. Secondly, *manoeuvre warfare* is an overarching approach to the conduct of military operations. It is more than the use of mobility or tactical manoeuvre, and the application of mobility does not necessarily imply a manoeuvrist approach.

3/2. Manoeuvre from the Sea

Two outstanding examples of manoeuvre from the sea in which the Royal Navy played significant parts were the landing at Inchon in 1950 during the Korean War and the employment of amphibious forces in the 1991 Gulf War. In September 1950, three months after the North

Korean invasion of the South, the Northern forces had driven the United Nations forces into an area around Pusan in the far south of the peninsula. US Marines, covered by the gunfire of two British and two American cruisers, stormed ashore at the port of Inchon near the South Korean capital of Seoul, which was soon recaptured. This surprise amphibious assault struck the Northern forces in the flank, cut their lines of communications and caused their rapid collapse and retreat. Only massive Chinese intervention saved the day for the communist cause. In the 1991 Gulf War two US Marine Corps brigades first carried out a *demonstration* landing in Oman, then *poised* at sea. The effect was to tie down five Iraqi divisions in defence of the Kuwaiti coastline. On both occasions Royal Navy warships assisted in providing escort and barrier defence. In the Gulf the Royal Navy also provided the key mine countermeasures capability.

Manoeuvre and Joint Operations

In its most effective form, *manoeuvre warfare* has both spatial and temporal effect. That is to say, it employs manoeuvre both to gain positional advantage and generate a faster tempo of operations than the opposition. The aim is to achieve a decisive initiative in the right place and at the moment of one's own choosing. In applying this approach the intention is to undermine the opposition's ability to co-ordinate an effective response, rather than to destroy all components of his military capability through incremental attrition. So, the true value of firepower is not measured by its aggregate potential but rather by its selective, targeted and surgical application against the opposition's critical vulnerabilities.

All forces have the potential to offer ways and means of enhancing the manoeuvrist approach. To do this most effectively, all must be allowed to play to their particular strengths. Maritime, land and air forces have different but complementary attributes: the *access*, mobility, versatility, sustained *reach*, resilience, *lift* capacity, forward *presence*, *poise* and *leverage* of maritime forces; land forces' capacity for shock action, protection and the ability to take and hold ground; and air power's ubiquity, speed, responsiveness and reach. These are the inherent strengths and they must be used to overcome relative weaknesses, both those that are themselves inherent and those that arise for reasons of circumstance or situation. Land forces, for example, may experience difficulties on their own in achieving a manoeuvrist approach because the terrain and physical features may severely restrict mobility. In such circumstances, a combination of airlift and maritime mobility may enable ground forces to move significant distances and re-deploy to maximum manoeuvrist effect, catching the opposition unawares. The maritime environment is especially conducive to manoeuvre of this sort, presenting land commanders with opportunities to get around their own traditional and situational difficulties by lateral thinking and action across environmental boundaries.

Joint operations are not simply a matter of forces from different arms of the armed forces operating in the same theatre. The real essence of effective command of manoeuvrist operations is to recognise the relative strengths and weaknesses (both inherent and situational) of each component of the force and to play each to its strengths in support of the others. By doing that, the value of a joint force is more than merely the sum of its constituent parts.

Maritime Manoeuvre

Maritime manoeuvre is the ability to use the unique access provided by the sea to apply force or influence at a time or place of political choice. As an element of joint operations, such use enables movement, concentration of fire-power, surprise or overt presence, to gain an advantageous position - the central precept of *manoeuvre warfare*. There are numerous examples of the ways in which maritime capabilities can contribute to joint manoeuvre, and to the projection of force to bring about the resolution of a problem on land, where it must, ultimately, be resolved. Some examples of how they can make a significant contribution to each phase of an operation or campaign, even when adequate host nation support is available, will give a flavour of their usefulness and flexibility.

Before the build up of friendly joint forces in theatre, the presence of maritime forces can be used to deter further escalation, especially against a friendly and adjacent host nation. Maritime forces can be used to deter an aggressor by deploying into a region at an early stage, at relatively low political risk and, if necessary, in considerable strength. This is the principal reason why the UK has always aimed to deploy its navy widely rather than keep it at home. It is not by accident alone that British warships and amphibious forces are so often in an *area of interest*, ready to make their impact at a time and precise point of political choice. Indeed, the freedom of the seas, freedom for use, freedom from boundaries and frontiers is why the sea is so valuable an arena for joint force manoeuvre. In preparation for subsequent operations, maritime forces can be employed to both gather intelligence and mount non-combatant evacuation operations (NEO), withdrawing civilians from a potentially hostile combat zone. As forces build up in theatre, they can demonstrate further resolve by launching discrete amounts of mixed land, air or sea force against key enemy targets, to prevent or impede a potential aggressor from using force. Importantly, they can do this with a measure of control over factors that might otherwise lead to major escalation. In other words, as well as supporting operations on shore, maritime power can stop crises ever happening or nip them in the bud.

Prior to the main offensive, maritime forces can help to shift the emphasis from defensive to offensive operations by disrupting enemy activity, especially by the use of *raiding* techniques into enemy territory. Developing techniques for inserting forces from maritime platforms directly to their operational objective is an important way of enhancing this capability. During the main combat phase of an operation the maritime component's full range of capabilities, in particular its ability to engage in precision attack against designated targets, can be brought to bear in support of forces ashore. Finally, when it comes to withdrawal, the ability of maritime forces to transport large numbers of personnel and heavy items of equipment out of theatre, and protect them in the process, could be a vital function. The problem of force extraction is a demanding one, particularly when under attack, and especially so if a force has to rely solely on its own assets deployed with it and under its control.

HMS ALBION (right) replenishes from RFA WAVE KNIGHT

Manoeuvre from the Sea as a Combat Function

The ground combat function of manoeuvre seeks a position of advantage with respect to the enemy from which force can be threatened or applied. An important role of maritime power projection forces, particularly amphibious forces, is to provide manoeuvre from the sea in this sense. Firepower can create the conditions for successful manoeuvre by providing the protection to cover movement into a favourable position, by disrupting or deceiving an enemy so that he cannot effectively react, or by exposing vulnerabilities that can be exploited by manoeuvre. Speed of manoeuvre at sea will often surprise opponents ashore. A maritime force can move in the order of 400 miles a day, whereas land forces without the benefit of air or sea lift will often be lucky to move 30 miles (even in the German 'blitzkrieg' attack on France in 1940, the maximum advance achieved was 75 miles per day).

Proactive and Reactive Choices in Campaigns

A maritime force projection operation is by definition a *proactive* operation in that it involves seizing the initiative by forward operations in which forces are moved to invite contact with the enemy. However, it is not necessarily offensive. The mission may be to effect withdrawal or evacuation. In contrast the task of achieving sea control will present the commander with both proactive operational and reactive options in which the initiative is retained by drawing the enemy into battle.

The *offensive* is a course of action that forces the enemy to fight, if only to defend his own position; the *defensive*, in contrast, is a posture which forces the enemy to attack if he wishes to fight. Both the offensive and the defensive are relevant at every level of warfare. Convoy, to take the classic example, is tactically defensive but operationally offensive in that it obliges the enemy to fight in circumstances of one's own choosing; his only alternative is to abandon his strategic objective. It is extremely dangerous to confuse the offensive as a policy or course of action, with the offensive mentality. It has always been highly desirable, and usually essential for victory, that the commander and his subordinates should be endowed with an offensive (or aggressive) mentality: a determination to win whatever the difficulties, a trait in ample evidence in the characters of all the great commanders through history. But this attitude of mind has nothing whatever to do with the actual method of warfare being employed. Indeed, the offensive mentality is as necessary in defensive operations as it is when conducting an offensive.

3/3. The Balance of Offence and Defence: Convoy

The use of convoy in both World Wars represents the subtle combination of offensive and defensive operations, as it was used to both protect shipping and defeat the submarine, aircraft, surface raiders and mining threats.

During the decades immediately before the First World War, technological developments seemed to make convoys obsolete because short-endurance, coal-burning steam ships would not be able to operate on ocean convoy routes. In the event, the growing threat from German U-boats, especially, after the adoption of unrestricted warfare, persuaded the Admiralty to introduce a comprehensive convoy system. The Admiralty presumed that that this form of U-boat warfare would be repeated at the start of the Second World War and therefore planned to introduce convoy at the outset.

During 1942-43, the peak of the Battle of the Atlantic, the concentration of shipping into convoys left much of the ocean empty, which made it difficult for the U-boats (largely lacking supporting air reconnaissance) to find their targets. The U-boats, operating in packs, wasted much of their time in operational areas fruitlessly searching for convoys (and during much of the war, only about 10% of convoys were located). If one member of a pack was successful in finding a convoy, the others were then obliged to travel at high speed (on the surface), making them vulnerable to detection and attack by aircraft operating offensively at some distance from the convoy. Over the next 2-3 days about 70-80% of the pack would make contact with the convoy, during which time the Allies could reinforce threatened convoys with additional sea and air escorts, whose aggressive tactics took a heavy toll on the diluted and disrupted U-boat concentration. These actions were supported by offensive operations over the U-boats' Bay of Biscay and Northern transit routes, mining of their bases and training areas, attacks on support vessels (such as minesweepers) and bombing of maintenance and industrial facilities.

> This anti-submarine strategy was thus based on defensive (but reactive and aggressive) tactics close to convoys combined with comprehensive offensive (proactive) operations, with the whole enabled by exemplary use of multi-source intelligence, operational analysis, rigorous and regular training, together with effective tactical development and some significant technological innovations.

To be successful in maritime combat a commander must seize and maintain the initiative to force a response to his actions, thereby ensuring that engagements take place on his own terms. In doing so, the commander should exploit, where possible, the advantages both of reactive posture (for instance concentration of forces around the shipping at risk to draw the enemy to destruction) or proactive operations (such as the *distraction* of enemy forces).

A classic proactive method of achieving *sea control* is to seek out the enemy to bring him to decisive battle thereby destroying his forces and eliminating his capability to challenge sea control. Other maritime operations can then proceed unthreatened. Historically this course was not simply a matter of *élan* but reflected Britain's qualitative and often quantitative superiority over its enemies. To be effective it will generally require a large *balance of advantage* in maritime forces. The enemy may also have the option of declining battle and operating a *fleet in being*. Bringing the enemy to a decisive battle may well be the most effective option. Arguably, despite the espousal of manoeuvrist principles, most naval warfare, where there is no territory to take or hold, is essentially a matter of *attrition*, although mounting enemy losses may ultimately have the desired effect of breaking his will to fight, as well as progressively reducing his physical ability to dispute the use of the sea. Battles are not the only route to victory but they matter because they offer the opportunity considerably to speed up the rate of attrition. As much may be achieved in an afternoon as in a year or more of generally successful warfare against an enemy who avoids decisive battle. By the same token, of course, battles are risky, for much may be lost instead of won. But, for the commander who is determined to win and has something like sufficient forces, battle is by far the quickest and often cheapest route to victory. Arguably, the Gulf War of 1991 was a classically offensive attritional campaign in every dimension of warfare waged: land, sea and air. That is not to ignore its manoeuvrist characteristics, which complemented the largely attritional approach.

Proactive methods, other than the offensive, can be considered under the concept of military containment, which constitutes constraining an enemy's forces and reducing risk in areas outside those in which sea control is required. Containment can be achieved by close or distant blockade, the implicit threat of force (as with submarines and mines) or by *distracting* an enemy's maritime forces by posing an explicit overriding threat to his critical interests. Reactive methods of achieving *sea control* comprise the direct *screening* of formations and convoys, and the use of single or integrated defensive barriers of sub-surface, surface and air forces.

Because of the huge expanse and diversity of the maritime arena and its environmental complexity, the variety of air, surface and sub-surface threats, and vagaries in detection and prosecution of targets, no single system or layer of protection is likely to be adequate. For this reason, *sea control* is usually effected by a combination of proactive and reactive methods depending on time and space considerations. Probabilities of effectiveness of the various methods are thus aggregated to provide appropriate levels of protection and risk. This principle of defence in depth is demonstrated most clearly in the *layered defence* of a formation of high value.

Conclusion

This chapter has been devoted to principles related to the military or combat governed use of maritime force. Many of these have application during sustained hostilities (war). However the principles of *sea control*, *power projection* and *maritime manoeuvre* have relevance throughout the spectrum of conflict and in many operations that fall well short of war. The next chapter goes on to discuss the various applications of maritime power in which the principles discussed in this chapter will be applied.

HMS ARK ROYAL in the LPH role, with Support Helicopters from the Joint Helicopter Command embarked, leads a Royal Navy Task Group in the Arabian Gulf

4

The Application of Maritime Power

The UK's maritime forces may become involved in an extremely wide range of operations in home waters and overseas, reflecting the utility of maritime power in most of the Military Tasks assigned to the Armed Forces. These operations are bounded by high intensity war fighting at one extreme and essentially philanthropic tasks at the other. This broad range of operations can be broken down into distinct categories, each demanding a specific approach to the conduct of operations. There are also important legal distinctions that provide the basis for legitimate involvement in maritime operations of which commanders need to be aware. There are three general categories into which the application of UK maritime power can be grouped: *military*, *constabulary* and *benign*.

The Military Application of Maritime Power

A *military* application is one in which combat is used or threatened or which presupposes a combat capability. All war-fighting tasks require the military use of force. Less obvious perhaps are the uses of military force in support of diplomacy and in which forces are used to coerce, persuade or signal a message. Although under these circumstances combat may not be used or even envisaged, it is the capability of the forces to win in combat that underpins their use.

The Constabulary Application of Maritime Power

Constabulary application is where forces are employed to enforce law or to implement a regime established by international mandate. Force is only employed in either self-defence or to the minimum level necessary to enforce the law. The ways in which force can be used will normally be prescribed in the law or mandate that is being enforced and reflected in the ROE promulgated for the law enforcement operation being conducted. There will be a general reluctance to employ force. Combat is not, therefore, the principal means by which the mission is achieved, even though the situation may warrant combat preparations to allow for self-defence and to facilitate the use of the minimum level of force to ensure compliance.

The Benign Application of Maritime Power

Military forces can contribute organized and self-supporting formations with specific capabilities and specialist knowledge to a range of tasks in which violence has no part to play in their execution, nor is the potential to apply force a necessary backdrop. Tasks such as *humanitarian assistance*, disaster relief, search and rescue and ordnance disposal, whilst they may occur as a result of conflict, generally take place in a benign or permissive environment.

The Military Tasks

The framework for the application of maritime power is established in the Military Tasks assigned by the Government to the UK's Armed Forces. These Tasks comprise standing commitments and contingent operations at home and overseas, demanding the full range of military capabilities. Maritime power will be applied across the spectrum of Tasks and each of the above categories may be encountered episodically in the course of a specific operation. The ability of our maritime forces to conduct high intensity warfighting confers upon them their effectiveness across the full range of Military Tasks, whilst their enduring attributes allow them to cope with the pace of change of the strategic context and so discharge new missions and tasks effectively as Defence Strategic Guidance changes.

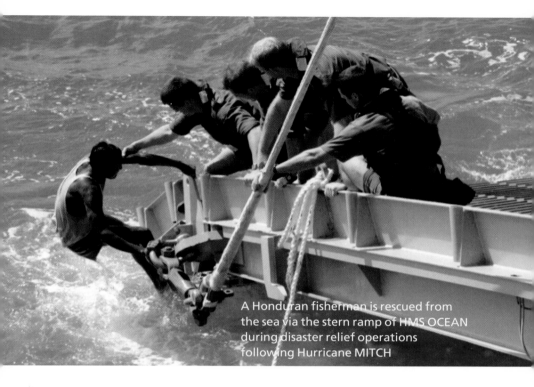

A Honduran fisherman is rescued from the sea via the stern ramp of HMS OCEAN during disaster relief operations following Hurricane MITCH

The Maritime Contribution to Standing Strategic Tasks

Maritime forces make a significant contribution to a number of Standing Strategic Tasks. At the heart of the UK's defence posture is the notion of deterrence, the purpose of which is to persuade a potential adversary away from a course of action that threatens British interests. It is applied at all levels, from the strategic down to the tactical, and the UK's armed forces in its entirety make up the nation's **strategic deterrent** by being capable of responding to a variety of threats. A critical component of this strategic deterrent is the strategic nuclear deterrent. The Trident D5 intercontinental ballistic missiles that constitute this instrument of strategic deterrence are deployed at sea in nuclear powered submarines, whose stealth makes them extremely hard to find and then destroy. They are not, therefore, liable to pre-emptive attack or counter-attack. Nuclear weapons deployed in this way have great reach and variable direction of attack. Trident submarines also have the flexibility to provide the sub-strategic component of our nuclear deterrence forces. This allows for the delivery of attacks that are more limited than those that would form part of a strategic nuclear response. They are an intermediate level of response that allows for a flexible and essential element of our overall deterrent posture, providing the linkage between strategic and conventional deterrence. The ability to deploy sub-surface launched land-attack missiles is a powerful conventional deterrent.

Maritime forces, by virtue of their forward deployment and sensor capability can make a significant contribution to **Strategic Intelligence**. There is a constant requirement for such intelligence in peacetime to monitor activity in areas of potential instability and provide sufficient warning of developing crises. If a crisis occurs, the intelligence requirement increases at the operational and tactical levels, requiring a more focused employment of in-theatre assets. Maritime platforms are frequently the first on the scene and can utilise the access provided by the sea and their sustainability to cover large areas with a degree of permanence.

Hydrographic surveying and geographic mapping and survey services are a defence responsibility because of the security aspects of providing hydrographic support for the strategic deterrent, anti-submarine warfare and mine countermeasures operations, and the need to maintain a survey capability for operations and emergencies. The Navy's Surveying Squadron provides specialist platforms to support this requirement (see Chapter 8), whilst all Naval ships make contributions to meteorological and climatic data collection.

The Maritime Contribution to Standing Home Commitments

Although UK's maritime forces spend significant periods deployed, they also contribute to a number of standing commitments in home waters. These include demonstrating British sovereignty and ensuring the integrity of UK's territorial waters and airspace, protecting UK's rights and interests

The nuclear powered submarine HMS VICTORIOUS, which carries
Trident D5 ballistic missiles as part of the nation's strategic deterrent

in the surrounding seas, port and route surveys and maritime counter terrorism. Some of these tasks were highly visible during the Cold War but their importance waned during the 1990s as the focus shifted to expeditionary operations in the Balkans, Africa and the Middle East. However, the upsurge in terrorist activity that manifested itself most tragically on 11 September 2001 resulted in the spotlight shifting back to the security of the UK and a reinvigoration of the involvement of UK's Armed Forces in the defence and security of the homeland. Many tasks remain unchanged, however, although some nomenclature has evolved since earlier editions of this book were published.

Since 1964, the waters adjacent to the UK have fallen progressively under extended and enhanced forms of domestic jurisdiction. In 1964 the UK established jurisdiction over its continental shelf and passed legislation creating safety zones around offshore oil and gas installations. These zones had the effect of extending criminal jurisdiction to the many exploration and production platforms operating today, principally in the North Sea. In the same year, inshore fisheries jurisdiction was extended to 12 nautical miles. In 1977, a 200 nautical mile extended fisheries zone (EFZ) was established and, in 1987, the UK extended its territorial jurisdiction from 3 to 12 nautical miles. The extension and enhancement of domestic jurisdiction within the UK's *maritime domain* has also had the effect of extending constitutional and administrative law principles and conventions to the same area. This has meant that those principles governing the use of the armed forces in providing assistance to civil authorities in the UK itself are also extended to the maritime domain.

In the UK, as in any well-established liberal democratic polity, there are strict legal controls imposed on the domestic activities of the armed forces. Whenever they operate they must do so in accordance with the law and in support, or at the behest of, the appropriate civil authority. The constitutional convention and administrative doctrine that governs the domestic use of the UK's armed forces falls under the general heading of **Military Assistance to Civil Authorities (MACA)**. MACA as a legal concept is sub-divided into three quite distinct categories. **Military Aid to the Civil Power (MACP)** is assistance provided for law enforcement and internal security purposes. Activities under this heading may necessitate the armed forces personnel involved carrying weapons and using authorised violence to achieve their objectives. Indeed, only those armed forces personnel involved in legitimate and correctly authorised MACP operations are permitted to use arms within the UK's domestic jurisdiction. **Military Assistance to Government Departments (MAGD)** is the use of the armed forces to ensure the provision of essential services, including during industrial disputes (eg the Firemen's strike in 2002-2003). Armed forces personnel used for MAGD tasks are emphatically not to be armed and MAGD operations must never be confused with MACP operations for that reason. Finally, **Military Assistance to the Civil Community (MACC)** is any form of *benign* assistance provided to the community at large, either directly or at the request of appropriate civil authorities, including other Government departments. All legitimate military activity having a domestic impact must fall under one of those three well-established legally significant headings.

All maritime MACP functions are, by definition, *constabulary* operations. They include: RN and RM patrols around the coast of Northern Ireland in support of the civil power in the Province; any military reaction to terrorist attacks on shipping or offshore installations within *territorial seas* or on the UK *continental shelf* (maritime counter-terrorism or MCT); any drug interdiction operations conducted at the request of HM Customs and Excise; and fishery protection patrols that are conducted to enforce fisheries legislation within the UK's EFZ.

MAGD has limited potential application in the maritime domain, although naval personnel can become involved in MAGD tasks ashore. However, there is a very wide range of activities that falls under the MACC heading conducted by the armed forces in the UK's maritime domain. The list includes: maritime search and rescue; salvage; ordnance disposal (there is a substantial amount of unexploded ordnance left in the waters around Northern Europe dating back to both World Wars. RN mine countermeasures vessels and clearance diving teams frequently respond to calls from the general public, particularly from fishermen); support for pollution control operations; hydrographic surveying operations (set amounts of surveying are conducted in accordance with formal inter-departmental agreements); and the provision of vessel traffic services in Dockyard Ports under the auspices of Queen's Harbourmasters.

The Maritime Contribution to Standing Overseas Commitments

Whilst always ready to conduct contingent operations when deployed, UK's maritime forces are routinely tasked in support of long-standing overseas commitments, including our commitment to international alliances and partners as a means of safeguarding UK interests overseas and the promotion of UK influence and support around the world. The forward deployment of UK forces contributes to the defence and security of our 13 Overseas Territories; maritime forces have particular utility in view of the number of island territories involved. UK forces are also deployed in a number of Permanent Joint Operating Bases (Cyprus, Gibraltar, Falkland Islands). Key alliances are supported, for example through participation in the activities of the Five Powers Defence Arrangements (FPDA).

One of the key missions is 'Defence Diplomacy', an SDR initiative that is very much in tune with the post-Cold War security environment, encompassing arms control, Outreach, confidence and security building measures and the promotion of British interest and influence abroad. Outreach activities are designed to contribute to security and stability in Central and Eastern Europe, particularly Russia, through bilateral assistance and co-operation with the countries concerned, whilst other activities cover military assistance to overseas military forces, such as the provision of personnel to British Military Advisory and Training Teams (BMATTs), and defence communities not otherwise covered by Outreach.

4/1. Defence Diplomacy - FRUKUS

Defence Diplomacy is a Military Task as part of our Standing Overseas Commitments. By its very nature, it suggests a co-operative and helpful approach to other states as a means of improving relations. In that sense it is generally benign in its application.

The Russia/UK/US (RUKUS) talks were initiated in the dying days of the Cold War at Adderbury in Oxfordshire and were originally unofficial and largely academic in tone. They involved representatives of the Russian Navy, the RN and the USN, as well as a number of academics and others with a naval interest. However, the success of the early Talks generated a momentum and they have emerged in more recent years as a regular, annual, official event involving all three navies, with each taking it in turn to host. In 1996 they were held in the UK, in 1997 the US Navy hosted them at the US Naval War College, Newport, Rhode Island and in 1998 they took place at the Kuznetsov Naval Academy in St Petersburg. Diplomatic discord in 1999 led to a lull in the annual programme. However, the success of subsequent diplomacy was displayed in July 2002 when reinvigorated RUKUS talks were restarted at the UK Maritime Warfare Centre in Portsmouth. During these talks a new programme of talks was produced that includes the French (FRUKUS), aimed at developing understanding and co-operation in the conduct of combined Peace Support Operations. Newport was the venue for the FRUKUS talks held in October 2003.

The aim of the original Adderbury Talks was to facilitate dialogue between East and West and they were, in that way, a form of unofficial confidence building measures. In contrast, the focus of the FRUKUS talks today is on achieving a practical and effective degree of multi-lateral maritime interoperability, by exchanging ideas and doctrine for use in multi-national Peace Support Operations. In that way they fit admirably within the Government's Defence Diplomacy initiative, with the accent on assistance and co-operation in an attempt to generate understanding and reduce tension.

Maritime forces can become involved in such activities across a wide spectrum. These include the traditional activities associated with maintaining presence and supporting diplomatic initiatives in peacetime (port visits being the classic example). However, in recent years, following the break-up of the Soviet Union and the dissolution of the Warsaw Pact in

HMS ST ALBANS arrives in the Baltic Port of St Petersburg for a goodwill visit

particular, there has been a concentration of effort on relations with the states of Eastern Europe. Some older Cold War initiatives remain in place with new focus, a good example being the FRUKUS Talks (see Box 4/1). However, the main thrust of Outreach activities has taken shape since the early 1990s. Personnel from the UK's maritime forces have visited all the European states of the former Soviet Union. Advice and assistance have been given, for example, to the Baltic States (who, prior to NATO accession, developed a tri-lateral mine countermeasures squadron - BALTRON - following advice from NATO navies), to the Ukraine, Georgia and Kazakhstan. The development of armed forces in new states presents a range of challenges. The UK's principal concern in providing advice and assistance is to help with the transition to balanced and responsible armed forces accountable to the political establishments in the new states. In providing such assistance we hope to achieve warm and positive relations with the states concerned and to develop military professionalism to the point where our maritime forces can operate effectively together and carry out humanitarian assistance and Peace Support Operations. The accent is on generating a sense of 'maritime community' amongst the armed forces of the region.

Anti-Piracy Operations are *constabulary* operations involving the exercise of universal jurisdiction on the high seas. Within territorial seas they are a coastal state responsibility. Where piracy is rife and pirates are equipped with modern weapons and craft, the task has the same characteristics and requirements as other forms of protection of shipping including, perhaps, the need for robust *sea control* measures. The other major form of criminal law enforcement task that is increasingly involving maritime forces is **Drug Interdiction**. The Atlantic Patrol Task ship, when operating in the West Indies, spends a substantial proportion of its time on-station involved in these operations, protecting the interests of dependent territories and complementing allies' (US, French and Dutch) efforts in the region. While anti-piracy and drug interdiction operations are the most obvious examples of low intensity law enforcement operations, other possibilities should not be discounted. These include the **Interception of Illegal Immigrants** and **Counter-Contraband** operations mounted to combat the smuggling of a wide range of illicit goods, including weapons and explosives (a good example of the latter being the RN operations mounted off the coast of Northern Ireland since the early-1970s). Operations to counter gun running may well be a part of a wider **Counter-Insurgency Operation**.

The maintenance of law and order in coastal states' maritime domains has generated a range of tasks, especially since the substantial extensions of coastal state jurisdiction resulting from the UNCLOS III negotiations and the **1982 UNCLOS** that emerged from them. For the UK, in its own maritime domain, such tasks performed by maritime and other military forces fall under the heading of MACA and are discussed above. Suffice it to say here, that any such operations within coastal states' relevant zones of maritime jurisdiction (be they UK, UK Overseas Territories' or foreign states') have to be conducted in accordance with the laws and other relevant legal rules and procedures enacted by the coastal state.

The Maritime Contribution to Contingent Overseas Operations

The most challenging operations undertaken by our maritime forces are deterrent, coercive and intervention operations overseas in response to conflicts or crises, in order to support other allies and partners, to protect our national interests, to maintain international security and stability or to uphold international law. It is here that the military application of maritime power is most likely to occur, although constabulary operations may be a part of the same or related operations, particularly during Peace Support Operations (PSOs) under an appropriate mandate. During and after such operations there may be a requirement to assist in the relief of human suffering. Our armed forces, whilst not specifically equipped for such tasks, have capabilities that may also be used effectively in the immediate aftermath of natural disasters. Any of these operations could result in the requirement to evacuate personnel to a place of safety, for which maritime forces are well suited.

Whilst the military applications of maritime power are governed by the principles of *sea control* and *power projection* that were explained in Chapter 3, they do not fall exclusively under either sea control or power projection headings. A degree of sea control is an enabling requirement for most tasks in *conflict*, including those that are also forms of power projection. Nevertheless, a useful distinction can be made between applications of maritime power at sea, of which sea control is the essence, and from the sea, which are broadly power projection tasks. A brief summary follows of the applications of maritime power at sea (essentially sea control and protection of maritime trade) and its use to project power ashore. More detailed discussions on the planning and conduct of maritime operations are included in Chapter 7.

Maritime power is applied at sea in both offensive operations conducted against enemy forces, and defensive operations conducted to protect friendly forces **(Force Protection)** and maritime trade. All involve **Sea Control** operations, which can be both offensive and defensive and may consist of elements of both. They may also contain aspects that are more

Part of a 3.5 tonnes seizure of cocaine worth £250M found on board the merchant ship MV YALTA by a boarding team from HMS IRON DUKE

akin to **Sea Denial**. Sea control operations will be conducted by any maritime task force, group, unit or element, all of which will aim to achieve an adequate level of sea control within their own areas of operations. However, **Area Sea Control Operations** are essentially geographic and are conducted using long-range surveillance and weapon systems over extended areas of sea.

4/2. Force Protection

Force Protection is defined as: "All measures and means to minimise the vulnerability of personnel, facilities, equipment and operations to any threat and in all situations, to preserve freedom of action and the operational effectiveness of the force".

Factors to be considered will include the nature of the threat, its intensity, the characteristics of the environment, the protection resources available, and the importance and urgency of each mission. Each situation must be regarded as unique if the chances for success are to be maximised.

Emerging technology and concepts, particularly in the fields of surveillance, information, and platform design, have extended the range of available protection techniques. Integrated operational deception and tactical distraction, new generation sea-lift vessels capable of high speed transit, and an imperative to seek out manoeuvrist solutions, can all be used to route vulnerable assets away from potential threats. Threat avoidance will be as important as the ability to respond to attack. If tactical contact with the enemy is unavoidable, sufficient combat power must be provided to the force to allow it a reasonable chance of success. Given the high value and scarcity of modern warships and the complexities of the environment in which they have to operate, careful judgements will need to be made by commanders about the utility of various force protection techniques. In certain circumstances, established methods such as convoying may prove as appropriate as they have in the past, especially in a single-threat environment, but they may not be the panacea that history suggests they should be. Fundamentally, the modern multi-threat environment, which includes *asymmetric* threats such as those that might be fielded by terrorists, renders rigid dogmatic resort to historically proven doctrine especially dangerous. In this instance, the best lesson of history is not to assume that previous solutions will necessarily apply but to retain an open mind and a flexibility of approach.

At the *operational level*, **Interdiction of the Enemy's Maritime Forces** hampers the enemy's attempts at reinforcement or manoeuvre from the sea and frustrates his sea control and sea denial operations. Interdiction operations can be conducted against shipping and aircraft at sea, in harbour, in the air or on land, through the threat or use of attrition.

Blockade is a combat operation to prevent access to, or departure from, a defined area of an enemy's coast and waters. It can be used operationally as a method of achieving sea control or sea denial through containment. Strategically, it may also be used as an extreme form of sanctions enforcement and as an operation against the will of a nation or regime, although it should be recognised that it may be less effective against nations that do not rely heavily on maritime imports and, to a lesser extent, exports. During full hostilities, it can prevent reinforcement, re-supply, and maritime trade, and thus deprive an enemy of the national material and moral resources necessary to continue hostilities.

Containment is achieved by posing a threat to an enemy's critical interests so that he must retain maritime forces in their defence. The threat to these enemy interests may take the form of a direct challenge to his sea control or power projection forces. Containment of the Soviet Navy, in order to maintain freedom of action in the Atlantic and Pacific, was an important component of the US Navy's Forward Maritime Strategy of the 1980s.

The establishment of **Exclusion, Identification or other Zones**, the legitimacy of which is only guaranteed and unambiguous under international law when authorised by the United Nations through a Security Council Resolution, have served both military and diplomatic functions. In conflict, they offer a means of simplifying sea control through the promulgation of an intention to maintain sea denial over a specific area. In diplomatic terms they are a way of enhancing coercive action by declaring resolve to use combat if necessary. Clearly, to be credible, they must be enforceable and the rights and security of third parties need to be safe-guarded.

Sea control **Barrier Operations** can be conducted where geographic or oceanographic features or operational constraints will channel or concentrate enemy forces. With modern long range surveillance, maritime forces may now be tasked to provide area sea control and static *Layered Defence* of these areas, though the difficulty of achieving area sea control should not be underestimated. Maritime trade is important to the UK, NATO and the European Union. In peacetime, naval forces maintain freedom of the seas for maritime trade by general presence and, on occasion, by *Freedom of Navigation Operations*. This is in addition to the specific requirement of providing security to air and *sea lines of communications* in support of a *joint* campaign.

4/3. Freedom of Navigation Operations

If a state's claim to extended territorial seas is not accepted, or a state attempts to restrict the use of the high seas or international straits, it may be necessary to use maritime forces to demonstrate intent to use those waters or to prevent a state from claiming customary rights in the future. Freedom of navigation operations are designed to influence a government and are therefore a form of naval diplomacy. They may be symbolic or coercive. In autumn 1963 the carrier HMS VICTORIOUS and supporting forces demonstrated the right and resolve to use the Sunda Strait between Java and Sumatra by conducting an overt transit during the campaign associated with Indonesian confrontation of Malaysia.

Maritime Trade Operations (MTO)

During operations, all levels of merchant ship activity need co-ordination and close co-operation between national military, civilian, commercial and government organizations to ensure the necessary level of liaison and safety is provided. This co-operation must be present in peacetime if the benefits are to be realised in an emergency, crisis or conflict. In certain situations UK maritime forces may be called upon to protect ships of many nationalities carrying cargoes of interest to the UK and its allies. MTO embraces this concept, incorporating various measures including *Naval Co-operation and Guidance for Shipping* (NCAGS) and the protection of merchant ships.

A Type 23 frigate
escorts an oil tanker in
the Arabian Gulf

MTO incorporates all matters associated with the worldwide movement
and harbour operations of merchant ships in which UK Government has an
interest. MTO is included in all aspects of Maritime Campaign planning
where merchant ships will, or may, affect maritime operations such as
embargo operations, deconfliction, reinforcement and re-supply,
asymmetric warfare, maritime safety issues, leadthrough of mined areas,
escorting, *accompaniment*, or *convoying*. MTO is effected through the
employment of a 4-tier graduated response from the onset of crisis,
maintaining a dialogue in peacetime to facilitate a smooth transition in
tension or conflict.

Naval Co-operation and Guidance for Shipping

NCAGS, which has replaced the term "Naval Control of Shipping (NCS)", forms an integral part of Maritime Trade Operations within the UK. Its mission is to provide support to military Commanders and merchant shipping in peacetime, tension, crisis and conflict through co-operation, guidance, advice, assistance and, where necessary, supervision. Additionally, NCAGS provides military guidance, advice or assistance in respect of participating nations' global commercial interests to enhance the safety of merchant ships and to support military operations. NCAGS provides military commanders with a series of tools for progressive implementation commensurate with the nature of any emerging situation. The size of the NCAGS organization and level of expertise required would be specific to an operation, as determined by the operational planning process. NCAGS staff are employed at strategic, operational and tactical levels. The organization is flexible and at readiness to operate within a wide variety of command structures and operational environments. The NCAGS response is tailored to the scenario and co-ordinated with other warfare disciplines.

4/4. Naval Diplomacy

The backing up of diplomatic negotiations, conducted in a period of tension, by the deployment of a naval task group able to pose an often unstated but self-evident threat, is a classical application of naval diplomacy. The deployment of the RN Task Force to the South Atlantic in 1982 was initially an example of naval diplomacy, with its steady passage south providing a clear threat of military force to back-up the diplomatic negotiations being conducted as an attempt to avert actual hostilities. Importantly, when the diplomatic efforts failed to achieve their aim (the removal of Argentine forces from the Falklands without the UK having to resort to force), the military threat was subsequently converted into actual military action. Arguably, the UK's resolve in 1982 will have provided subsequent such uses of naval diplomacy with additional coercive influence. The deployment of an RN aircraft carrier with US carriers to the Gulf in the winter of 1997/98 was a further example of coercive naval diplomacy, the aim of which was to persuade Iraq to comply with the needs of UN weapons inspection teams. On that occasion naval diplomacy appeared to work, although further pressure, including air strikes at the end of 1998, had again to be applied on Iraq in response to its disregard of UN Security Council Resolutions. Matters ultimately came to a head in early 2003, when coercive power projection operations failed and coalition forces conducted a deliberate intervention operation to depose the Iraqi leadership.

Doctrinally it is important not to confuse naval diplomacy with Defence Diplomacy (see Box 4/1). 'Naval diplomacy' is a term with a specific application. Defence Diplomacy is a Defence Policy Mission for the UK armed forces under which heading some naval diplomacy activities may well fall. However, some manifestations of naval diplomacy (as that in 1982) will be deliberately overtly coercive, even aggressive, in a way that Defence Diplomacy will never be.

Military force at sea contributes to **Naval Diplomacy**; the use of maritime forces as a diplomatic instrument in support of political objectives and foreign policy. It is the availability of force to back up and provide support to diplomatic efforts at various levels.

Naval diplomacy is designed to influence the will and decision-making apparatus of a state or group of states in peacetime and all situations short of full *hostilities*. It can be used on the one hand to support or reassure and can be a significant contributor to *coalition building*. On the other hand, it can be used to deter and coerce trouble-makers.

Doctrinally, there are several ways in which naval diplomacy can be brought to bear on international politics. When it is exercised in a general way involving deployments, exercising and routine operations in areas of interest, it is known as **Presence**. A traditional way of demonstrating *presence* is by foreign port visits to impress upon local populations the state's interests and involvement in the region. There is no threat of force; instead the vessel and her ships company act as ambassadors, whose function is to make a favourable impression on the local population. Warships are unique in their international acceptability, access capabilities and ability to make this kind of impact. The presence of a naval vessel in an area may be the primary symbol of national commitment - for example, HMS ENDURANCE in Antarctica. *Presence* is both a national and an Alliance task; indeed, the contribution of presence to stability and deterrence is considered to be so important that it has been adopted by NATO as a principle governing the use of maritime forces. The term *forward presence* is used to express a strategic decision to deploy forces for presence into or close to theatres of interest or concern.

Maritime forces can be used **Symbolically**, purely to signal a message, co-ordinated with other activities in an overall information campaign, to a specific government, while not in themselves posing any threat to an opponent or providing significant military assistance to a friend. When a stronger message is required, naval diplomacy can take the form of the employment of carefully tailored forces with an offensive capability. This can act as a signal of will and greater force to follow, or encouragement of a friend or ally by providing some reinforcement. The threat or use of limited offensive action represents a means of **Coercion**, a form of persuasion intended to *compel* a potential adversary to pursue a course of action that he would not otherwise be willing to take.

4/5. Symbolic Use of Naval Force

"In order to clothe the arrival of our new Ambassador, Lord Halifax, in the United States with every circumstance of importance, I arranged that our newest and strongest battleship, the KING GEORGE V, with a proper escort of destroyers, should carry him and his wife across the ocean." Sir Winston Churchill on a decision made in 1941 before the United States had entered the Second World War

(W S Churchill *The Grand Alliance*).

There may be occasions when the UK wishes to be in a position to influence events, particularly in the early stages of a crisis, but when specific policy objectives may be unclear beyond the need to declare interest and avoid *maldeployment*. In these situations **Preventative, Precautionary and Pre-emptive Naval Diplomacy** may be employed, with tailored maritime forces operating under carefully crafted *rules of engagement* poising in theatre for subsequent use when political objectives have been refined. In the language of PSOs, maritime forces may be significant contributors to *preventative deployments* for *crisis prevention*.

Embargo, Economic Sanctions and **Quarantine Enforcement** operations are normally carried out under international mandate, usually from the UN Security Council using Chapter VII of the **UN Charter**. As with other constabulary tasks, the level of force that may be used in enforcement must be mandated to ensure legality. Forces involved may be subject to counter-attack, so a level of overall local sea control may be required to ensure the protection of enforcement forces. These operations are normally used to restrict the egress of certain categories of cargo, with embargoes on arms entering states being of particular relevance in many cases. These tasks are distinct from blockade, which is a fully military application employed in war and which must fulfil the requirements of international law.

4/6. Maritime Operations in the Spanish Civil War

Modern maritime operations in support of diplomacy and humanitarian objectives are not new, but represent a return to the more traditional pattern of activities that pertained before the Cold War.

Good examples from earlier this century were the activities of the Royal Navy in the Spanish Civil War (1936-1939). British warships were used to prevent interference with shipping by Spanish warships not granted belligerent rights by the international community, to break illegal blockades, to deter Italian submarines from covertly sinking ships bound for Spain, to evacuate personnel threatened by one side or the other and to symbolise by their presence on patrol the principle of non-intervention.

Ultimately, if diplomacy breaks down completely, maritime forces may become engaged in **Combat Operations Against the Land** and **Support to Joint Operations** in a variety of ways. Maritime forces are capable of employing a range of amphibious operations that NATO doctrine has listed under four type headings: amphibious demonstration, amphibious raiding, amphibious assault and amphibious withdrawal (see the detailed discussion in Chapter 7). Maritime based aircraft can contribute to *air operations for strategic effect, counter-air, anti-surface force* (land and sea), and *combat support air operations*, all of which may be supporting joint campaign objectives ashore. Submarines and, indeed, surface ships armed with land attack missiles can contribute to attacks on important shore targets. Naval systems can provide fire support to all operations, increasingly with greater range, accuracy and lethality. Maritime electronic capabilities can contribute significant intelligence, area surveillance and communications, and naval missiles can provide air defence over littoral areas. Logistic support is also available to landed forces and structural and organizational improvements will enhance their capability for wider support of ground forces.

Maritime Force Projection capabilities (including special forces) may be employed as part of *sea control* operations to destroy enemy forces in harbours, ports and air bases, and their *command* and *control* systems and logistics. Alternatively, they can be used to secure a land flank for sea control forces.

Maritime forces can also assist in the **Protection of Joint Forces** or territory by providing a sea based defensive barrier or by holding down a flank. Conversely, they can expand the maritime flank or defend it against enemy manoeuvre from the sea. More specifically they can contribute to air defence, supplementing land-based forces or, within a *Joint Operations Area (JOA)*, supply comprehensive defence capability. Within this is the potential for sea-based forces to provide defence against theatre ballistic missiles, weapons of mass destruction and more static enemy indirect fire systems. Maritime forces can therefore provide support at all stages of a joint operation.

HMS RICHMOND providing Naval Gunfire Support to Royal Marines operating on the Al Faw Peninsula, Iraq

Peace Support Operations

Although not new, it is since the end of the Cold War that *Peace Support Operations* (PSO) have become ever more prevalent, with a consequent increase in the involvement of maritime forces. PSOs are multi-functional operations involving military forces and diplomatic and humanitarian agencies. They are designed to achieve humanitarian goals or a long-term political settlement, usually in support of an appropriate mandate. Applying the attributes of Access, Mobility and Versatility, UK's maritime forces may make a major contribution to these operations. PSO covers a wide range of operations that are linked by the key characteristic of impartiality.

4/7. Peace Support Operations - Maritime Tasks

- Intelligence/Information Gathering

- Active monitoring of a sea area for infringement of sanctions/embargo.

- Patrolling and monitoring a maritime cease fire line or demilitarised zone.

- Enforcement of sanctions/embargo.

- Supervising cantonment of vessels.

- Contribution of *organic* aircraft to enforcement of a *no fly zone*.

- Contribution of organic helicopters for in theatre movement of peacekeeping forces, humanitarian assistance and casualty evacuation.

- Contribution of ground forces to peace support operations.

- Maintenance of an integral amphibious capability in theatre to support peacekeeping forces, aid workers and other civilians.

- Maintenance of an integral amphibious capability in theatre to support peacekeeping forces, aid workers and other civilians.

- Provision of sea base, seaborne medical and other logistic and humanitarian resources where access by land is difficult.

- Environmental monitoring and patrol.

- Assistance to seaborne refugees.

- Provision of a neutral platform for peace negotiations.

- Mine countermeasures to provide access or contribute to a new peace.

The activities of forces involved in PSOs are conditioned by the diplomatic environment and complicated command and control arrangements that often apply. Operations will typically be carried out under the auspices of the UN or the Organization for Security and Co-operation in Europe (OSCE), although NATO, the EU and other regional organizations may also be involved. UK forces may be operating under the aegis of the UN, under national command in co-ordination with other UN forces or under NATO or other coalition partners. The hierarchy of military activity may not be clearly defined during PSOs. The presence of civilian UN authorities, civilian staff of non-governmental organizations (NGOs), the multiplicity of national and international *operational* and *tactical* headquarters in theatre, and the intricate and frequently ad hoc co-ordination arrangements between them will all complicate the situation.

Schoolchildren in Freetown, Sierra Leone, thank Royal Navy personnel who helped in the restoration of their school

Every PSO is different, although a situation requiring international intervention will normally develop through a period of decreasing stability during which the emphasis will be on conflict prevention. Early maritime presence, particularly by multinational forces, can have a significant deterrent effect. However, should deterrence fail and conflict occur, direct involvement might become necessary to coerce belligerents into full acceptance of the provisions of any subsequent peace agreement and/or mandate. If the level of consent and compliance is uncertain, the PSO will be one of Peace Enforcement, whilst the consent of all the major parties will allow Peacekeeping operations to be conducted. With increasing stability and a consequent reduction in tension, military forces can contribute to Peace Building, although the timescale to achieve this will depend on the scale and duration of the conflict in question. Whilst some PSOs may develop through the three phases of Implementation, Stabilisation and Normalisation , it is not necessary for this to happen and some, particularly if successful, may be restricted to one phase only. During these phases the tasks that may be undertaken are described in detail in *JWP 3-50 Peace Support Operations* and can be summarised as follows (see Glossary for definitions of each type of PSO):

Conflict Prevention

Conflict prevention activities are normally conducted under Chapter VI of the *UN Charter*. They range from diplomatic initiatives to **preventative deployments** of forces intended to prevent disputes from escalating into armed conflicts or from spreading. Conflict prevention can also include fact-finding missions, consultations, warnings, inspections and monitoring. Preventative deployments will normally need to possess sufficient deterrent capability to avoid a conflict and will therefore seek to overmatch the protagonists.

Peacemaking

Peacemaking covers the **diplomatic activities** conducted after the commencement of a conflict aimed at establishing a ceasefire or a rapid peaceful settlement. They can include the provision of good offices, mediation, conciliation, diplomatic pressure, isolation and sanctions. Military support to add weight to the diplomatic process may well be required. This was the case in the autumn of 1995, when aircraft from HMS INVINCIBLE flew sorties over Bosnia as part of the process of persuading parties to accept the Dayton Agreement.

Peace Enforcement

Peace Enforcement operations are **coercive in nature** and are preferably undertaken under Chapter VII of the *UN Charter*, when the consent of any of the major parties to a conflict is uncertain. They are designed to maintain and re-establish peace or enforce the terms specified in the mandate.

Peacekeeping

Operations undertaken under Chapter VI of the *UN Charter* with the consent of all the major parties to a conflict, to **monitor and facilitate the implementation of a peace agreement**. A long running example is the UN operation in Cyprus (known as UNFICYP) that, since 1974, has patrolled between the Greek and Turkish Cypriot areas of the island. Royal Marines have frequently provided forces since the operation commenced, in different circumstances, in the early 1960s. Such operations are principally engaged ashore, although there may be maritime aspects at the margins or involving the patrolling of rivers and other internal waterways, as in Cambodia in the early 1990s.

Peace Building

Peace building covers actions that support political, economic, social and military measures and structures, aiming to **strengthen and solidify political settlements** in order to address the causes of conflict. This includes mechanisms to identify and support structures that tend to consolidate peace, advance a sense of confidence and well being, and support economic reconstruction.

4/8. Yugoslavia - Maritime Peace Support Operations

The UK's contribution from the sea to UNPROFOR, SFOR, IFOR and KFOR in the former Yugoslavia included:

- fighter aircraft patrols (supported by shore based AWACS aircraft and air-to-air refuelling) in support of the No Fly Zone from a carrier in the Adriatic.

- reconnaissance and *close air support* to troops ashore.

- combat service support to the British contingents.

- embargo operations.

In addition to the value as a command and control and staging platform, the carrier's ability to position herself close to the operational area and minimise the effects of adverse weather made her organic aircraft ideal for short notice tasking together with her ability to position herself in the most favourable tactical situation. RN destroyers and frigates, acting under NATO and WEU command, helped to enforce the UN embargoes and, in the first two and a half years, NATO and WEU vessels boarded over 3,345 ships and diverted more than 653 suspected violators. Heavy equipment was moved to the theatre by sea and a Royal Fleet Auxiliary ship alongside in Split provided accommodation and ammunition and stores support. On two occasions RN ships were used as neutral territory to host meetings between warring factions; in one case this resulted in the lifting of the siege of Dubrovnik.

Humanitarian Assistance and Disaster Relief

As part of our overall security policy, Britain's armed forces have a history of contributing to regional stability by participating in *humanitarian assistance* and *humanitarian disaster relief* operations (HDRO) around the world.

Personnel from HMS SHEFFIELD repair hurricane damage on the island of Guanaja, off the coast of Honduras

Humanitarian operations are conducted to relieve human suffering. Military activities may accompany, or be in support of, humanitarian operations conducted by specialised civilian organizations. Maritime forces can provide a comprehensive logistics base and refuge offshore for humanitarian operations, with shipborne helicopters providing a versatile means of transport. Recent humanitarian operations include those conducted in the Former Republic of Yugoslavia and in Northern Iraq (where the UK contribution was led by 3 Commando Brigade Royal Marines), in both of which there was a military dimension – in contrast to the benign involvement of UK armed forces personnel and equipment in Central America in late 1998 (see Box 4/9).

The flexibility of maritime forces and their independent logistic support makes them particularly effective in disaster relief operations following hurricanes and tropical cyclones, local unrest or infrastructure collapse. The armed forces may in particular be required to provide disaster relief to the Overseas Territories, several of which are in the Caribbean where there is frequent hurricane damage. Maritime forces are especially important in the very early stages of disaster relief when they may well be the only assistance available to provide 'first-aid', such as fresh water, food, temporary shelter, fuel and electric power, while other agencies, including NGOs, mobilise longer term assistance. However, it is important to recognise that military forces are not well placed to provide long-term assistance; they are neither equipped for it nor very cost-effective over time. UK doctrine and considerations for HDRO are fully described in *JWP 3-52*.

4/9. Disaster Relief

In early November 1998, Hurricane Mitch caused great disruption and enormous loss of life in the Central American area, particularly in the Honduras and Nicaraguan regions. Mounting Operation TELLAR, HM Ships SHEFFIELD and OCEAN, carrying a mix of Sea King and Lynx helicopters and accompanied by RFAs BLACK ROVER and SIR TRISTRAM, 45 Commando and Dutch Marines, became fully involved in humanitarian relief operations in conjunction with other international military units. This involved moving up to 150 miles inland to assist the population until other international relief organizations arrived to take over.

All vessels on the *high seas* are required under international law to assist in **search and rescue**, and **salvage operations** may also be appropriate in some circumstances. In some cases, it may be necessary to carry out a degree of **marine pollution control**. This is also a particularly specialist task that military forces cannot cope with over extended periods or if the level of pollution is high - as it often is if it emanates from a stricken oil tanker, for example. Again, maritime forces may be extremely useful in the early stages of a crisis (carrying out initial surveillance or providing early command and control) and in some instances may even be able to provide specialised 'first-aid' equipment (the RN's offshore patrol vessels carry spraying equipment). After the initial stages of a crisis, however, military forces will need to make way for other agencies once the latter have arrived on-scene.

Many of these operations are both manpower and specialised equipment intensive. Disaster relief and salvage operations in particular may involve the entire ship's company of a frigate or destroyer and require a good deal of specialist equipment. Ships deploying to the West Indies, where such operations occur frequently, receive additional training and equipment prior to their deployment.

Evacuation of UK Citizens Overseas

In an increasingly uncertain world the protection of UK citizens and those of our allies abroad is an important task which may require a military assisted **Non-combatant Evacuation Operation** (NEO) to move them to a place of safety. Globalisation implies an increased interaction between people and organizations in different countries, resulting in large numbers of UK citizens travelling world-wide on business at any time. Proliferating humanitarian crises will increase the overseas commitments of NGOs, and consequently of any British citizens in these organizations. Increasing personal wealth and leisure time, together with improved communications and transport mean that the current growth in the number of British citizens travelling abroad for holidays each year will continue. Expanding adventure tourism will put more British citizens into unstable regions. Together with widening international commitments, such as an expanding EU, these trends imply a continued increase in the numbers of people entitled to UK protection abroad. Maritime forces may therefore be required increasingly to use their military potential to offer protection to UK citizens and others and effect their evacuation if the local Government Representative requests it. UK doctrine and considerations for NEO are fully described in *JWP 3-51*.

4/10. Non-Combatant Evacuation Operations

The use of maritime forces in evacuation operations was demonstrated during the civil war between government and rival factions in Aden in January 1986. The Royal Yacht BRITANNIA, later supported by HM Ships NEWCASTLE, JUPITER and RFA BRAMBLELEAF, evacuated 1379 men, women and children of 55 different nationalities from the besieged town. Many were evacuated by the Royal Yacht's own boats over an open beach.

Concluding comments

The mission of forces engaged in a particular campaign or operation may entail their use in more than one of the three ways (*military*, *constabulary* or *benign*) simultaneously or consecutively. For instance, disaster relief may require constabulary or military protection, depending on the nature and scale of any threat (such as looting or attempts to exploit civil disorder to seize power). Similarly, *constabulary* use may escalate into military use if there is a challenge of sufficient magnitude to the regime that is being enforced. What may begin as a constabulary task may deteriorate into peace enforcement or NEO, which are military or combat governed tasks. If a situation has deteriorated to the extent that terrorism or combat is being conducted by well-armed groups or irregular forces, the task of restoring order will require the military application of force. The legal basis for each of the three uses is different.

The perceptions of any potential or real opposition and of non-combatant civilians in theatre will drive decisions about whether a particular operation can be restricted to *benign* or *constabulary* application of force. As a result there are very real problems for military forces in a theatre in which forces from the same nation, coalition or agency are simultaneously engaged in different uses of force. For instance, it may be necessary for personnel and operational units from the same maritime *task group* in a single theatre to carry out combat operations against insurgents (*military* application) while enforcing a UN Security Council Resolution through embargo operations (*constabulary*) at the same time as providing humanitarian assistance/disaster relief (*benign*). The maritime commander in such circumstances will have to remain conscious of the distinctions, consider the ROE appropriate to each task and ensure that the conduct of each remains within the limits imposed by international law and the law of the country and coastal waters in which the operations are taking place. In such circumstances the military opposition may take action against those elements of the task group engaged in constabulary or benign tasks. These are complexities with which those who have operated in and around the Former Republic of Yugoslavia, Sierra Leone, Afghanistan and Iraq in recent years will be only too aware.

APPLICATION OF MARITIME POWER

MILITARY		CONSTABULARY	BENIGN
FROM THE SEA *Power Projection*	**AT SEA** *Sea Control*		
Strategic and Sub-Strategic Deterrence	Operations Against Enemy Forces	Embargo, Sanctions & Quarantine Enforcement	Disaster Relief
•	•	•	Assistance to Refugees
Coercion	Protection of Maritime Trade	Peacekeeping	•
•		•	Peace Building Operations
Combat Operations Against the Land		Anti-Piracy Operations	•
•		•	Search and Rescue
Combat Operations in Defence of Land Forces		Fishery Protection	•
•		•	Salvage
Evacuation Operations		Drug Interdiction	•
•		•	Ordnance Disposal
Conflict Prevention		Contraband Operations	•
•		•	Pollution Control
Support to Peacemaking		Oil and Gas Field Patrols	•
•		•	Hydrographic Surveying
Peace Enforcement		Maritime Counter-Terrorism	•
		•	Vessel Traffic Services
		Support to Counter-Insurgency Operations	•
		•	Military Assistance to Foreign and Commonwealth Governments
		Enforcement of Maritime Agreements	

Fig 4.1

A Type 22 Batch III frigate

RFA WAVE KNIGHT refuels the Type 23 frigate HMS SUTHERLAND

5

Maritime Logistics and Support

The purpose of logistic support is to ensure the provision, sustainment and recovery of forces, thus enabling the maintenance of combat capability and allowing the operational commander to deploy forces at the time and place of his choosing. Logistic support includes medical and repair facilities, movement of personnel, and the transport of the fuel, lubricants, ordnance, spare parts, food and other provisions, and the many stores required for missions. The sea will remain the principal transport medium for large, heavy and bulky items. Ships are, therefore, important joint *logistics* assets. The availability of shipping and the ability to transfer ashore may ultimately govern whether, where and when military operations can take place. However, the use of *sea lines of communications* to a campaign may be considered a critical vulnerability, and shipping may require protection, increasingly so against the threat of *asymmetric attack*. Similarly, at the *tactical* level, a formation's *organic* logistic shipping will invariably be essential to its mission and thus require special effort to be devoted to its protection.

The ability of ships to carry and transfer stores and fuel allows *maritime forces* to conduct self-sustained operations at considerable distances from fixed bases with little or no *Host Nation Support* (HNS) required. Indeed the sailor is so used to the level of organic logistics support that is provided routinely in a ship and its tactical formation that logistic considerations are intrinsic to maritime doctrine. For the operational commander, maritime and land logistics are not conceptually dissimilar, because the ability to use lines of communications along which a maritime force is *consolidated*, is comparable with tasks relating to seaborne support of land operations and to land *lines of communications*. In any event, logistic support is a fundamental activity in which resources and facilities must be pooled and focused to sustain a joint campaign in all its phases and environments. It is a tenet of joint *doctrine* that administrative services of common usage in the three Services can be provided by one Service for the use of others. At the operational level, logistic policy, planning and execution will be jointly co-ordinated.

Maritime logistics support to joint operations comes with two important advantages. *Joint sea basing* of logistics support optimises the 'footprint' ashore and allows that support to be landed in sufficient quantities as required without necessarily placing it all in a vulnerable and essentially immobile location. Sea basing also allows for the protection of logistics support, especially important in operational environments that may be affected by weapons of mass destruction (WMD) or *asymmetric attack*.

Logistics at the Strategic Level

At the *strategic level*, the logistics process provides the link between the resources of the nation and the military operations of combat forces. The creation of logistic resources (or production logistics) is almost entirely a civilian commercial process. Once they are manufactured, the employment of these resources in support of military operations (consumer logistics) becomes a military function, albeit one heavily dependent on civilian support. The integration of production and consumer logistic systems takes place at the *military-strategic level* and is the responsibility of the Chief of Defence Logistics (CDL). The determination of strategic requirements, procurement, planning of logistic aspects of *regeneration* capability, central storage and bulk distribution are all *military-strategic* logistic functions.

Logistics at the Operational Level

Maritime operational logistic functions are:

- the movement of logistics into, within and out of theatre;

- the establishment of logistic bases;

- the apportionment and allocation of logistics between subordinate commands; and

- the protection of logistics bases, on land, and along *sea lines of communications*.

In war, protection and distribution of logistics may constitute a major operation in its own right as a commander will want to ensure that his logistic plan is adequate to support his concept of operations. Logistic feasibility will frequently be the deciding factor in choosing a course of action. For this reason logistic planning will require the same attention as planning for warfighting, and must underpin all envisaged contingencies during each phase of the campaign plan. Detailed logistic planning is vital particularly during amphibious operations to ensure that manpower and equipment are integrated, accessible and flexible to match the tempo of operations set by the operational commander without the delays caused by the need to restow ships. This process is aided if the commander at each level has control over the allocation of the logistic support to the forces under his command. Complete unity of logistic command is desirable but difficult to achieve for two principal reasons. First, the harmonisation of production and consumer logistics is a continuous process involving a large number of organizations most of whom will not be under the control of the operational commander. He may therefore have little control of the supply side of his logistics. Second, there are particular problems associated with the control of logistics during joint and, especially, multinational operations. The establishment of the Joint Task Force Logistics Component under the Joint Task Force Commander (JTFC) with responsibility for logistic support, enhances unity of logistic command in national joint operations.

Multinational Logistics

Logistics during multinational operations have traditionally been, and remain, a national responsibility. This will inevitably be the case within ad hoc coalitions where there may be little standardisation between nations' equipments. However, NATO has developed Allied Joint Logistics Doctrine encompassing a principle of collective responsibility between member nations and Allied authorities, although specific national requirements, especially in ammunition resupply and the maintenance and repair of weapon systems, still limit the effectiveness of multinational logistics. The doctrine includes the establishment of a *Multinational Logistic Commander* (MNLC) to plan, co-ordinate and control all maritime logistic shore support and a Multinational Joint Logistics Centre (MJLC) to co-ordinate theatre wide logistic support for all components. Interoperability within an alliance is a prerequisite if one nation's logistic resources are to support another's, and considerable work in NATO's standardisation agencies is devoted to this end. Standardisation of fuel grades, replenishment rigs and connections allow for regular transfer of fuel between NATO nations and, indeed, between other nations that have adopted NATO standards. Medical support, supply of provisions and general stores, and non-specialist transport can generally be treated as common resources.

Logistic Principles

The principles of joint logistics are foresight, economy, flexibility, simplicity and co-operation. The need for foresight in logistic planning has been discussed earlier in this chapter, as has the requirement for co-operation between Services, nations and commands, particularly where control of logistics is not unified. Economy, flexibility and simplicity deserve special mention.

Economy

Logistics resources will usually be in short supply and sufficiency should be the objective of the logistician. It is possible to overplan as well as to underplan logistic requirements. Over-planning can consume resources that could be devoted to combat forces. Furthermore, an over-large logistic organization may require additional logistics staff who, in turn, will need logistic support, and the whole may draw forces for protection away from the main effort.

Flexibility

A logistic plan must be capable of responding to the inevitable changes in any operational plan. Equally, the logistic system that executes the plan must be capable of adapting to rapid changes of requirement. A large logistics organization geared to supporting a major campaign can acquire a momentum of its own and generate wasteful stockpiles of *materiel*, if it is not sensitive to change. It may also be necessary for an operational commander to take a calculated risk over logistic sufficiency, in particular where there are opportunities to exploit success or to maintain tempo. For example, he may allow the fuel and ammunition levels of a *naval force* that is exploiting success to fall below prudent norms in the expectation that consolidation forces will arrive. A flexible logistic system will minimise differences between operational and logistic tempo and therefore the attendant risk. It is relevant that a major reason for the planning of *operational pauses* in a campaign is to allow the consolidation of logistics and to avoid reaching *culmination* before success is achieved.

Simplicity

Any unnecessarily complicated aspect of operational planning will be prone to disruption. Logistic planning is in large part carried out by experts and can appear intractable to non-experts charged with assessment and execution. The principal non-expert may be the operational commander. A comprehensive, but simple, plan that accords with the direction given by the operational commander is more likely to gain approval and be correctly interpreted and executed.

Roulement

Consideration must be given at an early stage in strategic and operational planning to relieving maritime forces and personnel likely to be in an operational theatre for an extended period. Although ships, given sufficient logistic support, can remain on station almost indefinitely, the efficiency of personnel can be expected to decline during deployment. Furthermore, some aspects of maintenance may suffer if the tempo of operations is high. The rotation of ships and personnel on station to maintain a high state of *readiness* is known as *roulement* and is an important feature of the maritime component of a campaign plan.

Shore Support

Shore support, whether at home or abroad, provides the starting point for any maritime logistic chain. The home base will provide the main supply depots and dockyard facilities. Most supplies and repairs are obtained from the private sector under contract. Procurement of *materiel* must be carefully monitored both to ensure that adequate stocks of equipment and stores are available for transfer to the fleet and to avoid wasting resources in the production and retention of unnecessarily large stocks. When HNS is available, it may supplement afloat support by providing useful forward airheads and seaports for logistic and personnel movements to and from the theatre of operations, and forward operating bases for replenishment, maintenance and repair. HNS may help to economise on the need for logistics, but such support is not an essential feature of purely maritime operations. Indeed, a forward operating base may be no more than a sheltered anchorage for a support or repair ship. However, once troops are ashore, the significance and dimensions of the organization to co-ordinate and take advantage of HNS can increase substantially. HNS arrangements are often pre-planned in outline and formalised by inter-governmental Memoranda of Understanding (MOU). They are, nevertheless, not guaranteed to remain in force as the situation changes. Lack of HNS may cause the emphasis of an operation to remain with maritime logistics support.

Sustained Reach

No maritime force is complete without support vessels to provide fuel and other essential stores. An integral part of the Fleet, the Royal Navy's logistic shipping is organized as the *Royal Fleet Auxiliary* (RFA), manned by personnel employed under Merchant Navy articles, and whose officers provide afloat support expertise on Command staffs. Replenishment at Sea (RAS) from auxiliary ships enables naval forces to extend their reach world wide without the need to enter port. The RFA, supplemented where necessary by chartered vessels, gives British maritime forces a unique capability to carry out sustained operations at considerable distances from their home base, and the UK continues to maintain considerable investment in these ships; the effort is enhanced by in-theatre consolidation and the provision of air based supply. The mechanism for obtaining shipping from the commercial sector is well established and, in crisis, early identification of the need for chartered shipping is important if forces containing such vessels are to be formed in a timely fashion.

MV MAGDALENA GREEN, chartered in support of operations in the Arabian Gulf, with RFA FORT VICTORIA in the background

The Maritime Operational Logistics Pipeline

The sustained reach of maritime forces and the reach that they in turn provide to other forces are key components of maritime power. However, military and RFA support shipping form only a part of the maritime logistic system. Figure 5.1 shows the extent of the Operational Logistics Pipeline from the UK bases to the furthest forward fighting unit. The Pipeline may include an *Advanced Logistic Support Site* (ALSS) and, potentially, several *Forward Logistics Sites* (FLS) within the operational theatre. The establishment and maintenance of these sites, together with the provision of transport between them, will, in most cases, be a joint and frequently multinational requirement. The locations of the ALSS and FLS would be chosen to provide optimal support to the campaign and may need to move if the situation changes.

The pipeline must handle the movement of *materiel* and people into, within and from the operational area. Personnel may include casualties, refugees, displaced persons and prisoners of war. Segments of the pipeline may consist of air, land or sea transport, which could be supporting all three Services as well as multinational requirements. Priorities across commodities, services and nations will need to be established to cater for constraints on transport capacity.

5/1. El Alamein.

"Rommel greatly underestimated the importance of Naval co-operation during this campaign.....I was not in favour of the Alamein offensive because of the impossibility of maintaining the lines of supply."

(Vice Admiral Weichold, German Commander-in-Chief Mediterranean)

Supplying Montgomery

Montgomery's strategy at Alamein was entirely dependent on the safe delivery of supplies and reinforcements drawn from across the globe. The principal supply route ran from Britain and the United States, around the Cape of Good Hope and up through the Red Sea, a distance of 14,000 miles. During the five months leading up to the Alamein offensive 8th Army was massively reinforced and re-equipped via this route, with over 97% of cargoes and more than 99% of troops arriving without loss.

Concluding comments

The accurate preparation, sequencing and positioning of logistics in peacetime, and the seamless understanding between logisticians and warfare specialists at each level of command, are fundamental to the success of operations throughout the spectrum of likely tasks. Modern *joint* operations will only retain their effect when complemented by flexible, mission focused logistics drawing together single-Service, joint and civilian elements.

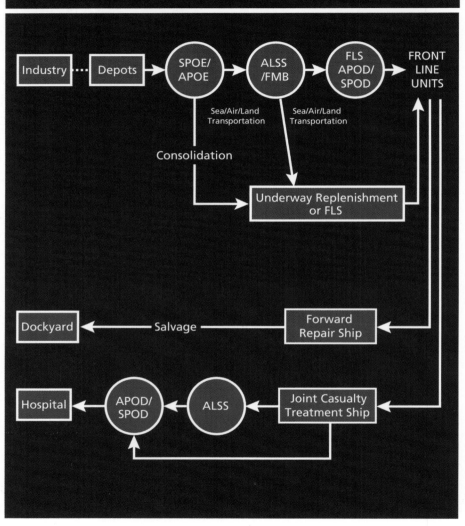

Fig 5.1

The Royal Fleet Auxiliary FORT GEORGE

(Left to Right) The Commanding Officers of HMS ARK ROYAL and HMS OCEAN and the Commander of the Amphibious Task Group are briefed by the Commanding Officer of 40 Commando Royal Marines on the progress of 3 Commando Brigade's operations in Southern Iraq, April 2003

Maritime Command and Control

Command is the authority granted to an individual to direct, co-ordinate and control military forces. *Control* is the actual process through which the commander organizes, directs and co-ordinates the activities of forces allocated to him. Command and control, supported by a system of people, information, and technology, enable the maritime force commander to apply military force effectively. Command and control governs all areas of maritime operations and new technology is broadening its scope and increasing its complexity. Nevertheless, its foundations remain constant: professional competence born of a high level of training and a thorough understanding of relevant doctrine, and an effective means of communicating information and directions through the operational chain of command.

6/1. The Nelson Touch

Nelson is well known for simple instructions, such as his use of the signal "close action" – usually interpreted as "engage the enemy more closely" – and his sentence in his memorandum before Trafalgar that "No captain can do very wrong if he places his ship alongside that of the enemy". It is easy to be misled by the apparent simplicity of these instructions. In reality they reflected a confidence that his subordinates were completely familiar with contemporary naval doctrine, amended sometimes by Nelson himself. Nelson, who was a great believer in delegation, expected his subordinates to use their intelligence, seamanship and understanding of his intentions to do much better in outmanoeuvring their opponents. Importantly he devoted much time and effort discussing with his captains how he pictured forthcoming battles. As a result, they were able to take independent action in support of Nelson's objectives, without further reference to him. Of course, if all else failed, they knew that there was a minimum that he expected of them and, if they had to resort to it, knew that they would not be judged "very wrong" in so doing.

NELSON explains his plan of attack on the eve of the Battle of Trafalgar

To be fully effective, commanders need to have a thorough understanding of the nature and conduct of military operations, the leadership attributes required, and the command and control processes through which they will direct operations. The latter requires an appreciation of the vulnerabilities and weaknesses in one's own command and control process and systems, as well as insight into the nature of an opponent's command and control.

The maritime command and control system encompasses all personnel, systems and resources throughout the maritime force, that support the flow and processing of information. It includes the functions of: intelligence, surveillance, target acquisition and reconnaissance (ISTAR); information processing; decision-making and display; communications; electronic warfare; cryptology; and information operations.

Higher Command of the Armed Forces

The command of each of the UK's fighting Services is vested in the Sovereign. The Secretary of State for Defence is appointed by the Crown after nomination by the Prime Minister and is accountable to Parliament. He is responsible for the defence of the Realm, is supported by the Defence Council and is advised by the Chief of the Defence Staff (CDS). The Service Chiefs of Staff are members of the Defence Council and are individually responsible for the fighting effectiveness, management, overall efficiency and morale of their respective Services. They report to the Secretary of State through CDS, but retain the right of direct access to the Secretary of State and the Prime Minister.

Operational and Tactical Organization

For operations mounted by the UK alone, overall command is exercised by CDS. *Campaigns* and operations are likely to be joint. CDS will appoint a *Joint Commander* (normally the Chief of Joint Operations, (CJO)) who will exercise Operational Command (OPCOM), from the Permanent Joint Headquarters (PJHQ), over the forces assigned to him. In theatre, a *Joint Task Force Commander* (JTFC) will be nominated, and he will exercise *Operational Control* (OPCON) through individual component commanders. Component commanders straddle the dividing line between the operational and tactical levels. They have a planning function within the JTFHQ that they discharge at the operational level with input to the joint campaign plan. In executing their component of the plan, they command at the tactical level.

This organization provides the essential unity of command required at the operational level. It also ensures that authority and responsibility for an operation are clearly defined, and appropriate expertise and experience is in place to provide effective command and control of assigned forces. This structure requires a trained and experienced joint staff drawn from the participating Services. This in turn necessitates regular exercises in joint command and control. Levels of command are illustrated in Figure 6.1.

Maritime forces are organized *functionally* for operations into a *task organization* consisting of a maximum of four levels: *task forces*, *task groups*, *task units* and *task elements* (see Figure 6.2). The use of these levels is flexible and they bear no direct relationship to levels of command or levels of planning.

6/2. Joint Task Force Commander and Component Commander Location

A JTFC will exercise command from the place he feels he can best influence events. Usually this will be in the vicinity of the region that operations will take place, namely in the Joint Operations Area (JOA). Factors considered when choosing the location of the JTFHQ include: the nature of the operation; the need to influence regional political leadership; the ability to reach-back to higher HQs; the protection of his HQ; the need for routine contact with locally based international and military agencies including non-governmental organizations (NGOs) and international organizations (IOs); and local infrastructure and facilities.

The JTFC may establish the JTFHQ on a suitably equipped warship for those occasions when the operation is essentially maritime or amphibious in nature, or when the infrastructure ashore is unsuitable. The JTFHQ may also be established afloat as a preliminary measure in advance of other elements of the JTF arriving and establishing a secure environment ashore.

Component Commanders (CCs) must strike the balance between the advantages of face-to-face contact with the JTFC and the need to exercise their tactical responsibilities, which may be somewhat detached from him. For the Air and SF components, the balance generally lies in favour of collocation with the JTFC. For the Maritime, Land and Logistics components, this is not so clear-cut; the judgement will depend entirely upon the circumstances. CIS enablers such as Video Teleconferences (VTC) have, to some extent, mitigated the disadvantages of separation but these do not replace the quality of understanding that arises through personal contact.

Communications

The exercise of effective command requires communications and the promulgation of sound doctrine. Modern communications present commanders with two challenges. The first of these is a consequence of effective communications and is the possibility of superior levels of command 'micro-managing' operations at lower levels. This is a tendency that is increasing, with tactical decisions having, at times, strategic effect and with even the political leadership being tempted to interfere in tactical decision-making. The second challenge comes as a consequence of too heavy a reliance on communications followed by subordinate levels lacking the necessary initiative when communications links are severed.

Micro-management undermines subordinate commanders' ability to seize the initiative when the opportunities arise. The ability to seize the initiative is fundamental to the application of a manoeuvrist approach to operations. However, the desire of superior commanders to apply a manoeuvrist approach, in which a range of disparate activities require co-ordination if effective systemic disruption is to be achieved, may lead them towards micro-management of forces under their command. The main message here is that commanders, in applying a manoeuvrist approach, should beware of an instinctive tendency to interfere, only doing so when not to do so would undermine the overall objective; balance, as ever, is the key.

Continuous superior interference in subordinate level decision-making will also have the effect of rendering subordinate commanders inexperienced in dealing with the challenges that arise when communications links are severed. The assumption that communications will be effective may also lead to complacency as far as doctrine is concerned. If communications were invariably effective, allowing superior commanders to micro-manage effectively, there would be no necessity for developing robust doctrine for the guidance of subordinate commanders in a position to exercise initiative. In brief, the danger is that the promise of communications may foster a neglect of doctrine.

The only response to these two opposing but connected challenges is to achieve a responsible degree of balance in command and control and for superior levels of command not to interfere routinely in the conduct of operations at subordinate levels. The balance should be somewhere between the contrasting approaches of Beatty and Jellicoe, allowing initiative to be taken by subordinates but with a responsible superior hand able to convey guidance when appropriate. Given the immediate impact that tactical decisions can have on strategic outcomes, achieving the right balance will not always be easy, but that will never be an excuse for over-bearing command and control.

Mission Command

A sound philosophy of command has three enduring tenets: timely decision-making; understanding a superior commander's intention; and a clear responsibility on the part of subordinates to fulfil the superior's intention. This requires a style of command that promotes decentralised command, freedom and speed of action, and initiative. The overall concept of *Mission Command*, one of the essential elements of the British Approach to Military Operations highlighted in **British Defence Doctrine**, will be applied in joint operations, including its employment within maritime forces. Mission command has the following key elements:

- A commander gives his orders in a manner that ensures his subordinates understand his intentions, their own missions, and the context of those missions;

- Subordinates are told what effect they are to achieve and the reason why it needs to be achieved;

- Subordinates are allocated sufficient resources to carry out their missions;

- A commander uses a minimum of control in order not to limit unnecessarily the freedom of action of his subordinates;

- Subordinates decide within their delegated freedom of action how best to achieve their missions.

6/3. Clarity of Orders. Harwood at the River Plate

Force G, under Commodore Harwood, engaged the German pocket Battleship *Graf Spee* on 13 Dec 1939 off the River Plate. His signalled plans prior to the battle were brief but made his intentions absolutely clear without stifling initiative:

"My policy with three cruisers versus one pocket battleship. Attack at once by day or night. By day act as two units. First Division (AJAX and ACHILLES) and EXETER diverge to permit flank marking. First Division will concentrate gunfire. By night ships will normally remain in company in open order."

Further orders were unnecessary.

Too great an emphasis on delegation in applying the principle of Mission Command could jeopardise manoeuvrist operations just as surely as will too great an emphasis on micro-management. Decentralised command and the application of too much initiative by subordinates will make co-ordination of effective manoeuvre difficult. Again, it is stressed that the key to success is achieving the right balance between control by superiors and subordinate freedom. An experienced and skilled commander will be one who recognises this command and control dilemma and achieves the necessary balance in his style of command that allows him adequate control while endowing his subordinates with sufficient freedom to use initiative. One should never underestimate the difficulties of achieving this balance; it is a fundamentally important skill for commanders to develop and will require a good deal of serious thought to get right.

Effective communication links that are secure and invulnerable to suppression, manipulation or degradation, are an essential means of effecting proper command and control. However, in some situations, certain ships may not be fitted with the necessary communications to meet the wider command and control needs of the force. This needs to be taken into consideration during the planning process and allowed for when assessing the degree of control and tempo possible within an operation.

No commander should be, or will wish to be, wholly dependent on umbilical communications links with higher commands ashore or afloat. It is essential, therefore, that commanders and their staffs have a clear understanding of the higher commanders' intentions so that they can take appropriate action in the absence of timely direction. This requirement reinforces the importance of decentralised execution. At the operational level, such understanding should include appreciation of national policy and the diplomatic and political environment in which operations are being conducted. As a general rule a commander and his staff should understand their immediate superior's detailed intentions, and the broad intentions of the commander two levels above him.

The command and control systems of a command ship together with the intelligence systems and communications connectivity supporting them are elaborate and comprehensive. They allow joint operational control to be exercised over a large theatre of operations from a platform that is self sufficient, mobile and flexible. However, the implications of the loss of such a capable unit needs to be addressed and contingencies arranged.

6/4. Command and Control and Doctrine in the Pacific

"The sum total of the American naval forces in the Philippine Sea area constituted the greatest assembly of naval might the world has ever seen or may ever see again - far greater than the strength that the Japanese Navy could muster in that area. And yet, mark you, there was no effective single command agency which could weld all our naval forces into a single fleet under single command; Admiral Nimitz did not have that authority, nor did General MacArthur; and no higher echelon could or would step into the breach. The details of the second battle of the Philippine Sea (usually referred to as the Battle of Leyte Gulf) will keep students occupied for decades to come. Obviously there were many things done which could have been done differently in the light of hindsight; obviously there were things left undone which could have been undertaken to great advantage. But to me, in retrospect, the vital and important thing is that, although not unified under a single authoritative command, all of those separated commanders were thinking in sufficiently like terms to construct a mosaic of tactical victories fitting together into a greater mural of strategic victory which effectively terminated Japanese sea power. There were gaps in communications and gaps in mutual understandings among the commanders, but the great principles of sea power had been inculcated in all of those commanders and were literally second nature to them, so that even without authoritative co-ordinated command, they instinctively moved in directions which were basically sound."

Vice Admiral Robert B Carney US Navy, *US Naval War College Review*, October 1948.

Rules of Engagement

Rules of Engagement (ROE) are issued to provide political direction, authorisation, guidance and instruction to commanders. ROE are the primary means of defining political limits to the use of military force and take the form of general policy indicators and directives, prohibitions and permissions. They can be instruments of *escalation*, *de-escalation* and the maintenance of the status quo. They are formulated and sought by military staffs at the operational and tactical levels and authorised at the political (grand-strategic) level following military and legal advice at the military-strategic level. ROE must be under constant review in order to ensure that they reflect changing military and political circumstances. Dormant ROE may be prepared and authorised for immediate use if certain contingencies arise. It is a military-strategic level function of the very greatest importance to ensure that ROE are crafted to allow effective use of military force, while providing proper protection. The operational commander in turn must ensure that he fully understands these rules, promulgates them throughout his force and is willing to make a robust case for alterations when circumstances change. It is a major challenge to create, in a few words, a vivid and succinct description of the changing situation, possible outcomes, and precise reasons for seeking new or amended rules. ROE are the basic tool for ensuring coherence between the political and military process, and should fit the mission as well as the capability of a force to ensure survivability. As a consequence, adequate time and training will be needed for ROE at all levels of military planning. ROE are likely to be major planning constraints and may shape significantly courses of action. During multinational operations variations in national ROE may be a principal constraint on the tasking of forces (See Multinational Operations below).

Naval Command, Control, Communications, Computers and Intelligence (C4I) Systems

Naval C4I systems are the information systems, equipment, software, and infrastructure that enable the commander to exercise authority and direction over assigned forces. C4I systems also help the commander to monitor and influence the actions of the maritime force through the chain of command. These systems support the following five basic functions:

- **Collecting** Gathering and formatting data for processing.

- **Processing** Filtering, correlating, fusing and evaluating data to produce a picture required for the commander to take appropriate action.

- **Disseminating** Distributing information for use or further processing, and distributing orders and instructions.

- **Displaying** Presenting information to the user in the most effective and efficient manner.

- **Protecting** Guarding information from an adversary's attempts to exploit, corrupt, or destroy it.

C4I systems encompass the hardware structure supporting the command and control process. Although highly automated, this structure should be designed very much with the 'user' in mind, giving them access to information and helping them make effective use of it. In modern warfare, advanced technology is essential for automating the collection, processing, dissemination, and protection of vast quantities of information. However, technology is not a means of taking the man out of the command and control process; instead it is used to enhance overall performance. Technology automates routine functions that machines can accomplish more efficiently, freeing commanders to focus on the aspects of command and control that require their experience, judgement, and intuition. It must be remembered, however, that while enhancements to C4I systems should upgrade the quality of the commander's information, more information is not always better information. C4I systems should:

- support all aspects of the commander's decision making process, from initial observation and orientation, to ultimate execution and validation.

■ enable maritime forces to integrate their efforts with those of others when appropriate.

■ monitor and exploit all dimensions of the battlespace, using all available sensors.

■ provide a coherent, accurate, and timely picture of the situation, scaled to the needs of the user.

■ allow information flow throughout the force: not just up and down the chain of command, but laterally as well.

■ be designed as part of an architecture that can integrate with other operational systems, software, and databases quickly.

■ support the maritime commander's efforts to exploit or attack the adversary's information systems and disrupt his ability to co-ordinate his forces.

C4I systems are vital for planning, executing, and sustaining a successful naval, joint, or multinational operation. All aspects of naval warfare operations, logistics, planning, and intelligence depend on responsive command and control. Integrating command and control requirements and plans with those for operations, logistics, and intelligence is essential. Experience has repeatedly demonstrated that command and control support staff should be brought in at the beginning of the operational planning process, and they must liaise continuously with those who will execute the operation.

Characteristics of Naval C4I Systems
Depending on the operational situation, maritime commanders may attach greater importance to some areas at the expense of others. Consequently, the order in which the characteristics of naval C4I systems are listed below is not intended to indicate their relative importance.

The Principal Warfare Officer on watch in the Operations Room of HMS OCEAN monitors the maritime picture on the Command Support System (CSS) and communications on the Coalition Wide Area Network (COWAN) during operations in the Arabian Gulf

Reliability Systems must be available when needed and perform as intended with low failure rates and few errors. Reliability is also assisted by: standardisation in equipment, procedures and training; the provision of appropriate levels of redundancy; availability of effective logistics support; and protection against computer virus attack, electromagnetic jamming, deception and manipulation. Systems should perform reliably, even in the most austere and demanding conditions.

Security Security, commensurate with the operator's requirements and the perceived threat from interception and exploitation, is essential. This may be achieved by employing appropriate security protection, including cryptographic systems, using transmission security techniques and educating and training personnel in security procedures. These measures must be kept under continuous review in order to counter any evolving threat.

Timeliness Information must be processed and disseminated between and within commands rapidly enough to maintain a high tempo of operations and ensure that the decision-making process remains faster than that of any opponent.

Flexibility Systems must be capable of being reconfigured quickly so that they can respond to any rapidly changing environment. This can be enhanced by intelligent system design and the sensible use of a diverse mix of fixed, mobile and transportable facilities, owned by both military and commercial organizations.

Interoperability In order to ensure that information can be exchanged amongst all commanders and forces involved in an operation, maritime C4I systems should be able to operate in joint and multi-national environments, integrating with other government departments and civilian organizations in theatre. Increasingly, the development of a network-enabled capability will be key in ensuring this.

Survivability Survivability can be attained by dispersal and protection of key nodes, physical and electromagnetic hardening, and redundancy of communications paths and information processing nodes.

Information Operations

Effective command and control are essential to success in modern operations. Information systems and command and control facilities must therefore be protected and maintained, since the whole system can be degraded through the loss or malfunctioning of one, or a small number of, components. Consequently, operations conducted against an opponent's command and control infrastructure and decision-making process play a key part in modern *conflict*. Information Operations embraces the components of the former Command and Control Warfare (C2W) (*electronic warfare*, physical destruction, *operational deception*, *psychological operations* and *operational security*) and Computer Network

Operations, co-ordinated with Media Operations and CIMIC. Amongst its objectives is the gaining of information superiority by exploiting, influencing, degrading confusing or destroying the enemy's command and control capabilities, while protecting friendly systems against such actions. Good intelligence and co-ordination between various elements in joint and combined forces are essential to its success.

Space

Modern command and control makes extensive use of space systems for communications and navigational accuracy; they are also a medium for critical, strategic and operational surveillance assets. The United States is a principal contributor of space systems to Alliance and coalition operations. Space is one of the *warfare environments*, along with the sea, the air, the land, the information environment and the electromagnetic spectrum. It can be an important enabler, which may not only be exploited by a sophisticated opponent but also by an increasing number of nations and interests serving, in part, proxy and commercial sources.

Multinational and Coalition Maritime Operations

In multinational operations there will be an additional dimension to the command and control organization. Multinational operations are conducted by *integrated multinational forces* and, by their nature, are complex. They involve forces with different national equipment and *doctrine*, often with specific political constraints on their employment. Close liaison between the various governments and their own individual services is required to ensure the achievement of common objectives. When national forces are assigned to a NATO operation, OPCOM and OPCON will normally be exercised by the Supreme Allied Commander Operations at the strategic level. The NATO chain of command has traditionally passed from the Strategic Commander (SC) through a Regional Commander (RC) to the operational formations. Under the *Combined Joint Task Force* (CJTF) Concept, a CJTF Commander may be appointed under SC or RC command. He will normally have OPCON of all the different participating national units. The CJTF Concept can also be used for purely European operations under EU command, and for operations in which other nations participate alongside NATO or EU forces.

6/5. Multinational Operations

The most likely scenario for military action by UK forces at the medium and large scale of operations will be as part of a coalition, perhaps under NATO or EU leadership, but increasingly US-led. Implicit in this statement is the recognition that the UK will provide significant, capable and self-sustaining contingents to the multinational components. UK will also assign a senior National Contingent Commander (NCC) to the Multinational JTFHQ. While a NCC can still be regarded as a fighting commander, this is not in the same sense as the JTFC. Although he is a key decision-maker and plays a pivotal role alongside the JTFC in building the coalition, he does not share the same command responsibility or authority in the multinational force as the JTFC. However, he must have the same level of understanding as the JTFC in order to provide effective advice, and will be required to make rapid and authoritative binding decisions on behalf of the UK. The NCC 'directs' the employment of UK forces in the execution of allocated tasks and will require OPCOM in order to achieve this.

The task organization inherent in the Maritime Component, and widespread adherence to standardised maritime tactical procedures amongst Allied navies, permits integration of multinational naval and amphibious forces down to unit level. Standing naval forces, such as NATO's Standing Naval Force Atlantic (STANAVFORLANT) may provide the nucleus of a larger multinational Naval Expanded Task Force (NETF). Other bilateral arrangements, such as the UK/Netherlands Amphibious Force (UKNLAF), provide multinational maritime forces in being.

Multinational Co-operation

Multinational military co-operation offers nations and coalitions both political and military advantages in the pursuit of their interests. National contributions must be judged by the full range of benefits they bring to a coalition, not solely by the capability of military forces provided. These operations also present a number of challenges that must be resolved if they are to be effective. These include different national security policies,

**HMS ILLUSTRIOUS and USS JOHN STENNIS in the Arabian Sea
with their air defence escorts**

force structures, and force capabilities, as well as a wide range of technological, equipment and procedural interoperability issues. To overcome these challenges needs considerable effort, focused particularly on those nations likely to be major partners in potential operations. Bodies such as the Multinational Interoperability Council (MIC), whose members comprise likely framework nations (UK, US, Australia, Canada, Germany and France), have been established for this purpose. Nations can prepare for multinational operations through political interaction, exercises and war games, personnel exchanges, port visits, cultural, legal and language training, and equipment standardisation programmes with potential partners. This preparation serves routine peacetime political and military purposes and provides a framework within which a multinational force could operate during a crisis or war.

Principles for Multinational Operations

Multinational operations must be directed toward a well understood and agreed-upon *objective*, and all partners must strive for unity of effort in its achievement. Adherence to these principles is vital for success.

Command and Control Organization

Organization plays a crucial role in the conduct of multinational maritime operations. It determines how the constituents of a *multinational maritime force* will interact with each other and with other non-maritime forces involved. Command and control terminology must be agreed and understood by the participants before a command structure is developed to meet the needs, political realities, constraints, and objectives of the participating nations. Command structures may range from highly to loosely centralised. In highly centralised command structures, the degree of command and control may approach that existing in individual nations. In looser command structures, the command relationship is more accurately described in terms of co-operation and co-ordination. There are three basic organizational structures, which may be used in combination:

- **Parallel Command** Forces operate under national command in the co-operative pursuit of coalition objectives.

- **Framework Nation Command** One partner is designated the overall commander and the other participants follow the concepts and direction of the framework nation, which may rotate among the partners.

- **Integrated Command** A single commander, with a staff composed of representatives from all member nations, commands the operation.

Key Factors in Multinational Operations

Multinational operations will require maritime commanders to consider a wide range of factors that may have a decisive impact on the cohesion and effectiveness of the force. The factors listed below are not placed in any particular order, although the need for shared doctrine must be considered of prime significance, as also must be awareness of differences of meaning or interpretation in ROE.

Commanders In all but the parallel structure, a Multinational Maritime Force Commander may be appointed. His authority is determined by the participating nations, and is often substantially limited. In any event he will have to establish unity of effort through consensus building and extensive liaison with the National Maritime Component Commanders designated by each participating nation. Achieving and maintaining a sufficient degree of interoperability will be a primary objective of the multinational command regardless of the structure chosen.

Shared Doctrine and Publications Shared doctrine and publications are fundamental to any successful multinational maritime operation. NATO has developed standardisation agreements and a body of doctrine publications over many years that ensure interoperability between Allied forces and between the components of a joint force. More recently, NATO has developed a set of multinational doctrine publications for use by Partnership for Peace (PfP) nations to allow them to participate in a range of operations alongside Allied forces. However, it may be necessary for contributing nations in a coalition operation to adopt the doctrine of the lead nation and adapt accordingly, although the enduring attributes of maritime forces and many years of co-operation between navies around the world means that any doctrinal differences in the maritime environment are likely to be small.

Language In the earliest stages of a multinational operation, agreement on a common language and terminology to co-ordinate coalition activity must be reached.

Liaison Officers Liaison officers improve the flow of information and act as bridges between cultures, languages, doctrine, and procedures. They are essential to the effective conduct of multinational operations, and the selection of suitably experienced officers, who have the requisite decision-making authority and the confidence of the commander for whom they are working, is critical.

Information Exchange   A multinational maritime force must have common situational awareness based on the effective exchange of intelligence and tactical data. This must include the location, disposition and movement of friendly, neutral and opposing forces, supplemented by information on electromagnetic emitters and the environment. In order to facilitate this exchange of information, communications planners must consider the need for equipment interoperability, common protocols and procedures, and the necessary levels of security required to protect information without hindering operations.

Force Co-ordination   Weapons safety, *Combat Identification (Combat ID)*, collision avoidance and air and water space management procedures are essential for combat effectiveness, to prevent mutual interference between ships, aircraft, and submarines, and to avoid friendly fire incidents. Multinational air operations are likely to require a particularly high level of co-ordination and the appointment of an overall commander for air operations may be necessary.

Rules of Engagement   ROE differences within a force may reduce operational effectiveness. Common or harmonised ROE should be sought as early as possible. All partners must, as a minimum, understand how each will apply force in support of the mission or in self-defence. This will avoid units being placed in situations in which differences in their ROE prevent them conducting properly co-ordinated responses.

Safety Issues The ability to conduct a variety of seamanship evolutions, operate and support helicopters, and conduct co-ordinated search and rescue operations are all important to the safe conduct of a multinational maritime operation.

Planning   Planning for multinational maritime operations focuses on developing and maintaining the ability of the elements composing the force to work together toward the objective. It commences with a directive from the authorizing organization detailing the mission, resources, and general command and control arrangements. The commander and his staff then analyse the mission and prepare an estimate of the situation that will address all aspects of the operation, including mission, situation analysis, and friendly and opposing courses of action. A best course of action is then selected and expressed in the commander's concept of operations that describes how and why he intends to employ his forces to achieve the desired end state. Once the concept of operations has been produced, the staff will develop the operation order, which gives detailed directives and guidance on all aspects of the operation.

Logistics A clear logistics plan will be required to support the operations plan. It must resolve national differences in logistical doctrine and capabilities, establish the responsibilities of each nation and the multinational maritime force commander, and detail a logistics organization.

Concluding Operations The success or failure of any multinational operation will largely be determined by the decisions made at the very beginning of the planning process. The objectives and desired end-state must be clearly stated and acceptable to all participants. Moreover, the perception of progress toward achievement of the desired end-state is important to prevent premature dissolution of the coalition. Establishing realistic measures of effectiveness will help maintain focus on the mission, and prevent mission creep as the situation evolves. Nations will decide individually when their participation in a multinational operation should end, and some may wish to terminate their participation earlier than others. Ideally, nations should inform partners of their intentions to end their participation as far in advance as possible. Before withdrawing, they should clean up the area of operations, meet all financial obligations, and provide a comprehensive turn over to follow-on forces or civil authorities. Finally, the lessons learned from the operation should be recorded and published for future reference and the relationships formed in the conduct of the operation should be maintained to ease future co-operation.

6/6. Failures of Command and Control at Antwerp

The problems which failures of command and control can bring are well illustrated by the history of British maritime operations against Antwerp. In 1809, in the greatest amphibious operation carried out by Britain to that date, almost 40,000 troops were sent primarily to capture the city and destroy the large French fleet and dockyard and, secondly, to divert Napoleon from his attack on Austria. The naval commander, Sir Richard Strachan, did not have the intelligence or doctrinal grasp to operate effectively with the lethargic land force commander Lord Chatham. This resulted in the occupation and eventual evacuation of the island of Walcheren at the mouth of the Scheldt with little else to show for the loss of over 4,000 men, all but 106 to illness. 135 years later, in 1944, ineffective operational direction saw the capture of the city of Antwerp totally neutralised by German retention of the Scheldt estuary. Only after a properly carried out maritime operation under effective joint command was Walcheren captured and access to a port, vital to the logistics of the Allied armies, obtained.

Concluding comments

If the command and control arrangements, including communications and doctrine, are inadequate or lacking in some way, an operation may be undermined and an entire mission placed in jeopardy. While an operation will never succeed by effective command and control alone, it will undoubtedly fail if the command and control arrangements break down completely. Command and control arrangements are, therefore, a very high priority when planning an operation.

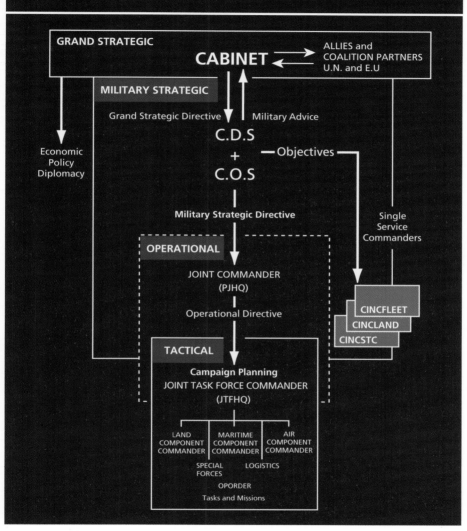

NATIONAL LEVELS OF COMMAND

GRAND STRATEGIC

CABINET ⇄ ALLIES and COALITION PARTNERS U.N. and E.U

MILITARY STRATEGIC

Grand Strategic Directive ↓ ↑ Military Advice

Economic Policy Diplomacy

C.D.S
+
C.O.S

— Objectives —

Single Service Commanders

Military Strategic Directive

OPERATIONAL

JOINT COMMANDER (PJHQ)

CINCFLEET
CINCLAND
CINCSTC

Operational Directive

TACTICAL

Campaign Planning
JOINT TASK FORCE COMMANDER
(JTFHQ)

LAND COMPONENT COMMANDER	MARITIME COMPONENT COMMANDER	AIR COMPONENT COMMANDER

SPECIAL FORCES   LOGISTICS

OPORDER

Tasks and Missions

Fig 6.1

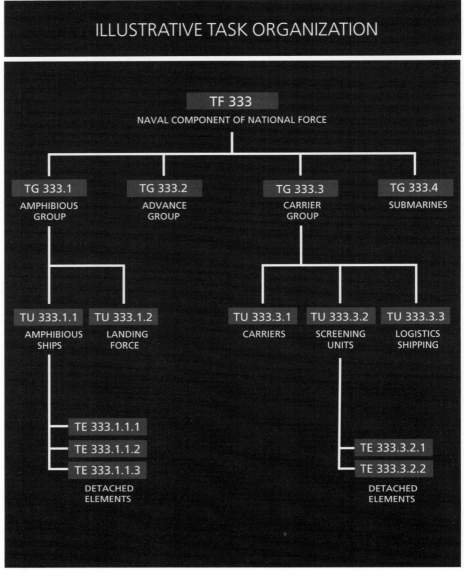

Fig 6.2

The Type 22 Batch III frigate **HMS CORNWALL** leads a multinational Task Group off the coast of Hawaii

Royal Marines embark in Sea King helicopters at night
on board HMS ARK ROYAL

Planning and Conducting a Campaign or Operation

7

The emphasis in this chapter is on the operational level of military planning and the conduct of maritime operations. As such, it deals with the sorts of issues with which the *Maritime Component Commander* (MCC) will be concerned and provides a link to operational and tactical level doctrinal publications, in particular **The Fighting Instructions**. The MCC straddles the divide between the operational and tactical levels, fulfilling a planning function on the *Joint Task Force Commander's* (JTFC) command team and commanding the activities of the maritime component of the force. In the former function he is working at the operational level and in the latter at the tactical. This chapter will concentrate on operational level planning considerations. However, it is not intended to provide detailed guidance on operational planning, which can be found in **JWP 5-00 Joint Operations Planning**, or to describe in detail planning tools such as the Joint Task Force Commander's Estimate. Rather, it sets the principles discussed in earlier chapters in a practical context. The relative importance of these will vary during the different stages of a campaign.

The Military-Strategic Aim

The policy objectives of military action will be decided at the *strategic* level by the Cabinet. The strategic *mission*, desired *end-states* and constraints for a particular campaign will be formed in the Ministry of Defence and issued in the form of a strategic directive from the Chief of the Defence

Staff (CDS). In the UK command system, the recipient and implementer of the strategic directive is the *Joint Commander*. For a NATO campaign the *grand-strategic* level is the North Atlantic Council (NAC) supported by the International Staff. The military-strategic level is the Military Committee supported by the International Military Staff. The Supreme Allied Commander Operations (SACO) is the NATO Commander at the top tier of the operational level.

In the majority of cases, the nominated UK Joint Commander will be the Chief of Joint Operations (CJO) at the *Permanent Joint Headquarters* (PJHQ). Having received his directive from CDS, he will issue his own directive (agreed by the Ministry of Defence) to the JTFC who will normally be supported by a MCC. The maritime, land and air components of a campaign must be integrated fully to execute a single joint *concept of operations* to fulfil the military and strategic aim.

Although maintenance of the aim is a Principle of War, a particular feature of maritime operations is that certain preventative, precautionary or pre-emptive tasks may be carried out when political and military-strategic objectives are unrefined and immature (see, in particular, the discussions about naval diplomacy in Chapter 4). Commanders should also be alert to the fact that political objectives can change during the course of a campaign. Indeed, once actual *hostilities* begin, a train of unpredictable events may occur with bewildering rapidity and may reshape and alter political objectives. Defining the aim and associated objectives are part of an iterative process as the results of specific operations and new intelligence are fed into the decision-making chain.

Conditions for Success and the End-State

In establishing his aim, a commander must consider what constitutes success. Certain types of task, such as many *constabulary* tasks, are a continuous process and there will be no easily measurable conditions for success, except perhaps the integrity of the environment or area to be covered. The same is true for some tasks of *naval diplomacy* such as *presence*, where the effects and success are rarely obvious except in retrospect and in the context of a larger political or military campaign.

However, for most *military* applications of force, success can be defined as meeting certain specific conditions. These conditions are referred to as the desired *end-state*. In classic military operations or in war, there are usually clear *military conditions*, such as control of territory, which can constitute military success. That said, success is more usually defined in terms of the elimination of the enemy's physical means of resistance and/or the collapse of his will. For *coercive* operations, military conditions often cannot be specified, and success is measured by compliance or acquiescence by the target government, power or regime.

In planning the maritime component of the campaign there are several issues the MCC and his staff need to take into account, using the Estimate Process as the basis for planning. There will need to be consideration of which factors will be relevant in the prevailing circumstances. This chapter deals with all these issues, concluding with a description of the phases and stages of the campaign.

Concepts of Operational Art

There are several concepts that are particularly useful when looking at joint operations and will certainly have relevance in any major operation involving maritime and other forces in a *joint* campaign in the *littoral*. Those of particular relevance are discussed below.

Centre of Gravity

The *Centre of Gravity* (CoG) is defined as those characteristics, capabilities or localities from which a nation, an alliance, a military force or other grouping derives its freedom of action, physical strength or will to fight. Examples that are frequently given include: the mass of an enemy army, the enemy's command structure, public opinion and national will, or an alliance or coalition structure. There may be both strategic and operational CoGs. Success at both the strategic and operational levels is achieved through identifying and controlling or destroying the enemy's CoG and protecting one's own. The concept is central to modern interpretations of *manoeuvre warfare*, discussed in Chapter 3.

Decisive Points

While it may be possible to defeat the adversary's Centre of Gravity (CoG) by direct attack, it is more likely that a series of co-ordinated actions will be required. Such actions are described as Decisive Points (DPs). DPs are arranged along various lines of operation leading to the adversary's CoG. A DP is therefore an event or action, the successful outcome of which is a precondition to unlocking the enemy's CoG. They need not necessarily constitute a battle or physical engagement, nor need they have a geographical relevance; they may be the elimination or denial of a capability, or an achievement such as obliging an adversary to engage in formal negotiations. The key is the effect that the actions have on the adversary. The acid test of a DP is that its removal from a campaign plan in the planning phase would prejudice the overall coherence of the plan and, during the execution, failure to achieve a DP would threaten the plan's viability.

The Culminating Point

An operation reaches its culminating point when the current operation can just be maintained but not developed to any greater advantage. To be successful, an operation must achieve its objective before reaching a culminating point. Successful defence may involve luring an attacker beyond his culminating point and then counter-attacking. During *linear operations*, the further an attacker advances, the larger the number of forces he requires to protect his lengthened *lines of communications*, while the defender may be correspondingly closer to his own logistic bases. *Attrition* and combat fatigue may also take their toll and contribute to culmination. Another factor that can bring a force to a culminating point is time.

7/1. Risk of Culmination in the Falklands Campaign

During the Falklands Campaign it was important for British forces to have completed the re-occupation before the combined effects of extended lines of communications, attrition of forces, possible dwindling of national will, cumulative material defects and the onset of winter might have brought about culmination.

The Planning Process

Doctrine does not supplant the need for good planning, but it aids the process of thought and eases the dissemination and understanding of the resulting plan. Furthermore, doctrine, coupled with a clear statement of a commander's intentions, allows subordinate commanders to adapt their missions in response to a changing situation. In developing his concept of operations the commander must analyse the enemy's situation, vulnerabilities, vital and critical interests and likely courses of action. The situation of his own and friendly forces should be examined along similar lines to that of the enemy. Any restrictions imposed upon the use of force, ROE, assumptions made and deductions drawn from the analysis must be noted.

The Commander's Estimate

This analytical process is formalised in the Commander's Estimate, which reviews several courses of action to accomplish a mission, and from which the operational plan can be developed. But such an estimate is only a tool aiding the commander to orchestrate the conduct of his campaign or operation. It is not an end in itself.

The estimate process is central to the formulation and modification of the campaign plan. There are six key stages of an estimate process for every type of operation. These are review of the situation, identification and analysis of the problem, formulation of potential courses of action (COAs), development and validation of COAs, COA evaluation and, finally, the commander's decision and development of the plan. More detailed descriptions of this process and the production of the operation order are contained in *JWP 5-00 Joint Operations Planning*.

Operational Level Factors Important to the Maritime Commander

The commander's concept of operations or 'design for battle' should serve to exploit his strengths to advantage and ensure that he seizes and maintains the initiative. He should always seek to limit enemy activity to reaction to his own actions, thereby ensuring that battles and engagements are fought in the manner, and at the place and time of his choosing. All these areas are pre-eminent in shaping the battlespace for subsequent exploitation. In orchestrating his campaign and designing his battles, the commander must also consider a number of important operational level factors. These are not ends in themselves. Rather, they assist the commander by allowing him to design his contribution to the campaign and then execute his concept of operations. These factors cannot be viewed separately. They are interdependent and produce a synergistic effect.

Command and Control A maritime operation involves the direction and co-ordination of many activities in all *warfare environments* in what may be a hostile or potentially hostile situation. Command and control must be robust, flexible and capable of dealing with a rapidly changing situation. It must permit swift decision making so that opportunities can be exploited as they are provided. Additionally, it must support the principle of centralised direction and decentralised execution, thus allowing and encouraging freedom of action within the overall concept of operations. (Command and Control is discussed in detail in Chapter 6)

Intelligence and Surveillance Success is often heavily dependent on the maintenance of a clear picture of the disposition of forces, known at sea as the *Recognised Maritime Picture* (RMP). Intelligence is an important contributor to this picture, particularly during the early stages of an operation when it may be necessary to seek political clearance for reconnaissance and intelligence gathering activities. Intelligence is not just a matter of information gathering over the duration of a campaign or operation. Strategic intelligence, which is of more long term significance than operational or tactical intelligence, is the product of continuous in-depth analysis of the political, economic, industrial and social characteristics of potential adversaries, as well as the military capabilities of any adversary and the characteristics of their armed forces and military leadership. Strategic intelligence is derived from a variety of sources and is used to inform and educate operational intelligence, which is more military in focus and specific to the theatre of operations. Operational intelligence needs the political, economic and psychological context for interpretation. Tactical intelligence mainly comprises the RMP, and has the narrowest and most detailed military focus. Strategic intelligence, collected over time,

A Royal Air Force Nimrod Maritime Patrol Aircraft

enables a commander to use judgement in planning a campaign in the absence of operational intelligence or tactical information, and allows subordinate commanders to act appropriately even when the RMP is sketchy. A commander should nonetheless seek to obtain as much intelligence and information as possible to inform his decision-making. This will require the optimum employment of his intelligence gathering assets. On the other hand he should not become a slave to intelligence gathering. There will always be gaps in a commander's knowledge, particularly in the matter of enemy intent, and a commander must be prepared to take decisions in situations of incomplete intelligence. Information that is available must be analysed, but commanders must be aware of the tendency, present in everyone, to make information fit any preconceptions.

Tactical Exploitation of the Environment A tactically exploitable knowledge of the environment based on superior technology is essential for both joint and maritime commanders. The *Recognised Environmental Picture* (REP) consists of foundation and dynamic information and is the environmental element of the Joint Operations Picture (JOP). The ability to maintain and exploit the REP, supported where necessary by *Rapid Environmental Assessment* (REA), is an essential part of a maritime force's range of combat capabilities. The REP and REA enhance operational capabilities by providing increased options for positioning forces to advantage, for example in theatre entry operations. Modern weapons systems continue to demand high resolution and accurate environmental information so they can be employed to best effect, particularly in the *littoral*, where there are likely to be different conditions over sea and land that must be taken into consideration.

A Sea Wolf anti-air missile launches from a Type 23 frigate

Protection The protection of maritime forces as an operational function is concerned specifically with preserving the combat power of the force. This can take a variety of forms: layered defence of high value targets; routeing to avoid enemy capabilities; deception to prevent successful enemy attack and, of course, the destruction or neutralisation of the enemy's combat power. The aim is to preserve one's own combat power so that it can be used to advantage in the manner, and at the place and time of one's choosing.

Application of Combat Power The combat power of a maritime force is a combination of its combat systems and its ability to bring firepower to bear effectively. Individual units must be given suitable tasks, and commanders the necessary direction so that they can co-ordinate their efforts to execute the concept of operations. All in the command chain must share a common purpose, and personnel must be imbued with the will to fight. Thus leadership and morale are critical elements of the combat power of a maritime force. A commander should seek to maximise the combat power of his force and then use it to advantage against his enemy. Crucial to success are an accurate assessment of the enemy's strengths and weaknesses, and a correct judgement as to how his own combat power can most effectively be brought to bear against the enemy's critical vulnerability to cause incapacitation or systemic disruption.

Logistic Support The operational function of Logistics is the planning and carrying out of the movement and maintenance of forces. It is both an enabler and a constraint and the logistic tempo should at least match the operational tempo. Good logistic planning is the art of the possible and must be an integral part of operational planning. Logistic considerations pervade all aspects of a campaign from deployment, to employment, and withdrawal. Operational *tempo* cannot be achieved without responsive and reliable logistic resupply. During a campaign, logistic support will usually be limited to some degree. Logistic priority must be given to support the *main effort* yet all elements of the force must be adequately provisioned including those engaged in *holding* or *economy of force operations*. A commander may require to surge his logistic support when the situation demands. Conversely the need to consolidate logistics may be a major factor in planning an operational pause. (Logistics are the subject of Chapter 5)

Shaping the Battlespace There is risk associated with any military combat operation. To minimise this risk and to ensure success, it is necessary to define and shape the situation in and around the operating area in order to prevent enemy action or other circumstances from disrupting the operation. *Shaping* of the battlespace is achieved by a combination of *Information Operations*, control of the electromagnetic spectrum, situational awareness, *interdiction* of enemy forces, and a responsive and agile force capable of acting faster than the enemy. Using these instruments the commander can create the conditions that will allow his operation to succeed and reduce risk and the operation of chance to a minimum. Shaping the *battlespace* can permit deception, distraction, *disruption*, pre-emption and *dislocation*. It allows a force to attack the enemy's cohesion and ability to react, whilst simultaneously carrying out operations at a tempo that the enemy cannot match.

7/2. Gallipoli - How not to Structure a Campaign

Allied maritime operations in the Dardanelles in 1915 are a case study in how not to mount a joint operation. They sought to exploit the potential for strategic leverage by passing a fleet through the Dardanelles that might have intimidated Turkey out of the war. The initial plan, to carry out the operation with ships alone, reflected the lack of a joint approach at the military strategic level. The original campaign plan underestimated the combat power of mutually supporting gun and mine defences, and was finally abandoned because of a failure to neutralise them sufficiently at the tactical level. When amphibious landings on the Gallipoli peninsula eventually took place inadequacies in command, and under-estimation of Turkish land forces, resulted in failure to achieve the ultimate objectives inland. A second wave of landings again established beachheads but was unable to exploit their successful deployment to objectives further inland. The result was stalemate on the ground and the landing forces were eventually withdrawn in a meticulously planned evacuation that was the most successful part of the whole affair. A campaign imaginatively conceived at the grand-strategic level failed because of strategic, operational and tactical errors.

Additional Planning Considerations

What follows is a collection of additional issues to be taken into account when planning an operation. They are not in any particular order of priority, nor is the list exhaustive.

Flexibility   Plans must be flexible to take account of the unexpected, especially in the light of enemy response. No operation ever goes strictly according to plan, which is why the planning process does not stop the moment the operation starts. The estimate process in support of the plan is a continuous one and will require frequent updating as events unfold.

Exploitation   The commander must plan to enhance the strengths of his force and work with the environment to exploit the opposition's weaknesses and his own success. The MCC, in the context of a joint operation, must be aware of his force's strengths and weaknesses, as well as those of the other components, in order that he can keep the JTFC aware of all possible options, remembering that the real value of joint operations is the extent to which each component can be played to its strengths as an effective element of a *manoeuvrist* campaign.

A Favourable Balance of Advantage   The defeat and possibly destruction of an enemy's forces will be a deciding factor during combat. In the process own losses must be considered. Society has become less tolerant of the loss of people in combat, both friendly and enemy, and large losses may not be politically acceptable. Furthermore warships are costly, may take weeks to repair and years to replace, while crews take time to train. Preservation of forces will be a factor in planning and restricting acceptable risk. To minimise risk, a plan should create the conditions for a highly favourable *balance of advantage* at the decisive act. Calculation of exchange ratios should consider both quantitative and qualitative factors.

Termination Termination of a campaign must be considered at the outset of planning. Planning must consider the conditions and the mechanism for withdrawal. Termination of an independent naval operation may be a relatively simple matter compared with that of a fully joint campaign involving extensive *sealift*.

Organization The *task organization* for a campaign must be appropriate to the mission, properly reflect command relationships, and preserve unity of command at the operational and tactical levels (see Chapter 6). Consideration must be given to the scale and experience of staffs and the capacity of headquarters facilities. Multinational operations bring particular problems, and mechanisms must exist for senior officers of national elements to exercise appropriate influence, to consult with political and non-governmental authorities, and to provide advice on national capabilities and political constraints.

Liaison with Civil Authorities and Non-Governmental Organizations
Close liaison and co-operation must be maintained with civil authorities in theatre to arrange use of port facilities, diplomatic clearance for passage through *internal waters* and *territorial seas*, staging of aircraft and overflight, control of aircraft movements for the safety of civil aircraft and activation of Regional *Naval Coordination and Guidance for Shipping*. Non-Governmental Organizations (NGOs) will also be important in many situations, especially those with a humanitarian assistance dimension. Civilian authorities, NGOs and International Organizations (IOs) will be key contributors to the Civil Military Co-operation (CIMIC) process, whereby the relationship between military and civilian sectors is addressed, with the aim of enabling a more coherent military contribution to the achievement of UK and/or international objectives

Media Operations Images of *conflict* can be brought directly into homes through television, the Internet, radio and newspapers as events are unfolding. The media are a powerful influence on public opinion at home, on an opponent and within the international community. A democratic government can only engage in combat while it has public support and the endorsement or acquiescence of the international community. Although it is possible to exercise some control over the news media at sea, this option must be taken advisedly. Unbalanced reporting can be a consequence of strict control afloat and free reporting from ashore. A commander must treat the media as an important element of his contribution to the campaign plan so that he can benefit from opportunities and manage negative aspects. A careful balance must be struck between the needs of security and the advantages of candour. However, in all cases, the commander should establish and disseminate his strategic aim and operational objectives with regard to the media so that it is not to his detriment.

Nuclear, Biological and Chemical (NBC) Defence If the use of chemical, biological, radiological or nuclear weapons is anticipated then the planning process will need to take account of any constraints this may place on maritime forces, especially in the littoral region. The psychological effects on personnel and public perceptions need consideration, as well as the provision and timing of personal protection equipment, clothing and prophylactics. In particular it will determine the balance of concentration and dispersal, as well as the need for a greater stand-off range and remote sensors and weapons.

Preparation Although ships and submarines are stored and manned for combat during peacetime, they are likely to require some additional reprovisioning before they deploy to ensure full stocks are carried. Preparation time will depend on the *readiness* of the unit. Some naval units may require to be brought forward from longer readiness, both to provide front line forces and to service any *roulement*. Preparation includes training, both specialist training for a particular environment or task, and group and force training in company (often termed *Combat Enhancement Training* (CET) and *Force Integration Training* (FIT)). The period of passage into theatre may be used for some *shakedown* and limited *work up* training. However, experience has shown that the collective performance of maritime forces can only be honed effectively by appropriately

Personnel train for operations in an NBC environment

structured staff-covered *operational sea training* or rehearsals in a realistic tactical environment.

Deployment Effective *crisis management* usually demands a rapid response. Force deployment times will vary with the distances involved and speed of transit. Speed and time are not, however, the only considerations in selecting methods of transport. Lead elements of ground forces may be able to deploy into theatre most rapidly by air if suitable airfields and ramp space are available and overflight rights granted, but seaborne transport will usually provide the quickest and invariably the cheapest movement of a substantial force of personnel and equipment.

Sustainability A sustained and tailored logistic train will be needed to support a campaign. Forces using sea lines of communications may need protection. See Chapter 5.

Unity of Effort A clear statement of the mission and commander's intent is essential. It may be necessary to designate some operations within a campaign as *holding operations*. Ideally there should be unity of command over all resources including logistics. Where command and control is complex, especially likely in joint and combined operations, there must be co-operation and co-ordination of activities to this end.

Tempo Tempo is the rate at which events are driven in relation to the enemy and the situation. Forces that can maintain high tempo, with fast decision-making cycles, can seize the initiative and exploit the weaknesses of the enemy. To achieve high tempo and keep the initiative, and to exploit success, a commander must be prepared to devolve decision-making. This can be achieved by *mission orders* that tell a subordinate commander what his task is and its purpose, without dictating how it should be done.

Simultaneity Simultaneity seeks to disrupt the decision making process of the enemy commander by confronting him with a number of problems simultaneously, such as attack or the threat of attack from several directions. He is denied the ability to concentrate on one problem at a time or establish priorities between problems. If simultaneity can be achieved, the enemy's decision making may be delayed or incoherent, allowing the operational commander to seize or maintain the initiative.

Iterative Planning It is rarely possible to plan in great detail beyond the first phase of a campaign because the outcome of that phase will shape subsequent phases. Part of the planning process must be a consideration of the "what ifs" or branches and sequels. Once the plan has been set in motion, the commander must constantly study the unfolding situation, and revise and reorder the plan as necessary.

7/3. The Maritime Component Contribution to a Joint Operation – The Gulf War 1990-91

A good example of the contribution of the maritime component to a joint campaign occurred during the operations against Iraq in 1990-91. The Royal Navy Task Group 321.1, part of Operation GRANBY, formed the maritime component of the overall UK Joint Force contribution to Operations DESERT SHIELD and DESERT STORM. First, the Group was closely integrated into the coalition embargo effort as it worked itself up for the expected hostilities. The maritime element of the campaign plan was in three phases:

1. Progressive sea control operations consisting of the neutralisation of the Iraqi surface fleet and maritime air forces. Sustained sea control, which included RN Type 42 destroyers providing Anti Air Warfare (AAW) protection well up threat at the northern end of the Gulf, was a prerequisite for subsequent phases. Sea control operations continued during phases 2 and 3 below.

2. A maritime contribution to joint air operations against Iraq provided by US carriers and cruise missile equipped surface ships and submarines. In this phase the Type 42 destroyers were an integral part of the US/UK AAW barrier for the coalition maritime forces.

3. A move inshore to the Kuwaiti coast with MCM forces completing the sea control task by clearing the way, both for battleships to provide naval gunfire support and amphibious forces to carry out operations, should they have been required. The Type 42 destroyers provided local area AAW protection to the force and this phase included the shooting down of a land-launched SILKWORM anti-ship missile by Sea Dart from HMS GLOUCESTER. The war began with air operations that were themselves initiated with a 72 hour surge (600 carrier sorties per 24 hours) and then continued at a reduced but still rapid tempo (400 sorties per 24 hours). Sea control operations continued with the destruction of an initial Iraqi air attack on coalition maritime forces and continued with attacks on Iraqi vessels, both in port and at sea. Royal Navy shipborne Lynx helicopters were especially successful against Iraqi Fast Attack Craft. With the threat to them largely neutralised, MCM forces were able to clear the way for bombardment and amphibious forces up to the shores of Kuwait. Surface escorts provided protection from the residual threat posed by coastal defence missiles. Fighting ceased before an amphibious landing could take place but the threat of such a landing had an important operational effect, *fixing* five Iraqi divisions.

Stages of the Maritime Contribution to a Joint Campaign

As a gross simplification there are typically seven stages of a maritime operation in support of a joint campaign: identification of a crisis; force generation; deployment; sea control operations; maritime force projection; sustainment of operations; and recovery/redeployment. In reality these stages will not be easily distinguishable; nor will they necessarily coincide with the phases of a specific campaign plan.

Identification of a Crisis

Initial indications that a crisis is developing will probably come from a variety of sources including strategic intelligence, wide area *surveillance* systems, and open sources such as the news media. Intelligence gathering and analysis can provide warning of changes in operating patterns, exercise and *work-up* programmes and communications volume, and allow for *strategic level* identification and evaluation of potential crises. Intelligence recovery is now a global science that involves close co-operation with allies, swift dissemination of assessed data, clear presentation and early background advice to commanders. Early assessment of the military capability of any potential adversary will play a significant part in assessment of the size and composition of forces needed to address a crisis.

Maritime forces operating in international waters can gather a wide variety of useful intelligence and provide a significant surveillance capability. Information gathered in this way is sometimes the only reliable source of evidence and, as such, is a critical element in identification and assessment of a crisis. Monitoring of shipping or air activity may be a preliminary phase to embargo or sanctions enforcement, or may support other constabulary tasks such as drug interdiction. Intelligence gathering and surveillance will continue throughout a campaign, although its focus will shift from the strategic and general in the early stages to the operational and tactical, and hence become more specifically military as the campaign develops.

Force Generation

The size and composition of the forces required to respond to a developing crisis will be shaped by:

■ the policy objectives and strategic concept of what the Government wants to achieve, how it wishes to act and, in a multinational operation, what the UK contribution should be;

■ understanding of the military *conditions for success* or *end-state* - what the military commander must achieve to be successful;

■ assessment of the threat - and therefore the combat power and levels of protection that may be required to achieve the aim;

- the forces available and their readiness - which will depend in part on the priority given by Government to the policy objectives;

- the time available to respond.

Among the factors that must be considered is the requirement for a robust, flexible, and responsive command and control system able to adapt to changing force levels and threat. In multinational operations, it must be able to integrate with the coalition command and control structure whilst meeting any national requirements. The potential duration of the campaign, the need to sustain or increase force levels, and logistic support requirements throughout the campaign will also have a profound influence on force generation.

Deployment

Deployment to a theatre of operations involves: mounting and sailing the force from home bases or often from their current locations forward deployed; passage to the area of operations; transit; and arrival in the theatre of operations in a posture appropriate to the threat and mission. Co-ordination of the deployment will require detailed planning, close liaison with diplomatic posts, other civil authorities, Allied military authorities and probably foreign government agencies. Consideration must be given to the legal position of the forces, selection of ROE and the use of civil transport such as chartered ships. The routeing of forces must be carefully considered to ensure their security.

The protection of shipping forming a part of a maritime force and providing strategic lift into theatre may take on the characteristics traditionally associated with the wider wartime task of protecting maritime trade and strategic SLOCs. This can take different forms and depends upon whether the aim is to deter attacks, or to defend against them. If the threat to shipping is sufficiently great, protection will require sea control methods (discussed below). Merchant shipping may benefit from wider sea control operations that will offer protection in the waters through which it will pass, or a specific sea control operation may be devoted to the shipping under threat using **Convoying**. Both concepts can be used within wider sea control operations if resources permit. When there is a severe risk to maritime trade, convoying is a method of reducing the scale of the sea control problem that has, in the past, proved effective. If shipping is gathered into convoys, the area and time over which sea control must be exercised for their protection is reduced to a minimum. Convoying complicates the attacker's task and concentrates escorting forces to enhance the effectiveness of protection. However, convoying is less likely to deceive the enemy or deny him intelligence about the position of friendly shipping. It is also disruptive to trade. The strategic or operational decision to convoy requires a careful weighing of the balance of advantage and the opportunities for drawing the enemy into decisive action.

If there is regional tension or where there is a threat of *piracy* or attack by irregular forces, maritime forces can be in theatre, demonstrating presence to deter attack. When the threat is greater, **Distant** or **Close Escort Operations** provide more specific protection. Maritime forces can provide surveillance against threats, be positioned in the vicinity of concentrations of merchant shipping (distant escort), or remain in direct proximity to selected ships (close escort). While conducting both close and distant escort, naval forces offer a measure of defence, but the concept is to deter attack through the threat of reprisals. In looser coalition operations, **Accompaniment** may be adopted, with warships ready to react depending on emerging circumstances. It will rarely be possible to escort and, thus, to defend every vessel, in which case measures must be taken to enhance the defensive capability of individual merchant ships.

Sea Control Operations

Wherever the freedom of action of the maritime force is challenged and, in particular, as it approaches the area of operations, there will be a requirement to establish levels of sea control that will be sufficient to ensure its protection and to enable subsequent operations. Without sea control, the ability of maritime forces to manoeuvre, concentrate for offensive action, apply leverage, project force ashore, and deny the same to an opponent, will be adversely constrained. Sea control is synonymous with dominance of the maritime battlespace, which allows the force's strengths to be used to advantage, while at the same time protecting its combat power. All maritime operations will require sea control and all the types of operations discussed in the chapter are either so much a part of sea control operations as to be indistinguishable from them, or are themselves dependent on sea control operations as a preparation for their conduct.

In open ocean, there is rarely, if ever, a precise geographical area of sea to defend in the way that distinct areas of land may be defended over time by ground forces ashore; maritime forces at sea do not 'hold ground' in that way. Rather, they take measures to protect themselves, in both their immediate vicinity and over wider areas which, since they are themselves moving, means that the areas over which sea control operations are concentrated will also move.

Notwithstanding this, **Area Sea Control Operations** are essentially geographic and are conducted using long range surveillance and weapon systems over extended areas of sea. Targets are principally enemy aircraft, ships and submarines that are transiting to attack positions. However, area sea control operations may also include defining and shaping operations. It is important that commanders responsible for area sea control take necessary measures to ensure that their activities do not conflict with those of other units and task groups that are passing through their area and which may well be conducting their own sea control operations in their immediate vicinity. Careful co-ordination of command and control is required to integrate a mobile force, to deconflict operations and to avoid mutual interference or *fratricide*.

Blockade can be used as a method of achieving sea control through sea denial by preventing access to and from enemy ports and harbours. To be recognised under international law, a blockade must have been declared and notified to all concerned, it must be effective, and it must be applied impartially to ships of all nations. The term 'blockade' has a clear legal meaning, therefore, which very definitely does not include embargo operations in support of economic sanctions of the sort approved by the UN Security Council. A blockading force has the legal right to seize in prize any merchant ship, either enemy or neutral, which attempts to run the blockade either inwards or outwards. The blockade can be either close, denying an enemy access to or from his ports, or distant, denying access to a sea area through which all ships must pass in order to reach the enemy's territory.

Containment Using their high transit speed, nuclear powered submarines can be despatched covertly ahead into theatre to pose a threat to enemy surface and submarine forces and valued land targets, and to tie down enemy forces in defence. Offensive mine-laying might be used to enhance containment, if available and if ROE allow. If friendly shore based and *organic* attack aircraft are within range and the ROE allow, they might *interdict* port facilities, airfields and command and control installations and enemy surface shipping.

Area and Barrier Operations In the past, attempts to defend sea lanes directly have always failed because the available sensors and weapons were not able to prevent attacking forces from penetrating the defences. However, there are some defined areas of water that may need to be cleared of hostile forces and subsequently protected against incursion. These might include straits, approaches, convoy assembly and dispersal areas, and the area selected for an amphibious operation or joint entry into theatre. Submarines and maritime patrol aircraft conduct surveillance of the sea areas through which friendly naval surface forces and logistic shipping will in due course pass, locating and tracking submarine and surface targets and interdicting these as ROE allow. Helicopters from the carrier group might assist with prosecution of submarine and surface contacts when within range.

Force Protection A maritime force, most of the elements of which will have a multi-role capability, will not only require self protection but will inevitably contribute to the overall protection of the Joint Force itself. To achieve this, maritime assets can be employed against the threat according to their individual and corporate capability creating a moving area of battlespace control, thereby protecting power projection forces and support. Force protection is achieved through the warfare disciplines:

Anti-Air Warfare (AAW) The protection of friendly forces from the air threat, irrespective of the launch platform, is achieved through the principles of: denying intelligence to the enemy; obtaining warning; applying defence in depth; and co-ordinating air defence activity. The

A Sea King Mark 7 Airborne Surveillance and Control System (ASaCS) helicopter from 849A Flight with its Searchwater surveillance radar deployed. HMS RICHMOND is in the background

maritime force will contribute to and benefit from the Joint Air Defence plan, using shore-based and organic Airborne Early Warning (AEW) and fighter aircraft and ships armed with surface to air missiles supported by Electronic Warfare (EW) systems. The inner layer of defence for a maritime force is provided by a combination of point defence missile/close in weapon systems and the use of Electronic Countermeasures.

Anti-Surface Warfare (ASuW) Protecting the force from the enemy surface threat is achieved through the same principles articulated above in AAW. Establishing a good surface picture, normally through the use of shore based Maritime Patrol Aircraft (MPA) and organic helicopters, will enable the MCC to deploy his ASuW assets to best effect, keeping the enemy at arm's length. A wide range of attack assets can be used: submarines with missiles or torpedoes; attack aircraft and organic helicopters armed with air to surface missiles, bombs, rockets and cannon; ships and fast attack craft (FAC) armed with surface to surface missiles, guns and torpedoes.

Anti-Submarine Warfare (ASW) The best form of ASW is for vulnerable platforms within a force to operate in a different time and space from enemy submarines. The operational level approach to the problem includes neutralisation of all aspects of submarine operations, such as their infrastructure, communications and support. Continuous efforts must be made to evaluate the location of all enemy submarines so that they can be avoided, through intelligence and sensible routeing. If vulnerable assets must enter an area of submarine threat, then a co-ordinated all arms approach must be taken. Space, air, surface and subsurface assets would be co-ordinated to deceive, distract, detect and destroy submarines. Nuclear powered attack submarines and MPA in support of the force provide the outermost layer of anti-submarine and anti-surface defence.

The next layer of anti-submarine defence is composed of frigates with long range towed array passive sonar, together with supporting MPA and organic helicopters, which also assist in the location and prosecution of submarine contacts. The innermost layers of anti-submarine defence are provided by helicopters, using passive and active sonar, and then surface ships using hull mounted sonars.

Mine Countermeasures (MCM) The most effective MCM is to avoid mined areas. Exploratory MCM will be required by dedicated MCM vessels to determine the extent to which mines have influenced the available maritime manoeuvre space. Once the size and shape of the minefields have been established, task groups may either avoid the area or dedicated

A Royal Australian Navy Sea King flies past HMS SANDOWN conducting mine clearance operations off the Iraqi port of Um Qasr

mine clearance tasks may be conducted. However, it must be assumed that mine clearance operations rarely match the pace and tempo of modern campaigns and emphasis necessarily has to be on exploratory operations.

Advance Sea Control Operations (Shaping Operations) During the transit phase, an advance sea control group may be despatched to complement anti-submarine and anti-surface static area operations. These forces may also be used to establish elements of sea control in any *holding areas* to be used by power projection forces as they poise offshore. Before an amphibious operation it may be necessary to conduct prolonged littoral sea control operations to eliminate any threat from FAC and shore batteries and to reduce the risk from mines and conventional submarines to an acceptable level. During these operations MCM vessels are vulnerable to enemy attack and their protection will be an important consideration. In preparation for an amphibious landing *advance force operations* may involve MCM operations, *Rapid Environmental Assessment*, the insertion of special forces for *reconnaissance*, *surveillance* and possibly direct action and the landing of *naval fire support* controllers.

Sea Lines of Communications (SLOC)   Although mentioned already above (under Deployment), it is worth stressing that sea control operations must provide for the protection of reinforcement and resupply shipping, providing support to the entire national intervention force.   Once the maritime task force is on station, this protection may require a separate operation involving the *escort* or *screening* of important units and, perhaps, full convoying.   This could involve the employment of significant resources across extended distances, with particular emphasis on passage through straits and other natural choke points where the threat is likely to be greatest, especially from unconventional or asymmetric attack.

7/4.   Protection of Sea Lines of Communications; 1990-91 and 2003

During the build up of combat power and logistics before the Gulf War in 1991 it is estimated that there were times when there was one ship carrying combat materiel every 50 miles between Norfolk Virginia and Kuwait. The loss of any one of these ships would have had an enormous impact on operations, psychologically if not necessarily physically, and the resource implications of re-tasking maritime forces for escort duties in the wake of such a loss would have been enormous. In the event, the potential threat from attack along the route from a small number of nations sympathetic to Iraq's cause failed to materialise. In 2003, fewer ships were involved in the build up of UK forces and the deployment took place in a much shorter timeframe.   However, in the wake of terrorist attacks against the USS COLE and the French merchant tanker LIMBURG off Aden, force protection along the SLOCs, particularly against the threat of *asymmetric attack*, was given a high priority, and escorting forces were tasked accordingly in a number of choke points, where the threat of attack was considered to be greatest.   Initially RN frigates and destroyers provided protection in the Straits of Gibraltar, until NATO maritime forces were made available as part of the wider ACTIVE ENDEAVOUR anti-terrorist operations in the Mediterranean. Allies who did not commit ground troops to operations in Iraq nevertheless contributed to force protection by escorting coalition shipping through the Straits of Bab-el-Mandeb and the Straits of Hormuz as part of wider "Global War on Terrorism" operations. Had the threat from attack been present along the whole 6000 mile route, or had allied escorts not been made available, then the RN DD/FF force would have been extremely stretched, and would have had to divert combat power from the front line. The uninterrupted flow of coalition shipping may have been affected or possibly the alternative to route round the Cape of Good Hope would have had to be considered. Both of these options would have threatened the UK's ability to rapidly generate and deploy forces to meet an exacting military plan. This was not, however, the case for naval and amphibious forces themselves, which were able to self deploy and engage in combat with integral sustainment, underlining the flexibility of maritime forces for early deployment and the provision of a theatre entry capability.

Afloat Support Forces engaged in sea control operations will need afloat support which will either benefit from the wider sea control regime or will require its own layered defence. This support need not necessarily be independent of that provided to power projection operations. The replenishment of forces that are operating in outer layers of defence or on area operations need careful planning as time off task while in transit and during replenishment must be minimised for both combat units and auxiliaries. For operations of long duration organic afloat support must be consolidated; *consolidation* shipping will also use the SLOCs.

Maritime Force Projection Operations

With the establishment of appropriate levels of sea control, maritime forces are able to project force ashore and may be employed in a number of ways, including NEOs, amphibious operations, maritime air support, and surface and sub-surface land attack. A robust command and control system, which in the case of amphibious operations must be capable of deploying ashore, gathering intelligence, concentrating combat power, and generating influence over the battlespace, are critical functions for force projection operations.   Co-ordination and *synchronisation* with land and air operations will be required.

Non-Combatant Evacuation Operations (NEOs) An early concern once forces have started to arrive in theatre may be the protection of UK and other uninvolved citizens. NEOs can involve maritime forces, either alone or as a part of a joint force. When airfields and commercial ports are not available, an independent naval operation may be necessary. Maritime forces may also be used to poise in theatre as a precaution should an evacuation become necessary as a result of local instability. The host nation may be able to provide for the security of the evacuation, in which case the UK or coalition forces would provide assistance to the process. In extreme cases an evacuation may be effected through the mounting of an amphibious raid. Maritime based forces will land, secure and defend beachheads and airheads, establish mustering points for evacuees and the routes linking them, move the evacuees to safety and, finally, withdraw. Maritime forces are well suited for NEOs in that they are self-sustaining, require little or no in-country or host nation support, and have the capability to respond rapidly to any deterioration in the situation.   The decision to evacuate nationals is the responsibility of the local British Ambassador, or other Head of Mission, whose staff will normally give instructions to evacuees.   Command and control arrangements must integrate that Mission and any SF contribution. National and NATO Joint Contingency Plans and Joint Planning Guides include contingency plans for evacuation.

Amphibious Operations An Amphibious Task Force (ATF) is the focus for the projection of amphibious force ashore, normally operating in conjunction with a Carrier Task Group. The full campaign may include operations to secure initial *access* to territory, manoeuvre from the sea, raids, demonstrations, withdrawal and redeployment of the Landing Force, adjacent operations and subsidiary landings. Amphibious operations are amongst the most complex of all military activities, as many units are co-ordinated across all the operational environmental boundaries. The four principal types of amphibious operation are:

Amphibious Demonstration This is an operation conducted to illustrate capability or to deceive an enemy into a course of action unfavourable to him. A credible threat must be posed to a land commander that then requires him to allocate sufficient forces to counter that contingent risk. Demonstrations can be used as components of shaping operations and exploiting operations, prior to or during an amphibious assault. The demonstration is perhaps the most elegant expression of amphibious capability. The limited liability offered by poising at sea, both in a military and political context, provides a unique form of leverage which can easily and rapidly be converted into combat action ashore.

Amphibious Raiding   Raids involve the temporary occupancy of an objective followed by a pre-planned withdrawal. As with all amphibious operations, raids can be used to increase the tempo of a campaign, shape the battlespace or create opportunities for subsequent operations. In many circumstances, the raid will be the method of choice for the joint, maritime or amphibious commander.   Raids offer precision violence, minimal risk, and avoid the requirement to invest substantial combat power ashore, including the associated logistics commitment, for extended periods.

Amphibious Assault This is the principal type of amphibious operation. It is distinguished from other types in that it involves establishing, with some permanence, a force on a hostile or potentially hostile shore. The purpose of an assault is to secure operational objectives in support of the campaign's main effort, or in preparation for subsequent operations ashore such as the introduction of follow-on forces. Amphibious assaults exploit the full effects of maritime combat power and can be conducted across the full depth and breadth of the littoral battlespace, to find, fix, strike and exploit an enemy. They are most effective when the landing force can have a disproportionate impact on heavier forces that are impeded by local conditions such as adverse terrain, climate or infrastructure.

Amphibious Withdrawal The withdrawal involves the extraction of forces by sea in naval ships or craft, or the re-embarkation of a landing force into its parent shipping, from a hostile or potentially hostile shore, as part of a pre-planned evacuation or after the seizure of amphibious objectives. Withdrawals are complicated by the necessity to reload tactically and reconfigure the landing force in its parent shipping, often when time and space is at a premium. The amphibious withdrawal is the principal means of reconstituting the amphibious task force at sea, thus bestowing operational level capability.

7/5. Examples of Amphibious Operations

Demonstration: Gulf War 1991
In the 1991 Gulf War two US Marine Corps brigades first carried out a demonstration landing in Oman, then poised at sea. The effect was to tie down five Iraqi divisions in defence of the Kuwaiti coastline.

Raid: St Nazaire, March 1942
In the early hours of 28 March 1942 an amphibious raid destroyed the Normandie Dry Dock in St Nazaire. The attacking force consisted of the old destroyer HMS CAMPBELTOWN, 18 coastal craft and a force of commandos. Approaching by stealth and deception the force achieved complete surprise until five minutes before CAMPBELTOWN rammed the dock gate. The charges in the ship and the destruction achieved by the commandos crippled the dock for the rest of the war. This had the effect of inhibiting use of the German battleship TIRPITZ in the Atlantic, as well as having a strong psychological impact on both sides.

Assault: D-Day 6 June 1944
The D-Day operation in Normandy on 6 June 1944 was the largest amphibious assault ever undertaken and signalled the commencement of the decisive phase of World War II. The build up of combat power in the first month was impressive. By the end of the first day some 156,000 men had been delivered ashore (23,000 of these by air) with initial supplies and vehicles. One week later nearly 430,000 were

ashore with over 100,000 tons of supplies and 62,000 vehicles. After a month, these figures had risen to nearly 1,000,000 men, 650,000 tons of supplies and over 180,000 vehicles.

Withdrawal: Hungnam, December1950

In November 1950 China entered the Korean War and X Corps of UN forces was isolated around the port of Hungnam. From 5-24 December UN navies conducted a successful amphibious withdrawal which embarked 105,000 troops and 91,000 civilians. Because of the availability of specialist amphibious shipping it was also possible to withdraw 17,000 vehicles and 300,000 ton of supplies. This meant that the units removed could be immediately re-deployed. This had the operational effect of stabilising the front-line and the strategic effect of preventing an escalation of the war.

All amphibious operations will consist of a number of separate phases, some of which will run concurrently. These include:

■ planning to establish the most suitable time and place to conduct the operation;

■ embarkation of personnel, vehicles and equipment in ships to reflect the intended scheme of manoeuvre developed during the planning phase.

■ rehearsals to test the adequacy of plans, timings, combat readiness, familiarity with the plan and communications.

■ movement of the components of the ATF from the points of embarkation or a position of forward deployment to the Amphibious Objective Area (AOA).

■ shaping operations to shape the battlespace for the ATF comprising supporting, advance force and pre-landing operations.

■ the amphibious action (demonstration, raid, assault or withdrawal).

Elements of 42 Commando Royal Marines embarked in HMS OCEAN demonstrate a surface assault on a beach in Sierra Leone

Support by Organic Air Aircraft from a carrier task group will contribute air defence of the battlespace (*counter air*), *anti-surface force*, and *combat support* air operations in association with land based aircraft when available. Maritime air operations should be integrated with those of other components through co-ordination or control by the Joint Force Air Component Commander (JFACC), who could be maritime and/or afloat, when the JFACC is established in theatre. The carriers will embark aircraft from Joint Force Harrier if the operations require their assets. Similarly, rotary-wing aircraft from the Joint Helicopter Command embark in amphibious shipping as necessary. Organic aircraft may themselves require support from shore-based assets such as tanker aircraft.

Surface and Sub-Surface Land Attack Surface and sub-surface land attack missiles will also provide the primary means of organic long range attack, particularly in the early stages of a conflict, and have particular utility for coercion. They will subsequently complement other air interdiction forces. Naval fire support may conduct advance bombardment and will complement landing force artillery once this is landed. It is also available to other ground units operating in the littoral region.

Sustainment of Operations

Once the focus of an intervention campaign moves ashore, the emphasis of maritime force operations will shift from being enabling to being supportive. Maritime forces can contribute to all the components of capability required for the conduct of operations ashore. In particular, the focus will be on enhancing the manoeuvrist characteristics of land operations by intelligent application of the principal attributes of maritime forces, especially their ability to enhance manoeuvre and apply force where it is least expected. Additional tasks are likely to be protection and logistic support: protection of units using the sea lines of communications, of the maritime flank, and of logistic support to forces ashore and afloat through *Joint Sea Basing*, sustainment by *sealift*, and an alternative supply to *Host Nation Support* (HNS). Lengthy operations may require *roulement* of units; a common technique enabling both the relief of forces in place as well as the introduction of differently configured forces.

Campaign Termination, Recovery and Redeployment

It is likely that once the end-state of a campaign has been reached, effort will be directed at achieving increased stability as well as the hand-over of responsibility to regional organizations, non-governmental organizations (NGOs) and International Organizations (IOs). Elements of the JTF might find themselves engaged on tasks designed to improve stability, even if other elements of the force are still engaged in combat. As military operations draw down, transit to another stage, or even to another campaign with different objectives, the force will usually adopt one of two broad options: facilitating the transfer of authority to civilian authorities; or act as an occupying force. Military resources may also be diverted at any stage to assist with Humanitarian Assistance operations either in the form of life saving or in life-sustaining aid.

The recovery and/or redeployment of forces at the end of a successful campaign will need to be planned as carefully as the deployment to the area of operations. Indeed there may be the added complication of recovering unusable equipment, and a political requirement for a speedy extraction and return. Moreover, if conditions for success have not been achieved, and an amphibious withdrawal is to be made in the face of continuing or escalating conflict, it will be even more problematical. There may be a need to increase combat power ashore to stabilise the situation before withdrawal can take place. Command and control will be difficult and fragmented. A JTFHQ (Afloat) may provide the most secure and capable communications to assist in this respect, and there will be a requirement to provide protection and logistics, including medical support, both for the maritime forces supporting the withdrawal and for the forces being withdrawn. Protection of a withdrawal, like a landing but in reverse, requires the establishment of necessary levels of sea control.

Royal Navy Sea King Mark 4 helicopters and a Royal Air Force Chinook recovering to the flight deck of HMS ILLUSTRIOUS during operations in the Indian Ocean

Personnel closed up at Action Stations in the Operations Room of HMS OCEAN

Maritime Fighting Power and Operational Capability

8

The applications of maritime power (discussed in Chapter 4) encompass a wide range of operational situations from peacetime activities to full *hostilities* in high intensity situations. The majority of possible applications are *military* (combat governed), even though the actual pattern of employment of the UK's maritime forces may seem to suggest that it is either *constabulary* or *benign* application of maritime forces in operations that tend to dominate the Fleet programme. No apology is necessary for this because it is the ability to continue action through to combat if necessary, and the message maritime forces convey as a consequence, that confers upon them their effectiveness in a very broad range of peacetime activities. Not least, of course, is their effectiveness in applying naval diplomacy as a means of keeping the peace and thereby avoiding the actual use of the full range of their military capabilities.

It is vitally important that the UK's maritime forces maintain an appropriate level of Fighting Power and *Operational Capability* (OC) in order that their military attributes can be brought into effective play in support of UK national interests. Both Fighting Power and Operational Capability mean more than simply the ships, aircraft, their weapons systems and other equipments that exist on the 'inventory'.

The Chiefs of Staff are responsible for delivering to the Secretary of State, through CDS, the overall Fighting Power of their respective Services in a way consistent with obtaining the optimum mix of attributes for joint operations. In turn, the operational Commanders in Chief are responsible for delivering OC. For the bulk of the UK's maritime capability, the responsibility for delivering maritime OC rests with the Commander in Chief Fleet. However, both the Army's CinC Land Forces and the RAF's CinC Strike Command also have to ensure that relevant elements of their own forces can operate effectively in the maritime environment as part of a joint force.

A Merlin helicopter on the flight deck of HMS IRON DUKE

Fighting Power, therefore, is a means of expressing the overall capability of our Armed Forces taking into account all those factors that go to contribute to their effectiveness over time. Operational Capability is virtually synonymous with Fighting Power but is the way this is assessed by the Commanders in Chief within their commands. There is a difference between the two in that there is a great deal that goes into supporting, training, equipping, guiding and directing the Armed Forces that does not fall within the ambit of the Commanders in Chief. Importantly, OC is also relevant across all the components of Fighting Power. Equipment in service falls under the responsibility of the Commanders in Chief, but that yet to be delivered or that in long-term maintenance does not. Maritime tactical doctrine is a part of the Conceptual Component of Fighting Power, but is the responsibility of the Commander in Chief Fleet, who delegates responsibility for its development to the Maritime Warfare Centre.

The Components of Fighting Power

Fighting power defines armed forces' ability to fight and achieve success in operations. It is made up of an essential mix of three inter-related components: conceptual, moral and physical. None is invariably more important than the others - although it matters not how advanced one's platforms, weapons and sensors are if the people manning them lack motivation, training or adequate leadership. The Components of Fighting Power are summarised diagrammatically in Figure 8.1 overleaf.

The Principles of War, Doctrine and Concepts (The Conceptual Component)

The conceptual component provides the thought processes needed to develop the ability to fight. It comprises both lessons from the past and thinking about how the Armed Forces can best operate today and in the future. The conceptual component of fighting power consists of two areas: the body of thought about how we conduct current operations, comprising the Principles of War and doctrine; and the body of thought about how we aspire to fight in the future, comprising future concepts. It is the combination of the Principles of War and doctrine, applied with imagination and initiative by their commanders, that provides the

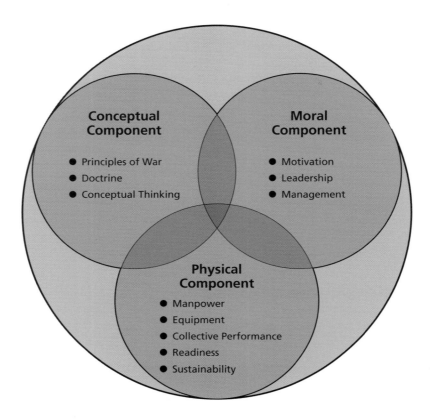

Fig 8.1: The Components of Fighting Power

intellectual force driving the UK Armed Forces' fighting power in current operations.

The Principles of War were discussed and illustrated in Chapter 1. Also mentioned in that chapter was doctrine, four categories of which provide guidance to the Armed Forces: joint doctrine; higher level environmental doctrine; single Service doctrine; and NATO doctrine. Those forms of doctrine of relevance to maritime operations are:

Joint Doctrine

This is contained in the hierarchy of Joint Warfare Publications (JWPs). *British Defence Doctrine* is the highest level of joint doctrine. It focuses on the military strategic level of war, but contains comment on both the grand strategic and operational levels. The principal operational level publication is *JDP 01 Joint Operations*, with *JWP 3-00 Joint Operations Execution* and *JWP 5-00 Joint Operations Planning* also being key documents. Warfare at the military strategic and operational levels is inherently joint; so too is the doctrine relating to it. While not all operations at the tactical level are necessarily joint, there is a large body of joint tactical doctrine that represents the bulk of the joint doctrine hierarchy.

Single Service Doctrine

BR 1806 is the highest level of doctrine produced by the Royal Navy. It is perhaps best described as the RN's perspective on joint doctrine at the military strategic level. Some elements of tactical doctrine are also, by their nature, exclusively single-Service. They remain the responsibility of the single Services, with the development of maritime tactical doctrine being the responsibility of the Maritime Warfare Centre.

NATO Doctrine

NATO is by far the most important security arrangement for the UK; it is the principal organization through which the UK conducts military activities. A substantial amount of operational and tactical level doctrine is produced by NATO, with both the RN and the RAF relying heavily on it as the guidance for their operations.

Conceptual Thinking

There is a further essential element that assists with the development of Fighting Power into the future. It is concerned with innovation and ideas for developing future capabilities and better ways of operating in a continually fluctuating strategic environment. The development of concepts for future operations is vital for both force and doctrine development. Without it, the Armed Forces could not maintain Fighting Power, including equipment superiority, over time. In thinking about the future of warfare and the forces necessary to cope with its challenges, the

UK uses a capability based approach. There are seven fundamental defence capabilities required to deliver Fighting Power. These are:

- A robust and responsive means of **Command** (the authority for the direction, co-ordination and control of military forces).

- A process to **Inform** the command (the acquisition, collation, processing, management and distribution of information).

- A means to **Prepare** forces for employment (all the activities needed to define, resource and deliver fighting power for operational employment, within readiness criteria laid down in policy).

- Measures and resources to **Project** and recover in a timely manner, a force that is appropriately packaged for the objective it is pursuing.

- The means to **Protect** and preserve fighting power, principally on operations (involves countering wider threats, natural, human and technological).

- The ability to **Sustain** the force (the maintenance of the necessary level of fighting power required to achieve objectives).

- All of which are necessary in order to discharge the prime function, namely to **Operate** by conducting military actions, primarily in combat (including movement, supply, attack, defence, and manoeuvre).

These fundamental defence capabilities are inter-related and mutually supporting, and none of them should be considered in isolation.

People (The Moral Component)

Ultimately it is people that realise fighting power. The UK has highly skilled and fully volunteer Armed Forces with a history of excellence in performance. Their world-recognised strengths require time, effort and resources if they are to be developed, maintained and exploited to the nation's advantage. The moral component of fighting power is about persuading our people to fight. It depends on good morale and the conviction that our purpose is morally and ethically sound; these promote the offensive spirit and a determination to achieve the aim. There are many things that contribute: training, confidence in equipment, firm and fair discipline, self-respect and a clear understanding of what is going on and what is required. With all of those in place there is clear potential for military success. To draw it out, however, requires motivation, leadership and management.

8/1. The Ethos of the Royal Navy

The Royal Navy ethos is a set of characteristics and values that differentiates our servicemen and women. It serves to shape and direct personnel in the effective execution of the unique tasks and responsibilities that help to deliver maritime capability.

It is defined as: "The enduring spirit derived from our people's loyalty to their ship, unit or team, sustained by high professional standards and strong leadership, that gives courage in adversity, and the determination to fight and win."

Motivation

Motivation implies a determination for getting things done. It derives from a personal commitment to an idea, a sense of purpose, and a feeling of belonging. In many people there is an instinctive desire to do what is right and good. One means of generating motivation, therefore, is to ensure that our Armed Forces believe in what they are doing. A sense of purpose is achieved when that belief is linked to the individual's involvement in its pursuit. Involvement is a stronger source of motivation for most people when they feel themselves to be a part of a team, all members of which provide the others with support. In military units, given the challenges inherent in war fighting, the need is to go beyond mere team-building, to develop genuine comradeship that will endure even as the violence and fear of war, death and injury begin to bite deep into the individual's consciousness. It is pride in belonging, best described by the term 'esprit de corps' in relation to unit identity but which, at a higher level, includes a belief in patriotic duty. Being highly motivated in peacetime is one thing; to retain that motivation in the face of battle requires a profoundly deep commitment to one's comrades, one's unit, one's country, and to the cause for which one is fighting.

Leadership

Leadership at all levels is the principal element in the maintenance of morale. Without good leadership, morale will undoubtedly crumble in the face of adversity. All leaders must accept their responsibility for maintaining morale and the fighting spirit of those under their command. Military leadership is the projection of personality and character to get subordinates to do what is required of them and to engender within them the confidence that breeds initiative and the acceptance of risk and responsibility. Born leaders are rare, but leadership potential can be developed by training, experience, study of the methods of great leaders in the past, and a knowledge of military doctrine. Through these, individuals develop their own style of leadership and no two people will necessarily lead in exactly the same way. Leadership starts with self-discipline. It is a continuous process throughout training and daily life. Leaders promote this amongst their subordinates by: decisive action; precept and example; advice, encouragement and admonishment; and by giving subordinates every opportunity of contributing to operational and tactical success.

It is the Commanding Officer who must stamp a leadership style on the ship or other unit under his command. But he is not the only person onboard or within the unit who must be trained to lead. A ship's company is divided into departments, sub-departments and sections. At each level, strong leadership will contribute to the effectiveness of the team and the smooth functioning of the ship. Leadership at all levels is a principal element in the maintenance of morale.

An outstanding characteristic of all great leaders is their refusal to be dominated by circumstances. While not challenging the inevitable, they use events around them to achieve their own ends, rather than modify their ends to keep pace with the tide of events. Personal qualities present in a successful leader are:

■ an open mind which is receptive to all possibilities;

■ the ability to grasp the essentials important to success;

■ firmness and speed in decision, largely acquired by thinking through during quiet periods what action should be taken if different circumstances arise;

■ calmness in crisis; the courage to withstand mental stress and strain, and the refusal to be distracted by bad tidings;

■ the ability to explain clearly what he wants to achieve and why, so that he can be effectively and appropriately supported by his peers and subordinates;

■ boldness; a good leader must be successful to retain the confidence of his subordinates, and success will not come from faintheartedness;

■ a readiness to accept and discharge responsibility at all times; the mere acceptance of responsibility without the determination to fulfil it by executive action is useless;

■ the ability to generate mutual trust, respect and confidence between himself and subordinates, peers and superiors.

- ■ the ability to convince subordinates at all levels that he has their best interests at heart by a mixture of wide and sympathetic understanding of human nature (supported by a sense of humour), an understanding of the strengths and weaknesses of individuals, and meticulous and impartial care in dealing with their affairs.

- ■ the confidence to delegate in the knowledge that his intentions have been clearly expressed and well promulgated.

- ■ capacity for accurate risk assessment.

Management

Management is no substitute for leadership but is a vital element of the moral component nevertheless. It is about making the best use of resources. It is an attribute of command that cannot be overlooked because it is fundamental to efficiency and, of course, relates to two Principles of War, economy of effort and sustainability. In those senses, especially in relation to logistics, it also has a bearing on the physical component of fighting power. It is regarded as an element of the moral component, however, because without good management of resources and the provision of sufficient administrative support, the maintenance of morale and the motivation of the force would be rendered considerably more difficult. The measure of good management is the achievement of the right balance – neither an over-abundance nor a shortage of resources, either of which would undermine the concentration of effort on the main objective.

Challenges

Life at Sea Within our maritime forces, large numbers of sailors, marines, airmen, soldiers and, indeed, civilians have to live and work in very close proximity to each other. The ship or submarine, which is their home for extended periods in peace and conflict, is a cramped and often uncomfortable space. The maritime environment is featureless, tiring and demanding. Patterns of life during peacetime exercises differ little from those during hostilities. Historically, maritime warfare has been characterised by long periods of inactivity, surveillance and search followed by short bursts of intense combat. Concentration and alertness must not be allowed to drop during quieter periods. People, weapon systems and sensors must be integrated into a composite team.

On board HMS OCEAN a Royal Marine of 9 Assault Squadron writes a Mothers Day card

Morale The maintenance of good morale is one of the *Principles of War*. It is based on recognition of the needs of the individuals who collectively form the team, and it manifests itself in the will to win. Morale promotes the offensive spirit and determination to achieve the aim. Good morale is based on: a shared sense of purpose; clear understanding of, and belief in, the aim; discipline and self-respect; confidence in equipment; training; and well merited mutual trust and respect between those in and under command. The naval systems of command and its long standing Divisional

System provide a clear framework for effective leadership and support for the individual within the ship, or unit. Supportive public opinion at home is also vital to the maintenance of morale. The presentation, by the media, of the conduct of an operation and of the personalities involved, can assume great significance. The ability of the operational commander to provide a clear, confident and credible message to those at home is crucial, but he must balance the need for security with that of accurate reporting from the operational area. Operational success provides the quickest and most effective boost to morale for those at war but outstanding leadership will sustain high morale when all other factors are against it.

Discipline Military training instils discipline from the outset. Ideally, rather than being imposed from above, discipline rests within the individual. From self–discipline stems the spirit of teamwork and the willingness to be led. Many of those who have no personal experience of the modern, professional armed forces tend to assume that their efficiency and ability to achieve their success is due to a rigid, disciplinarian's approach to getting things done. Nothing could be further from the truth. Ultimately, in the tightest and most demanding operational circumstances, orders need to be given and carried out with a sense of urgency and without question. However, those circumstances are few and far between and the essence of sound military organization is achieved by instilling in people a discipline based on co-operation and teamwork. This must involve a willingness to: challenge superiors when appropriate and to accept such challenge from subordinates; maintain an open mind and to apply free thought responsibly; and accept also the need to act with others in a co-ordinated fashion by subordinating one's own personal desires to the higher needs of the Service.

Combat Stress and Fatigue Every commander must know how hard to drive his force, ship or unit. It must not be spurred beyond the limits at which people lose their powers of recovery. Undue mental strain often leads to physical exhaustion and undue physical strain to mental eccentricities. Combat stress is inherent in warfare but it can be tempered by an individual's physical and moral courage and by his confidence in a sound and well-expressed plan. A commander must have a firm knowledge of the dangers and warning signs of unrelieved combat stress. Effective leadership, self-control and confidence in the team all combine to help limit the natural fear of violence. A commander must also consider his own fatigue, for it is essential that his energy, mental and physical, should be conserved for crucial periods. He must ensure he has adequate and regular periods of rest and reflection, avoid over immersion in matters of detail that are the job of his staff and delegate as much as possible to subordinates. He should issue clear and concise orders and leave his staff to work out the details. This creates a more responsive force, gives subordinates vital experience essential for their own development, and preserves the vital force of the commander for when it is most required.

The Means to Fight (The Physical Component)

The physical component of fighting power is the means to fight. It has five elements; manpower, equipment, collective performance, readiness and sustainability. It is, therefore, a combination of the ships, land vehicles, aircraft, associated weapons and sensors, and other equipments, the people that man them and the training they undergo to fight, both as individuals and as members of operational units, in order that they can be deployed in good time and sustained to achieve the tasks assigned by HM Government.

Manpower

The servicemen and servicewomen that comprise our armed forces, both regular and reserve, are highly trained and skilled volunteers. They go through a rigorous selection and initial training process that gives them an essential grounding for the further professional development and collective training necessary to turn them into effective combatants. The UK's Armed Forces have been involved in active operations throughout the period since the Second World War and have accumulated a wealth of experience, with many of those with that experience still serving. They are highly regarded internationally. Nevertheless, their skills need to be nurtured, developed and retained. No matter how successful they might have been in the past, their effectiveness can so easily be undermined by changing economic, social and political factors and by significant shifts in the values of society as a whole.

The manpower component of maritime OC is dependent upon the right numbers of competent personnel available to deploy so as to meet the required maritime tasks. In seeking to satisfy this remit, the manpower requirement should include an appropriate mix of skills that are balanced against the key strategic capabilities. Furthermore, this manpower base and the associated policies need to be flexible enough to meet surge demands and be able to reconfigure to meet the changing operational environment.

Equipment

The UK's Armed Forces go to war and fight with the equipment they already have and British doctrine reflects this. However, a fundamental part of maintaining fighting power is the procurement of the best and most effective equipment that can be afforded, the aim being to maintain a technological advantage that represents a war-winning capability. The conceptual component of fighting power includes the development of concepts to inform and guide the UK's equipment programme and to develop fighting power into the future. It is essential that those in the Defence industries understand the British Approach to military operations in order that they can better anticipate the UK Armed Forces' equipment needs. Equally, interaction with industry enables the Armed Forces to achieve a better understanding of the capabilities that might be employed by potential adversaries.

Operational capability depends on the availability of an appropriate range of equipment for those tasks that maritime forces are likely to meet. The ships, aircraft, weapon systems and sensors need to be of a suitable mix, available in sufficient quantities, and reliable, given the conditions in which they are likely to be employed. There are both national and multinational reasons for the UK to possess a spread of maritime assets with a range of combat capabilities; what has traditionally been referred to as a *balanced fleet*. Independent national operations require the complete suite of maritime warfare capabilities, at both the operational and tactical levels.

It is not possible to create robust coalition formations capable of high intensity combat at short notice from an assembly of disparate national capabilities. Although *maritime forces* can easily be brought together to form a multinational force for tasks in which there is a low risk of combat, a fully integrated fighting force requires a period to work up from basic levels of inter-operability to full OC under the direction of an experienced commander and afloat staff. Within NATO the problem of creating major multinational fighting formations is simplified because it is probable that the United States will provide the core capabilities for a *NATO Task Force* or *NATO Expanded Task Force*. For a European Union or other coalition operation, in which the US has chosen not to participate with combat forces, these core capabilities must be provided by other nations. The UK, as the leading European maritime nation, would be able to make a significant contribution in the allocation of forces to such an operation. It is one of very few nations able to provide the core building blocks, such as a carrier task group and amphibious force, to a multinational maritime formation. It can also contribute a tried and tested, comprehensive, afloat command and control facility. This range of capabilities enables the UK to make an effective contribution to multinational operations, giving it the authority significantly to influence decision-making within any maritime coalition, be it allied or ad hoc.

The principal platforms and units that are available within the UK's maritime forces represent a well-balanced and independently capable collection of capabilities. That collection consists of the following.

Nuclear Powered Ballistic Missile Submarines
Nuclear powered ballistic missile carrying submarines (SSBNs) deploy the TRIDENT D5 missile system that provides *strategic* and *sub-strategic nuclear deterrence* for the UK and NATO.

Aircraft Carriers and Their Organic Air
The RN's aircraft carriers (CVS) are substantial contributors to sea control, power projection and to the overall command and control of maritime operations. They operate a mixed and flexible air group consisting of short take-off and vertical landing (STOVL) jet fighter attack, reconnaissance and *close air support* aircraft from Joint Force Harrier, as well as anti-submarine and Airborne Surveillance and Control System (ASaCS) helicopters. The

Royal Air Force Harrier GR7s embark in HMS ARK ROYAL. Royal Navy
Sea Harrier FA2s are in the background

exact composition of the carrier air group (CAG) will be tailored to the
mission of the force. Organic air provides the ability to conduct
independent air operations when it may not be possible to use bases
ashore, coupled with the mobility to find clear flying conditions and to react
rapidly when the force is close to the combat zone. CVSs provide essential
command and control capabilities for a Maritime Component Commander
(MCC) at the tactical level. At the operational level, when suitably
augmented, they can provide a *Joint Task Force Headquarters* for a national
JTFC, or embark a NATO/EU *Combined Joint Task Force* (CJTF) Commander.
If required, a carrier can also be used to carry units of a Landing Force for
operations of limited duration as an LPH (see the section on Specialist
Amphibious Shipping below). Operating as an LPH, aircraft carriers can

embark a tailored air group (TAG) made up entirely of helicopters from the Joint Helicopter Command for support of amphibious and land operations.

Nuclear Powered Attack Submarines

Nuclear powered attack submarines (SSNs) are capable of high transit speeds and sustained underwater operations. They constitute a principal sea denial system having anti-submarine capabilities and an anti-ship capability using torpedoes and anti-surface missiles. When fitted with land attack missiles, SSNs have a power projection capability of considerable range and penetrability, with important uses for deterrence and coercion. SSNs can gather intelligence and insert and recover special forces. They can operate independently or in conjunction with surface forces and contribute to the protection of the strategic nuclear deterrent.

Specialist Amphibious Forces

The UK's specialist amphibious forces represent a comprehensive range of capabilities, fully able to operate independently if required, but also eminently suitable for integration with other UK forces and those of other nations. There are three essential elements to this amphibious package.

3 Commando Brigade Royal Marines A mandatory element of an amphibious capability is a *Landing Force* organized, trained and equipped for amphibious operations. This is provided by 3 Commando Brigade Royal Marines and consists of three *Commandos* (with tracked, wheeled or dismounted organic mobility), a light artillery regiment (Royal Artillery), two combat engineer squadrons (Royal Engineers), a logistic regiment, light and support helicopters from the Joint Helicopter Command, a landing craft squadron, a command support group with air defence, an EW capability, strategic communications and a long range patrol capability.

Amphibious Shipping The specialist shipping provided to give the landing force strategic mobility and operational manoeuvre consists of:

Landing Platforms Dock (LPDs). Two Amphibious Force command platforms equipped with landing craft and a flight deck;

Landing Platform Helicopter (LPH). One specialist LPH in service, plus a CVS operated as an LPH if required;

Landing Ships Logistic (LSLs). Five platforms for specialist amphibious lift;

Landing Ships Dock (Auxiliary) (LSD(A)s). Four LSD(A)s are being built to replace/supplement the LSLs.

In a potentially hostile environment these vessels can provide the transport and initial offload of the assault echelons of a landing force, in a tactical posture, without recourse to harbours and airfields. They provide the launch platforms for assaults and raids by landing craft and support helicopters. LPDs have the necessary command and control facilities for a brigade size operation, and are capable of landing a two company group surface assault, as well as heavy battle winning equipment (such as *armour*) and landing force vehicles and equipment. The LPH can accommodate a full commando and deploy half the helicopters required for a two company group assault landing. LSLs and LSD(A)s provide the specialist amphibious *lift* needed to load, sustain and deliver rapidly elements of the UK Landing Force tactically configured including troops, Combat Support and Combat Service Support, additional to that provided by other specialist amphibious shipping. They also have helicopter spots, LSD(A)s have a dock, and LSLs have stern offload ramps and carry *Mexeflotes*, which are large, powered pontoons capable of offloading heavy stores and *materiel* from amphibious shipping and chartered shipping (see discussion below). The LSD(A)s have the ability to conduct concurrent surface and air offload without needing to rely on a beaching capability.

Landing Force Movement Assets The process of projecting a landing force from the specialist shipping involves the use of aircraft and landing craft. The facilities available within the maritime force includes raiding craft, landing craft, Landing Craft Air Cushion (LCACs), Mexeflotes, and support helicopters that are embarked in the amphibious shipping. These assets can be transferred to the landing force on completion of a landing, thus providing it with tactical mobility in the absence of amphibious shipping. Helicopters enhance *tempo*, increase the Landing Force

Commander's options, contribute to the tactical mobility of the force and, in particular, improve the force's ability to achieve depth in the initial phases of a landing.

Frigates and Destroyers

Frigates and destroyers (FF/DD) are multi-purpose combatants with an emphasis on ASW or AAW, but with capabilities in many disciplines, including the ability to provide fire support to forces ashore. They are the smallest units that are deployed autonomously for extended periods for military tasks, and their numbers and capabilities allow them individually to cover a wide range of *military*, *constabulary* and *benign* tasks. They are particularly useful in establishing maritime presence. They are also versatile building blocks for larger formations, essential defensive elements of task groups, and contributors of organic helicopters to a force.

The Lynx helicopter from the Type 42 destroyer HMS MANCHESTER off the island of Montserrat in the West Indies

Mine Countermeasures Vessels

Mine countermeasures vessels (MMs) include vessels capable of minesweeping and minehunting. In home waters they operate in the approaches to harbours and choke points where they are used to maintain the flow of shipping and access to the open ocean for SSBNs. When operating in support of force projection, they are an important element of task groups, particularly in advanced sea control operations and as part of an amphibious Advance Force prior to an amphibious landing. MMs are used to establish the presence and extent of mining. They then provide mine clearance if required to enable other maritime operations to take place. MMs require a measure of forward support, a tasking authority and a degree of protection when operating in a surface or air threat environment, if they are to be deployed effectively for an extended period.

Hydrographic and Oceanographic Vessels

Hydrographic and Oceanographic Survey Vessels (SVs) provide the capability to conduct specialist Military Data Gathering (MDG) in support of maritime operations, including the nuclear deterrent. Hydrographic, oceanographic and meteorological information is then used to produce charts and other products which underpin both safety of navigation and formulation of the Recognised Environmental Picture (REP) for subsequent

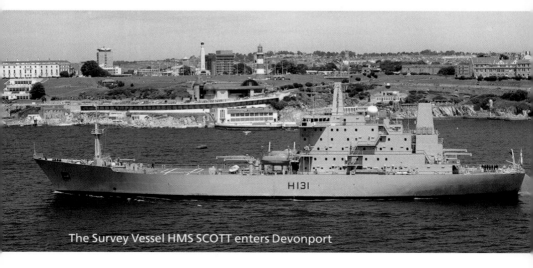

The Survey Vessel HMS SCOTT enters Devonport

exploitation by maritime units. *Rapid Environmental Assessment* (REA) involves the mission specific collection of essential environmental data to ensure that the REP is sufficient to meet the requirements of a particular operation. SVs can also provide MCM Tasking Authority facilities. SVs require a measure of forward support and appropriate force protection when operating in a sub-surface, surface or air threat environment.

Patrol Vessels

Specialised vessels and MMs are deployed routinely on patrol around the UK, chiefly on constabulary tasks, to protect economic interests and ensure the good order and security of the *maritime domain*. They include units of the Fishery Protection Squadron and those assigned to duties in Northern Ireland. For fishery protection, the ships are operated under contract to the Department for Environment, Food and Rural Affairs (DEFRA) to patrol UK waters to protect UK fishing vessels and to enforce fisheries regulations. Ships assigned to duties in Northern Ireland make the maritime contribution to counter terrorism in that Province. The Ice Patrol Ship makes annual deployments to Antarctic waters to demonstrate British interest in the region and to provide assistance to the British Antarctic Survey; it also undertakes hydrographic survey and meteorological work.

Shore-Based Aircraft

The speed of transit, wide sensor and communications fit, ability to cover large areas and substantial capacity for weapons, make maritime patrol aircraft (MPAs) important contributors to both ASW and ASuW. They are particularly useful for area ASW operations, surveillance and reconnaissance and search and rescue, and may be well-placed to provide some C2 capabilities. Other shore-based aircraft can contribute to the combat capabilities in a range of tasks such as reconnaissance (multi-sensor – EW/SIGINT and IMINT), surveillance and control (AWACS), air-to-air refuelling, air defence, attack and logistics resupply.

Afloat Logistic Support

Afloat logistic support provides for the direct organic replenishment of fighting units and is required for any operation where a self reliant maritime force must be sustained at distance from shore bases. Ships of the *Royal*

The Antarctic Patrol Ship HMS ENDURANCE

Fleet Auxiliary provide fuel, stores and ordnance while maintenance can be carried out by a Forward Maintenance and Repair Organization (FMRO) often deployed in a Forward Repair Ship (FRS). Many auxiliaries carry helicopters that can be integrated into a formation. Specially equipped ships may be required to receive casualties if extensive combat is envisaged. Freighting support is required to move supplies from the main support area (usually the UK) to *Forward Logistics Sites* and to consolidate organic logistic shipping (see Chapter 5). Chartered shipping is also used for this task and can be modified to carry helicopters.

Chartered Shipping

An Amphibious Task Force will normally include chartered shipping to complement the lift provided by specialist amphibious shipping. Chartered shipping may include transports for personnel (passenger vessels), vehicles (Ro-Ro ferries), hospital ships, container ships, water ships, tankers and specialist lift shipping, such as semi-submersibles to transport additional landing craft or even MMs.

8/2. Maritime Task Groups and Force Packages

Aircraft carriers, amphibious shipping with an embarked Military Force, logistic shipping, submarines, frigates and destroyers are all able to provide combat capabilities to whichever commander has need of them. All can operate independently but will normally be grouped with other forces in an appropriately packaged Task Group.

A Task Group's size and its mix of vessels will depend on the scale and the nature of the tasks it might need to undertake and the functions required to meet those tasks. The capabilities required for a specific operation will be an output of the joint estimate process. However, a key asset that would have a profound impact on its ability to influence joint operations would be an aircraft carrier. An amphibious element, including an LPH, together with a balanced range of frigates, destroyers and submarines, including a TLAM fitted SSN, would represent a comprehensive and highly capable range of maritime force projection capabilities. Other forces, including MCM and hydrographic surveying units, can be added to a Task Group to ensure its ability to conduct entry operations. The key to success is to put together a force package tailored for the needs of the operations in which it will be required to perform. The reconfiguring of an aircraft carrier's air group, by flying aircraft independently out to meet it when it is already forward deployed, is an excellent example of how this can be achieved.

The operations of a single Task Group will usually be concentrated geographically. However, if maritime operations within a campaign are geographically dispersed, they may require either the single Task Group to split or the deployment of more than one Task Group, with different capabilities. It may be necessary, for example, to have one concentrating on the security of sea lines of communications for deployment into theatre, where a second will be operating in direct support of ground forces ashore.

An appropriately constituted maritime Task Group will be able to provide support for operations right through the spectrum, from warfighting to peace support, from high intensity to low and through all phases of an operation. Just as important, it will be able to alter its posture rapidly, moving from low intensity to high intensity with relative ease. Indeed, because of the way that maritime forces deploy fully worked up and with their full suite of capabilities, they can even switch from ceremonial diplomatic activity during a formal port visit to intense military activity in the short time it would take to sail and settle into Defence Watches; a matter of hours not days. This means that their presence anywhere in the world, for whatever routine peacetime activity, provides their political masters with a ready source of military leverage that can be brought to bear in a wide range of crisis circumstances.

Collective Performance

Collective performance is the ability to apply current tactical and operational doctrine in the full range of maritime operations. It requires the possession of a body of doctrine for maritime operations that allows for the effective employment of the force. There also needs to be a range of operational contingency plans. Ultimately, there must be a level of collective competence specific to the role of maritime forces, for the full range of operations required to meet those tasks listed in Government policy. It is important to recognise that collective competence in maritime forces encompasses more than just that which the term 'maritime doctrine' implies. It includes the competencies necessary to power a warship and run it and its weapon systems, none of which are the business of maritime doctrine, which is to do with maritime tactics and operations. The warship is, in general, the smallest tactically relevant element of a maritime force; collective performance is about how that warship floats, moves and fights. A ship's company is a cohesive body of men and women, all of whom have a vital function to perform in delivering combat power. Essentially, collective performance is achieved through training; not just that training associated with maritime tactical doctrine but also that to do with maintaining weapons systems and power plants and personnel support services.

The quality of the UK's military training is respected world-wide and is one of its armed forces' greatest strengths. Training builds proficiency, cohesion and teamwork. It ranges from individual training for each member of the maritime force, to the conduct of large exercises involving full maritime task forces that test command and control and the application of doctrine.

In the Fleet the expected level of OC to be achieved is laid down by CinCFleet Staff. Each unit must have a high proportion of its personnel at the standard laid down in the Operational Performance Statement (OPS). To achieve that, individuals must have achieved the standards laid down in the Training Performance Statement (TPS) for the billet they fill on the ship's Scheme of Complement (SOC). This will depend on their own career training and development and those elements of Pre-Joining Training (PJT) deemed necessary for their billet. Once they have joined their ships, individuals will require an amount of On Job Training (OJT) to raise their level of competence to that of the OPS.

As individuals, the men and women filling the billets on the SOC need to be trained as a team in order that the ship operates as a whole effectively. The ship's departments will have training programmes and serials to complete, including Command Team Training (CTT) for those responsible for applying tactical doctrine in the operational environment. Each ship will undergo Operational Sea Training (OST), on successful completion of which it will become a fully operational unit within the Fleet, available for all appropriate tasking. Further training for the ship will include Area Capability Training (ACT) which will enhance its ability to perform its primary warfare function (an ASW frigate, for example, will spend time on ASW training in deep water). Finally there are Joint Maritime Courses (JMCs) and major national and NATO exercises that involve units operating as an integral part of a maritime task group to enhance joint and multinational interoperability.

Training enables operations to continue effectively in the confusion and stress of combat. The maintenance and demonstration of operational effectiveness through exercising is an essential part of the deterrent value of our armed forces. Teamwork is essential within a ship if it is to be efficient and effective in combat. But the requirement for good teamwork extends beyond the individual unit. It is also crucial within a force, where each unit must understand its contribution. If the task group has an international dimension, the task of developing interoperability and forging corporate team spirit is equally important but more difficult to achieve. One of the basic building blocks is the establishment of standard tactical and operating procedures. Units must continually hone their skills in these procedures to maximise their contribution to the force. Further, training in a joint environment, and with forces from other nations alongside whom ships and task groups will expect to operate is key to optimising combat effectiveness.

Realistic training maintains fleet operational effectiveness by preparing units, task groups and task forces for war. Maritime task group and individual crew training specific to the scenario and threat should continue during passage to a theatre of operations, thereby ensuring a high state of readiness on arrival. Such Combat Enhancement Training (CET) and Force Integration Training (FIT) may be invaluable for a multinational force, whose individual units have little or no experience of operating together. Military training on passage is less easy to achieve; the landing force and the individuals within it must be fully trained before deployment to theatre.

Commanders must have a clear grasp of current *doctrine* so that they can fully comprehend their orders and execute them effectively. A thorough knowledge of doctrine will also allow commanders to take decisions in accordance with the intentions of their superiors even when they are out of contact with higher levels of command. Commanders must use judgement. They must not follow doctrine slavishly but must learn from the lessons of their own experience and be prepared to deviate from established doctrine when required, explaining their reasons for doing so to their subordinates.

Readiness

The ability to deploy combines the physical process of transit into theatre with the readiness to do so in as short a time as possible and the willingness to prosecute the task upon arrival. By their nature, crises spring up unexpectedly in equally unexpected places. Timelines are likely to be short. Government policy lays down readiness criteria for the Armed Forces, in which priorities are listed and forces allocated differing levels of required readiness. The readiness details are themselves a part of policy and not doctrine, but a commander's responsibility to meet them is a doctrinal imperative. This responsibility is discharged through the commander ensuring that the unit's preparedness and motivation are appropriate and match the readiness state.

Sustainability

Sustainability is about:

■ the holding of sufficient combat supplies, equipment, spares and other essential stores;

■ the ability to deploy with the levels of stores needed for an operation and within acceptable time scales;

■ the ability to deliver re-supplies to required locations in good time;

■ the ability to treat and evacuate casualties; and

■ the ability to reconfigure the manpower pool to deploy sufficient reserves of trained manpower and materiel to allow a force to sustain operations, if necessary for extended periods.

The military-strategic and operational aspects of logistics support have already been discussed in detail in Chapter 5; the importance of sustainability is at the core of the UK armed forces' approach to logistics. In manpower terms, sustainability is achieved through having a flexible pool of trained, professional, regular servicemen and servicewomen capable of meeting deployment in a timeframe that achieves the tasks laid down by Government, and by having well trained and prepared Reserve Forces capable of augmenting their regular colleagues if operations are mounted for extended periods or if specialist skills are needed in specific circumstances.

Conclusions

At first sight it might appear strange to link system capabilities and personnel matters in a single chapter but this is precisely the association that typifies combat at and from the sea. High technology equipment, complex command, control and information systems and highly trained and motivated personnel must function in harmony under conditions of stress and battle damage if maritime power is to be applied effectively. Individual vessels, landing forces and aircraft are partners in the business of sea control and power projection whose capabilities must be meshed to bring success. Similar partnerships must exist between force, group and unit commanders, and, within each unit, between the people and the equipment they operate.

Operational capability, the essential components that go to make it up and the detailed means by which those components are delivered, all constitute the real effectiveness of military forces. A military force may have the most advanced and sophisticated technology at its disposal, but if it has badly motivated people, an inadequate approach to teamwork and an inability to maintain operations over time, it will fail to achieve its potential. The UK's maritime forces are of a high quality and are capable of delivering because they have achieved a balance of all the components of operational capability.

8/3. MARITIME FORCES IN JOINT OPERATIONS – A SUMMARY

The essence of effective joint manoeuvrist operations is to apply force across environmental boundaries, using the strengths of all components to compensate for each of their inherent or situational weaknesses.

A maritime force is able to conduct **manoeuvre**, provide mobility and countermobility and contribute to the control of an area of influence. Manoeuvre is, of course, more than just mobility. A maritime Task Group's ability to poise off a coast ready to provide an instant or rapid response to developments ashore is entirely in keeping with manoeuvrist principles and aims, to achieve an opportunistic and unpredictable approach that will confuse the enemy. The ability to apply force in keeping with manoeuvrist principles ranges from the very overt use of ground attack aircraft (RAF Harrier GR7s embarked in a CVS) to the covert insertion of special forces. Included in the range of possibilities is the use of amphibious forces, applying appropriate capabilities when and where needed.

In the provision of **fire support**, a Task Group can deliver fire using carrier based aircraft, surface and submarine launched long range precision attack missiles, and medium range gun munitions. The intended future combination of the LPH, HMS OCEAN, and attack helicopters will considerably enhance fire support options. In this sense, a maritime Task Group represents what a soldier would refer to as a 'combat support function' which can process and engage ground targets, integrate fire support and even assess its effectiveness using aircraft to conduct battle damage assessment.

The **protection** of forces ashore preserves their fighting potential. A Task Group formed around an aircraft carrier can provide air defence (both offensive and defensive counter-air) and protection for ground forces in the form of both Close Air Support (CAS) and Air Interdiction (AI). The LPH or an aircraft carrier with a specifically configured TAG, as well as other ships, submarines and craft, can extend protection through the ability to recover combat personnel quickly if they come under serious threat. However, as well as taking precautions against conventional threats close to land such as mines and fast inshore attack craft, the increased likelihood of terrorist action means that ships in harbour, operating in littoral waters or transiting through choke points must take additional precautions against the threat of *asymmetric attack*.

Interdiction operations are usually conducted on a joint basis at the operational level. In this context, maritime Task Groups may be providers of air capability but also have the potential to provide EW support. They can contribute to the control of **the electromagnetic spectrum** by determining and managing their own use of the spectrum and by taking action to help deny the enemy the use of it. Domination of the spectrum contributes directly to finding the enemy and, through deception, improving the effectiveness of manoeuvre. Of particular value are SSNs, destroyers and frigates fitted with Communications Electronic Warfare Support Measures (CESM) equipment and links into intelligence support from our allies via satellite, although any warship fitted with an EW capability has a significant ability to support operations ashore.

The **command and control** function for operations ashore can be based at sea. Although not an aircraft carrier's principal role, the UK's CVSs have the facilities for a JTFHQ (Afloat). In principle, an essentially land orientated operation can be commanded by the Joint Task Force Commander entirely from the sea, although the Land Component Commander is likely to feel more comfortable exercising his command from a location ashore. The Air Component Commander and key elements of his headquarters would collocate with the JTFC with the other elements in a Combined Air Operations Centre (CAOC) ashore. Nevertheless, the JTFHQ (Afloat) may have important advantages, particularly in the early stages of an operation or during withdrawal when its mobility, security, and command and control fit, combined with a collocated source of support helicopters, may make it a compelling solution.

Closely related to the command and control function, a key feature of maritime forces is their access to sophisticated, high data rate (satellite) communications, which represent a powerful capability for receiving **information and intelligence** and accessing shore based information networks and intelligence databases. With an appropriately configured staff, this joint intelligence product can be collated, processed, supplemented by the local picture and disseminated over maritime and land based communications links.

A maritime Task Group may be the means by which an intervention force **deploys**, in particular in effecting entry into theatre and conducting movement within it. This is an important possibility, with a maritime force typically able to move significant quantities of troops and materiel, once embarked, in the order of 400 miles in 24 hours. Finally there is the *joint sea basing* of forces and logistics for use ashore when and where required. Support helicopters using an aircraft carrier, an LPH or an LPD as an operating base are able to provide combat service support to **sustain** operations ashore through all stages of a campaign. *Sustainability* is "the ability of a force to maintain the necessary level of combat power for the duration required to achieve its objectives".

No weapons platform is able to offer universal application. Some, however, offer such a broad range of applications across so many types of operation that their potential value is considerable. Perhaps no other contains so much joint potential as an aircraft carrier. It has utility in all three environments within a theatre of operations, in both the delivery of combat capability and its command and control. It is emphatically not merely a maritime asset; it is joint, in terms of both the capability it can deliver and the operational environmental impact it has. There has been a tendency in the past to regard aircraft carriers as naval units, purveying naval aircraft almost in competition with the RAF. This is erroneous and blinkered thinking. There can be no doubt at all that aircraft are best and most easily operated from properly equipped land bases. However, they are not always available. That being the case, aircraft carriers should correctly be seen as 'joint airfields' operated by the RN for all three Services, and even other nations - although, of course, the difficulties of achieving such implied multinational interoperability should not be underestimated.

The development of the Joint Force Harrier concept has seen RN and RAF Harriers operating as a cohesive whole from the carrier base. Looking into the future, this force will continue with the F-35 Joint Combat Aircraft (JCA), which will be the replacement aircraft for both the Sea Harrier F/A2 and the RAF's Harrier GR7/GR9.

HMS ILLUSTRIOUS with her air group of Royal Navy Sea
Harriers and Royal Air Force Harrier GR7s on deck

An artist's impression of the Type 45 destroyer HMS DARING

Future Maritime Operations and Concepts

9

The Royal Navy is a unique combination of land, sea and air capabilities merged into a single, adaptable and dynamic force. As we move to the future we need to build on this flexibility to create an ever more Versatile Maritime Force, shaped toward projecting power wherever the Nation requires it. Informed by higher level policy, and set in the context of the contribution made by the maritime component in future joint operations, concepts must be continually developed to ensure that UK's maritime forces can meet the wide ranging demands of the evolving strategic environment. This third edition of *BR 1806* has migrated the Royal Navy's previous operational concept, MCJO, into current doctrine. This chapter introduces the Royal Navy's vision of the Future Navy (FN), the factors that shaped the vision, the mechanism for its delivery and the operational concept for its employment.

Policy Framework and the Future Strategic Context

The baseline for the UK's armed forces is the *Strategic Defence Review* (SDR) of 1998, which defined a range of missions and tasks that the forces would undertake in the future. A *New Chapter* to SDR (2002) was written following the terrorist attacks in USA on 11 September 2001, which confirmed that we were going in the right direction but also recognized that we needed to refocus some capabilities against the complex, dynamic and elusive threat presented by international terrorism.

The latest **Defence Strategic Guidance** (2003) developed a new framework of Military Tasks (see Chapter 4). This work was informed by the Joint Doctrine and Concepts Centre's **Strategic Trends** (2003), which provides a coherent view of how the world might develop over the next thirty years in ways that could alter the UK's security. Significant trends include increased turbulence world-wide with persistent low intensity threats. Terrorists and/or hostile states will have more destructive power with which to threaten the UK homeland and overseas interests. New technologies that could be used by future adversaries, such as biotechnology, will proliferate, and it is likely that there will be new nuclear and WMD powers. There will be increasing competition for scarcer natural resources, aggravated by the effects of climate change as a result of global warming, and there are likely to be increasing calls for humanitarian intervention and assistance overseas, particularly in sub-Saharan Africa.

Two further pieces give high level context for how we are to operate in the future. The **UK Joint Vision** (JV) paper addresses the requirement identified in SDR to have '…a clearer long term vision of the way in which we expect our forces and their methods of operation to develop…'. It gives broad guidance on the capabilities our forces will need in order to fight in the described manner successfully and introduces a **High Level Operational Concept** (HLOC), describing how we expect our forces to fight in the period beyond 2015.

The Nature of Future Operations

UK policy and the strategic trends outlined above are likely to result in the deployment of UK forces more often than we had envisaged, and further afield than Europe, the Gulf and the Mediterranean, which had been identified in SDR as the primary focus of our interests. Forces are also more likely to be employed in defence of the homeland against *asymmetric* threats. Overseas operations will probably be multinational in character, albeit with a limited number of nations with the ability to lead them, and frequently in complex terrain such as mountain regions and urban areas. The asymmetric terrorist threat will result in a more diffuse and dispersed battlespace and operations against terrorist targets are likely to require smaller scale insertions of combat power. What is abundantly clear is that there remains a requirement for a wide and flexible range of military options, including rapidly deployable forces with strategic lift and the means to gain access to crisis areas, with sufficient force protection, including along the Sea Lines of Communications. Conventional weapons must have a capacity for precision and penetration so as to minimise incidental damage, as even low casualty rates will be politically difficult to accept over a protracted period. Media attention will continue to increase the degree to which military operations are exposed to public scrutiny. Operations may well be difficult to terminate and withdrawal may become as difficult a part of them as entry.

JV notes 4 key differences between how we do our business today and how we will do it in future: we will seek swift strategic deployability; we will prosecute **Effects Based Operations** (EBO); Information Operations (Info Ops) will be of increased importance; and there will be a growing emphasis on *Deep Operations*. Drawing on JV, the HLOC describes the UK Armed Forces as being agile, empowered by **Network Enabled Capability** (NEC) to give situational awareness within a variable resolution battlespace. The two key emerging themes from these papers, EBO and NEC, are expanded upon below. Both are in their infancy but promise much and should be embraced by the Royal Navy in order to realise the step-change in effectiveness that they offer.

Effects Based Operations and Network Enabled Capability

The UK's Armed Forces, and thus the Future Navy, are heading towards EBO enabled by a broad and robust NEC. The pace of change in this area, led by the United States, has continued to accelerate and in future it will be less useful to measure combat power in crude terms of numbers of platforms and people than in terms of our ability to deliver specific *effects*.

Future military operations will place increased emphasis on influencing the mind of an adversary, and EBO approaches this goal by seeking to co-ordinate the activities of all National players. Once the Grand Strategic objectives have been identified (the **Ends**) the various **Ways** of achieving them are assessed and, following this, are allocated to the relevant instrument of National Power (Economic, Military, Diplomatic – the **Means**). This approach will then cascade down each chain. Successful EBO rely on identifying the effects that will lead to campaign success and on deploying the optimum mix of capabilities with which to achieve them. However, EBO will not reach its full potential without NEC.

NEC envisages the provision of a single, robust UK communications architecture and comprehensive joint information management procedures that are compatible with close allies; it is seen as key to the UK's future expeditionary capability. At the operational level NEC will allow powerful new combinations of combat power, principally through shared situational awareness. Further to this, NEC will enable enhanced joint and integrated planning and should aid agility by avoiding unnecessarily early commitment to a particular course of action.

9/1. Effects Based Operations – The Ends, Ways and Means

Effects are achieved by firstly determining the Ends (what objectives must be achieved in order to bring about campaign success). For any given objective, there will then be a number of Ways in which to do this (options or courses of actions, dependent upon our will and approach (or that of an adversary), which describe how these objectives could be delivered). Finally, for any particular course of action, the Means are the specific capabilities that may be used (and applied across the strategic environment). Thus it is the selection of the Ends (the objectives), the Ways (the options) and the Means (the capabilities) that collectively determine the Effect that is to be delivered.

The Future Navy Process

The Future Navy Process (FNP) enables the strategic management of the Royal Navy across the Lines of Development (LoD: Personnel and Individual Training; Equipment; Sustainability; Collective Training; Structures;

Concepts and Doctrine), as directed by the First Sea Lord and the Navy Board. Its aim is to develop and deliver the Navy Board's vision for the Royal Navy of the future (the Future Navy (FN)). The FNP both informs and is guided by the Departmental Force Development and Definition process and this symbiotic relationship ensures that the outputs of the FNP are coherent with Joint thinking and benefit from single Service and Joint advocacy. The 3 elements of the FNP are **The Future Navy, The Future Maritime Operational Concept** and **The Naval Strategic Plan**.

The Future Navy

The *Future Navy* paper sets out the military strategic concept for the Navy in the 2015 (+) timeframe. It provides the enduring vision for the Royal Navy, acting as a headmark for the strategic Force Development and planning processes. At its core lies the concept of the Versatile Maritime Force (VMF) with an emphasis on warfighting and power projection, but which is capable of contributing to the differing scales of effort defined in MOD policy guidance through an ability to configure a force, formation or unit to allow it to operate successfully and cost effectively across a range of missions and tasks.

The VMF will deliver global reach and presence with afloat and shore sustainability. It will conduct contingent Joint operations overseas, gaining assured access to the theatre of operations for the maritime based Joint Force, and enable or deliver rapid maritime and Joint effects. It will also achieve or contribute to decision superiority. The VMF will make a significant and decisive contribution to UK's maritime security, support Other Government Departments and protect the maritime expeditionary capability. Importantly, the VMF must be fully interoperable with the Future Army, Future Air Force and other potential national and international military and civil partners in future Joint or Coalition operations.

To meet the pace of change the VMF will be sufficiently agile to meet the full spectrum of future operational tasks. The VMF will deliver the effects for which it will be optimised earlier, faster and with more precision and discrimination than before. It will be responsive, robust, flexible and well suited to the challenges of a rapidly changing strategic environment. It will continue to offer political choice to decision-makers as an instrument of Government. It will be inherently adaptable for the future and must retain the hallmark of the Royal Navy; that is its qualitative edge.

The Future Maritime Operational Concept

The *Future Maritime Operational Concept* (FMOC) describes, at a high level, how UK's maritime forces will fight in the 2015 (+) timeframe. Effects and capability-based, and enshrined in the manoeuvrist approach to warfare, the FMOC paper identifies those capabilities that will be brought to the Joint battle from the maritime environment. FMOC has evolved directly from MCJO, which in turn built on many enduring principles of maritime doctrine. It should therefore come as no surprise that the principles of FMOC have similarities with much of the revised doctrine in this edition of *BR 1806*. FMOC does, however, move conceptual thinking forward significantly in considering operations in the Information Age, and provides a framework to enhance the linkage between strategy and task – the contribution of tactical combat to the overall strategic aim – consistent with an Effects Based Approach. Carefully chosen effects, co-ordinated and integrated across the battlespace, will permit the generation of high tempo and rapid application of combat power with smaller deployed forces.

Agility will be a force characteristic by design across the LoD and will embrace the attributes of Responsiveness, Robustness, Flexibility and Adaptability, aiming to create a maritime capability that moves quickly and efficiently to meet future challenges. FMOC identifies how the VMF, with utility across the spectrum of conflict, will operate in a joint and multinational battlespace. The VMF will achieve this through five Core Maritime Roles (CMRs). Maritime Force Projection (comprising Maritime Strike and Littoral Manoeuvre), Theatre Entry (for the Joint Force) and Flexible Global Reach (sustainability and endurance to operate in the geographic regions identified in UK defence policy) embody the expeditionary focus of future capability, whilst UK Maritime Security addresses the contribution to the defence of the UK and home based protection of our Fighting Power. All are enabled by the last CMR,

Networked C4ISR (Command, Control, Communications, Intelligence, Surveillance and Reconnaissance).

FMOC describes a maritime capability that will contribute significantly to the Joint force of the future. Using traditional attributes of global reach and persistence, the Joint Commander will be provided with a potent mix of jointly configured theatre entry and strike capabilities, either as the vanguard for a mission or as a supporting force. The inherently large capacity of maritime transport units will continue to ensure that the sea remains the medium for the majority of strategic lift for any sizeable Joint force, complementing swifter but smaller capacity airlift capabilities. Increasingly joint in perspective, the VMF will be a truly dynamic entity.

The Naval Strategic Plan

The *Naval Strategic Plan* (NSP) lies at the heart of the Royal Navy's planning process. It states the First Sea Lord's strategic intent for the next 15 years and is effectively the routemap to the delivery of the FN. It reflects a Navy that has adapted well to the rapidly changing strategic environment of recent years and has a clear vision of how it needs to evolve in the future. The delivery of the FN and development of the VMF's capabilities are closely linked to the future concepts of the MOD as a whole using six "Pillars" (People, Equipment, Sustainability, Collective Training, Structures, Concepts and Doctrine) that mirror the MOD LoD. This ensures that the Navy's plan is closely aligned with central policy. Each pillar has a 2 Star officer as Sponsor and 1 Star lead who act on behalf of the Navy Board to develop the actions and achieve the improvements necessary to maintain a World Class Navy into the future. In addition, the First Sea Lord has personally appointed teams of "Champions" (each team has a 1 Star officer or civilian equivalent and a Warrant Officer) to help drive progress within each Pillar. An annual review of Pillar progress provides regular and detailed insight for the Navy Board on the strengths and weaknesses of the FN and VMF. This in turn informs consideration of strategic requirements and priorities in the MOD Annual Planning Round.

Conclusions

Much can change between establishing a new concept, such as FMOC, and bringing into service the capabilities needed to support it. World events and changes in policy may require substantial revisions of the concept or, *in extremis*, a completely new concept. The Future Navy Process mirrors the vision of the Future Navy itself in being agile and able to respond rapidly to such requirements. Nevertheless, some constants are likely to remain.

HM Forces will continue to act as a force for good in the world. In the new strategic circumstances, the philosophy of Manoeuvre Warfare remains appropriate and it demands the integration of all six capability elements (Air, Maritime, Land, Logistics, C4ISR, SF). All of this draws upon the traditional worth of maritime assets – flexibility, low political risk, access, reach, mobility and sustainability – allowing maritime power to be employed across the range of crisis and political activity, and conferring the ability to send an extensive range of signals.

Maritime forces will make critical contributions to future joint operations, which will frequently and ultimately involve operations against and on the land. Maritime power allows the projection of force to be carried out at minimum political and military risk, whilst easing the force protection problem. It allows for the exercise of Joint Task Force Command from offshore unless and until it is more sensible to move ashore, an attribute that the future digitisation of the battlespace will further enhance. Maritime power also makes a major, if not essential, contribution to the logistic sustainability of the joint force. Lastly it allows considerable in-theatre tactical manoeuvrability, at any stage in a campaign.

The changed military and political world is one for which the inherent flexibility of maritime power might have been designed. But it is important to stress again that maritime power does not mean naval power in the narrow sense. It means the use of the sea to deliver sea, land and air power to where it can most usefully be applied; to provide transport, mounting bases, airfields for all comers, stores depots, barracks, fire support, and refugee havens. It is a thoroughly joint contribution to a necessarily joint endeavour.

In summary, the sea is a pre-eminent medium because, above all, it provides access at a time and place of political choice. By history, tradition and skill the UK is better placed, certainly than any other European nation, to exploit this medium and to develop a strategic doctrine of warfare based on the joint use of the sea. The resultant theory is rooted in traditional virtues yet highly relevant to, and congruent with, modern needs, operational and tactical doctrine and providing as much strategic choice and operational flexibility as is likely to be possible. Ultimately, maritime forces can only realise their considerable potential when integrated fully into a joint force, through which operational value is increased beyond the mere sum of its constituent parts.

HMS VICTORY, Nelson's flagship at the Battle of Trafalgar

From Trafalgar to Today

A Bibliographical Essay on Doctrine and the Development of British Naval Strategic Thought

A fine example of empathy between commanders and mutual comprehension working at all levels is the executive order given by Lord Barham, First Lord of the Admiralty, to Lord Nelson for the final phase of the campaign of Trafalgar. The order told Nelson to sail in the VICTORY, collecting other ships on passage down the Channel, to take command of the squadrons of Admirals Calder and Collingwood, blockade Cadiz, reinforce Gibraltar and reorganize an enlarged area of command. Nowhere does the order tell Nelson how to perform these tasks. Rather, the order begins, "...as your judgement seem best..." and ends, "...from the opinion we entertain of your conduct and abilities... you will proceed to form the best system of so extensive a command that circumstances may admit of ...". These two phrases are, of course, the key to understanding the order and its successful outcome. Such an order was only possible because Barham and Nelson were each confident that they were following a common strategy and that they shared the same doctrine, that both knew what the other meant and could be relied upon to act accordingly, using judgement and experience. The order was written in less than 250 words.[1]

BARHAM'S INSTRUCTIONS TO NELSON (5th SEPTEMBER 1805)

"Your Lordship, being already in possession of our several orders for the government of your conduct as commander-in-chief in the Mediterranean, you are, in addition thereto, hereby required and directed to proceed with the VICTORY and the ships named....whose captains have orders to place themselves under your orders, to the Bay of Cadiz, where you may expect to find Vice-Admiral Collingwood and Vice-Admiral Sir Robert Calder, and the squadron of HM ships under his command. You will take such measures for the effectual blockade of the ports of Cadiz and San Lucar, as to your judgement shall seem best.

"After leaving such number of ships under the command of Vice-Admiral Collingwood for the blockade of Cadiz, as that service may require, you will proceed to Gibraltar, and take the most effectual measures for putting that garrison and the port thereof, so far as relates to the naval department, into the best possible state of defence, by allotting such a force thereto as may secure the trade of HM subjects in passing and repassing the Gut.

"And whereas, from the opinion we entertain of your conduct and abilities, we have thought fit to extend your command to Cape St. Vincent, you will proceed to form the best system for the management of so extensive a command that circumstances may admit of at the time."

Similarly, shared doctrine within the fleet enabled Nelson to bring his ships into battle on the morning of Trafalgar with a minimum of signals. Indeed, even the famous signal, "England expects..." was nearly never made because Captain Blackwood of the EURYALUS told Nelson it was unnecessary as the whole fleet seemed very clearly to understand what they were about. A mile away in ROYAL SOVEREIGN Collingwood, when he saw the signal, remarked that he wished Nelson would stop signalling "...as we all know well enough what we have to do...".

More than 125 years later, on 12th December 1939, two British and a New Zealand cruiser converged in the South Atlantic and Commodore Harwood issued his orders in a terse signal: "My policy with three cruisers versus one pocket battleship. Attack at once by day or night. By day act as two units. First Division (AJAX and ACHILLES) and EXETER diverge to permit flank marking. First Division will concentrate gunfire. By night ships will normally remain in company in open order". At 0616 the next morning, having sighted the German GRAF SPEE, AJAX and ACHILLES attacked as one division and EXETER hauled out of the line to attack from a different bearing. From then until the bitter action was broken off, when GRAF SPEE was chased into a neutral harbour, no other tactical signals were made, the three cruisers manoeuvring as necessary to clear their lines of fire on the German. It is a striking proof of the high state of training and understanding within the Royal Navy at the start of the Second World War that one of the first major actions could be fought on the basis of a signal just a few lines long and that nothing needed to be added during the battle.[2] It is clear, whether it was Harwood and his Captains, Barham and Nelson, or Nelson and his band of brothers that they all shared a common purpose and corporate body of knowledge. Today such knowledge is defined as doctrine.

Just as doctrine is about achieving a common level of understanding of tactics, operations and strategy so that commanders and planners will act instinctively and correctly in the wide variety of situations which they are likely to meet, that admirals will know how their captains are likely to act in any given situation, and captains will know what their superiors would wish, so it is also important to realise what doctrine is not. Doctrine, while it is authoritative, is not a substitute for judgement and experience, though the degree of judgement needed or experience available may vary with circumstances. Doctrine is not dogma: as the first edition of **BR 1806** said, it "...must evolve as its political and strategic foundations alter and in the light of new technology, the lessons of experience and the insights of operational analysis ...". The use of doctrine credits the individual, wherever he or she is in the chain or command, with a wide measure of initiative. Doctrine is not absolute, but is derived from first principles, but these principles themselves are not unchanging: for example, the tactics of the Grand Fleet at Jutland were not appropriate to winning the anti-submarine battle in 1917. Similarly, Western naval strategy in the Cold War is no longer useful when general war in Europe seems unlikely.

At the tactical level doctrine does tend to be specific to its context and to consist of a definite list of recommended actions. In the Royal Navy this tactical doctrine has hitherto been contained in *The Fighting Instructions*, although the adoption of NATO tactical doctrine for the majority of maritime operations has allowed this publication to be re-scoped recently to provide guidance for the Maritime Component Commander and his subordinates. When tactical doctrine is not understood, ships are lost. For example, in December 1941 Rear Admiral Sir Philip Vian's flag captain hesitated in turning the force to counter a torpedo threat, and the flagship, NAIAD, was sunk.[3] At the higher, operational and strategic levels doctrine is much more interpretative. On another occasion Vian, who was one of the greatest British fighting admirals of the Second World War, displayed his understanding of operational level doctrine by disobeying orders. During the hunt for the German battleship BISMARCK in May 1941, Vian was ordered to close on the Commander-in-Chief, but realising that his was the only force which could make contact with the enemy before night-fall, Vian chose to shadow and attack the BISMARCK.[4]

THE LOSS OF HMS NAIAD

"Time elapsed before the signal was seen; and almost as it was received I saw a torpedo track approaching NAIAD, which was too close to avoid. I say almost, but indeed there were seconds in which the helm could have been put over. As I was on the bridge, Grantham asked me which way to turn the Force, just as the alarm belatedly came through. I momentarily deliberated: fatally. The torpedo exploded in the exact spot in which a single hit could sink a cruiser of the DIDO class, that is, on the bulkhead between the two engine-rooms. A few yards either side, which an immediate alteration of course would have ensured, would have lodged the torpedo in one engine-room only"

In the American war in the Pacific during the Second World War there was no single unified command but the several commanders were all thinking in sufficiently like terms to construct a strategic victory from a mosaic of individual battles.[5]

Clearly, those in command, preparing themselves for command or contemplating a career leading to command need to be well read. British armed forces are apolitical, so while individuals need to be aware of domestic and international politics and of current affairs, a discussion of these subjects is necessarily outside the limits of this essay. They need however to understand the origins of strategy, its development and historic context. However, if doctrine is about achieving a common level of understanding of strategy, operations and tactics, and, if the Royal Navy has been successful for many years in those very activities, do not the senior officers of the Royal Navy already have, and always have had, a thorough understanding of these issues?

Rather surprisingly in 1890 *The Times*, in reviewing Captain Mahan's first book, ***The Influence of Sea Power upon History, 1660 to 1793***, was able to thunder that "... the book is almost a pioneer in its class, for, strange to say, the literature of the greatest Naval Power in history has no authoritative treatise on the principles of Naval Warfare...". Mahan gave statesmen and sailors alike, American, British and many others, the first general theory of sea power in modern times. The concept he gave was that being a great power meant being a sea power and that being a sea power meant commercial and naval strength. Mahan was quickly translated into many languages, and in the German navy the Kaiser made it compulsory reading. However, Mahan's elegant, if protracted, theories were traduced into the idea of a decisive battle between opposing fleets after which one side or the other would be left in command of the seas:[6] this is a crude version of Mahanian theory.[7] Mahan's ideas have been tarnished by this interpretation and the value of his work diminished. Today, for example, among the hundreds of titles all available from the US Naval Institute Press, Mahan is out of print. In any case, pure Mahan can be difficult to access, though one way to come to grips with Mahan's theories is through John Hattendorf's edited selections of *Mahan on Naval Strategy*.[8]

The American Mahan, even if he is the best known, is not and was not the only author to formulate a theory of sea power: his British counterpart is Sir Julian S Corbett. In *The Education of a Navy: the development of British naval strategic thought 1867-1914* Donald Schurman gives a more balanced view than *The Times* in 1890 of the development of British thinking about sea power and naval strategy. Schurman analyses the works of the Colomb brothers (one so verbose that Fisher called him "column and a half"!), Sir John Laughton and Admiral Sir Herbert Richmond, as well as Mahan and Corbett. Amongst other ideas Schurman recognises that thinking about warlike activity has been dominated by concepts which give land forces priority over naval forces and that naval personnel who do think about these things have tended to keep their thoughts to themselves. When analysing the works of Corbett, Schurman extracts two critical points, that "...it was unanimity of purpose and universality of strategic understanding that stamped the English sea moves with success ... naval officers worked from an agreed body of common doctrine..." and "...that a common knowledge of theory opened up channels of communications between leaders in the military forces and their political masters when all had drunk at the same fountain of knowledge ...".[9]

Eric Grove edits arguably the best edition of Corbett's *Principles of Maritime Strategy*. Corbett recognised the primacy of politics in directing war and developing appropriate strategies. He also distinguished between "...maritime strategy, the principles which govern a war in which the sea is a substantial factor ..." and "... naval strategy, that part of it which determines the movements of the fleet when maritime strategy has determined what part the fleet must play in relation to the action of the land forces...". Famously, he went on to say that "... since men live upon the land and not upon the sea, great issues between nations at war have always been decided - except in the rarest of cases - either by what your army can do against your enemy's territory and national life, or else by the fear of what the fleet makes it possible for your army to do...".[10] Corbett's ideas were greeted with some scepticism by contemporary senior naval officers - he was even blamed by some for the failure to achieve decisive battle at Jutland - but his ideas of limited warfare and joint operations are much more in kilter with present ideas of expeditionary warfare. In conclusion, John Gooch is probably right in his view of the contribution of Mahan and Corbett to naval thinking, that "...Mahan's theories have worn less well than Corbett's ... but together the two men stand as the founding fathers - as well as rivals - of modern maritime strategic thought...".[11]

On the plane of pure theory of strategy, in Peter Paret's *Makers of Modern Strategy: from Machiavelli to the Nuclear Age* Mahan is the only naval strategist to be awarded individual treatment.[12] In *Masters of War: classical strategic thought* where George Handel compares Sun Tsu, Clausewitz, Jomini and others including Machiavelli, Mahan is only mentioned three times and Corbett never.[13] More recently Handel has ranked Sun Tsu, Thucydides, Machiavelli, Clausewitz, Jomini and Mahan as amongst the greats and Corbett as first among the also-rans. This interesting observation deserves a separate discussion since many of these authors are only known to us through aphorisms and obscure sound bites. Briefly, Sun Tsu was not translated until early in the 20th century and had no influence on the others; Thucydides never wrote about strategy directly so his ideas are only available by inference and implication; Machiavelli was a medieval statesman whose principal interest was in statecraft; Jomini (who certainly influenced Mahan in his early years) wrote in French and is today unfashionable, and Clausewitz never finished his *On War*, which was only translated from German into English in 1874, i.e. after the first "modern" wars of the 19th century. On Clausewitz's premature death his wife managed only to partly finish his work - a fact which some hold to be the reason why academics prefer him, since they can argue over what they think he would have said. So, even if Corbett is only first of the second division of military and naval philosophers, then he is still first amongst the useful strategists.

In the genus of maritime and naval strategy, there are many good books, some of which have been popular in their time and whose authors have contributed specific ideas to the body of theory. However, since strategy and hence doctrine is affected by circumstances it is not surprising that few authors have been able to divorce themselves from their contemporary context, whether it is the dominant technology in use or the politics of the day. This is a besetting sin of, and should be a warning to, all retired admirals and captains, a sin committed by authors down the years such as Custance, Grenfell,[14] Richmond,[15] Scholfield,[16] Gretton,[17] Roskill,[18] and even Mahan. For example, few authors writing in the 1980s towards the end of the Cold War could envisage a world without two or more superpowers in confrontation. Hence the advice of one eminent scholar that it is not worth reading anything written before 1989.

The two books on Mahan and Corbett which have been already mentioned come from the Classics of Sea Power series, edited by John Hattendorf and Wayne Hughes for the Naval Institute Press at Annapolis. This series also makes available to us much foreign thinking on the evolution of naval strategy and operations, including the Russian S.O.Makarov,[19] the French Raoul Castex,[20] and the German Wolfgang Wegener.[21] Other British authors in the same series include Philip Colomb,[22] and Charles Calwell,[23] as well, of course, as several American authors. For another, non Anglo-Saxon view of the world there is *Maritime Strategy and Continental Wars* by Rear Admiral Raja Menon, Indian Navy.[24]

In the Cold War strategy did tend to ossify, perhaps not unexpectedly since even in the late 1980s confrontation between superpowers seemed to be a permanent state of affairs. During this period and especially towards its end the US Navy developed a maritime strategy, which can be interpreted, in a crude way, as Mahanian. Good reading on this subject is Norman Friedman's *The US Maritime Strategy*,[25] and the subject is brought up to date and developed by Stewart Fraser in *US Maritime Strategy: issues and implications*, a short paper from the Centre for Defence and International Security Studies at the University of Lancaster.[26]

For the Royal Navy the Cold War was a lean time, its low point the 1981 Defence Review and the resignation of the then Navy Minister, Keith Speed. It did not help that in the circumstances of the time the then Secretary of State for Defence was probably right to commit British forces to the Continent and to disinvest in the Navy. Coincidentally it is possible to chart the rise of British naval, strategic thought. Sir James Cable had already published, in 1971, his first edition of *Gunboat Diplomacy* about the limited application of naval force (and is remarkable not least for its anticipation of the newly introduced British concept of *defence diplomacy*), but he was largely ignored by a service preparing for general war against the Soviet Union.[27] *Gunboat Diplomacy* is already a classic work that has been reprinted and updated in Britain and America several times, the latest in 1994. Then in the black night of the 1980s there were two or three landmark publications. Geoffrey Till, now professor and dean of academic studies at the Joint Services Command and Staff College, edited a volume, *The Future of British Sea Power*, proceedings of a conference in 1983, which opened with an important statement about the Government's policy towards the Navy by the new Secretary of State, Michael Heseltine.[28] In the same year Sir James Cable published *Britain's Naval Future*, which looks increasingly perceptive in its arguments for a stronger maritime strategy.[29] Then in 1986 Rear Admiral Richard Hill brought out *Maritime Strategy for Medium Powers*, which recognised Britain's reduced role but also began to introduce new arguments and concepts such as *reach*.[30]

In this revival of interest in maritime history and strategy, other modern writers not mentioned elsewhere in this essay are Jan Breemer, Michael Duffy, Barry Gough, Andrew Lambert, Nicholas Lambert, Williamson Murray, Norman Polmar, Michael Pugh, Nicholas Rodger, David Rosenberg, and Jon Sumida (this list of names is only meant to be indicative). There have also been several good anthologies about sea power, one being *Seapower and Strategy*,[31] edited by Colin Gray and Roger Barnet, and *Maritime Strategy and the Balance of Power*:[32] though both were published in 1989 and thus overtaken by the end of the Cold War, they provide good, coherent surveys of the subject. One more anthology is the 1995 *Navies and Global Defense: theories and strategy*, published in Canada and less well known than it deserves.[33] Another valuable contribution to debate is Geoffrey Till's 1994 *Seapower Theory and Practice*, in particular his own perceptive essay *Maritime Strategy and the Twenty First Century*.[34] In this essay, which has stood the test of time well, Geoffrey Till argues that the changed global security environment means back-to-basics for strategists - and thus for doctrine writers - and he predicts more use and utility of navies in the 21st century. However, perhaps the most significant post-Cold War work is Colin Gray's *The Leverage of Sea Power*, published in 1992 and reckoned to be essential reading for anyone thinking about the role of maritime power.[35] Gray's central thesis is that sea power grants the ability to control the geostrategic terms of war and that the state or coalition of states which most effectively harnesses sea power wins wars.

In the last few years strategic and doctrinal thinking in the world's navies has evolved rapidly. From India Admiral Raja Menon has already been mentioned, and Australia too has proved a particularly fertile ground for new ideas about maritime strategy and security, two leading authors being James Goldrick and Sam Bateman. Naturally however the evolution has been most marked and most fertile in the world's largest navy and the influences on and the process of making strategy have been very well described in David Rosenberg's essay on making modern naval strategy.[36] Most notably, "*... From the Sea - Preparing the Naval Service for the 21st Century*", a joint United States Navy/US Marine Corps paper was published in 1992 and its successor paper in 1994 "*Forward from the Sea*". The former paper describes how, in the changed strategic environment, the attention of the US Navy and Marine Corps would shift towards littoral warfare and manoeuvre from the sea: the latter assesses the two Services' contribution to the totality of American armed power. These two American papers give a high level concept compatible with the post Cold War era from which strategy and then doctrine can be derived: they have also had a considerable influence on British naval thinking. In 1996 the Commander in Chief Fleet, Admiral Abbott, argued that territorial defence was no longer necessary to Britain and Europe, who with allies in and out of NATO must now be ready to project visible and useable power in order to deter, dissuade, protect mutual interests and, if necessary, credibly coerce.[37] In *Dimensions of Sea Power: strategic choice in the modern world* it was argued that the qualities and capabilities of a maritime strategy are particularly suitable for use in the unpredictable and confused situations which might threaten Britain's interests, whether these are vital, secondary or altruistic.[38] Then Brigadier Rob Fry perceived broad and enduring rhythms of strategy, and suggested that Britain's declared foreign policy must be active and occasionally militant if it is to be relevant and credible, that there was a growing consensus among professional military and defence-academics that future operations are likely to be expeditionary, and that a "maritime national strategy" was the appropriate response to the changed geopolitical environment.[39] This strategy, which emerged afresh from the British government's Strategic Defence Review (SDR) in 1998, is no other than the British way in warfare, for which Captain Sir Basil Liddell-Hart is best known (though in fact he synthesised the views of others including Herbert Richmond). For a historical overview of the British way in warfare see David French's book.[40] The past First Sea Lord, Admiral Sir Jock Slater, assessed that the changes which have taken place since 1989 caught the grand strategic mood of the time to which the Royal Navy responded with its concept of the Maritime Contribution to Joint Operations.[41]

The SDR marked the end in Britain of a period of post Cold War thinking. It marked a significant and historic shift in British Defence policy, away from a continental commitment back to a more maritime, expeditionary role for British armed forces. Certainly the Royal Navy and Royal Marines, which during the Cold War sometimes had difficulty in putting their case, emerged well from the SDR. In particular, several influential articles by senior officers in the RUSI journal have marked the changes and have armed the Navy with a new and more powerful rationale for its doctrine. What is now needed is a unifying theory to digest the changes that have taken place since the end of the Cold War and to encapsulate the present state of theory about maritime strategy. One candidate for this is clearly Cable's latest book, *The Political Influence of Naval Force in History*, in which he examines the use of naval force for political purposes and concludes that naval - he means maritime - force is attractive to politicians because it is easier to limit and control, inflicts no collateral damage, can poise and sustain a threat without perpetrating any warlike act, can deploy without commitment, or wait, gain time for diplomacy and withdraw without loss of face.[42] In short, the adoption by politicians of a maritime strategy allows them flexibility and choice.

One book deserves a separate category of its own, and that is Andrew Gordon's *The Rules of the Game: Jutland and British naval command*.[43] Gordon's book has probably been sold and read more widely amongst officers of the Royal Navy than any other book in recent times. It is a fascinating and controversial book that can be read and enjoyed at different levels. While dealing with the events and the personalities leading up to the Battle of Jutland in 1916, it is, as the subtitle warns us, about the development of the minds of and the mindset of senior officers and their approach to the problems of command, whether their actions should be ruled by doctrine or dogma. In *Rules of the Game* Gordon characterises commanders as rat-catchers or regulators, though in actuality any commander may have a mixture of both styles. It is an important book because it is the most recent and probably the best analysis of a fundamental problem that lies at the heart of all doctrine and strategy: how to encourage initiative and flexibility while maintaining effective command and control. In other words, how to institutionalise sound doctrine without turning it into rigid dogma. There are no black and white answers.

Other books to look out for are *The Changing Face of Maritime Power*, the proceedings of a conference held at the former Royal Naval College Greenwich to mark the translation to the Joint Services Command and Staff College, and *New Dimensions: the Royal Navy, maritime manoeuvre, and the Strategic Defence Review*, a collection of essays by distinguished military and civilian authors who assessed the impact of the SDR one year on from the announcement of its findings.

For a salutary memoir of operational command at sea in a major war, *Destroyer Captain*, by Roger Hill, cannot be bettered.[44] Hill took part in Russian convoys, nursed OHIO into Malta at the end of Operation PEDESTAL, and grounded his ASDIC dome off the beach on D-Day. At the end of the war, exhausted and disillusioned, he emigrated to New Zealand and became a dockside stevedore. His often harrowing account of the war illustrates many of the command issues raised in *BR 1806*, and should be read as much by those who will direct naval operations from shore, as by those who command at sea.

This has been no more than a catspaw of wind across the surface of a huge subject. One of the purposes of this essay is to indicate that the subject is constantly under development and that there is yet more that can be read about and written upon sea power and maritime strategy. A score of authors and their books, essays and articles have been mentioned in the text and more in the footnotes, and many of the books listed have their own bibliographies. However, just as students and practitioners, senior officials and politicians need to make up their own minds about what is an appropriate strategy, what doctrine should be associated with this, and how it should be applied in changing circumstances, so they should make up their own minds about what is the best to read on the subject. While the expert is presumably already well-read, it is suggested that the novice might wish to start with reading the essays in RUSI, then read Gray, Gordon, Hattendorf on Mahan, and Grove on Corbett, Fraser, Till, and Cable's latest book. A suggested short reading list therefore is:

THE RUSI ARTICLES

Admiral Sir Peter Abbott: *The Maritime Component of British and Allied Military Strategy*

Brigadier Rob Fry: *End of the Continental Century*

Admiral Sir Jock Slater: *The Maritime Contribution to Joint Operations*

BOOKS

Colin S. Gray: *The Leverage of Sea Power*

Andrew Gordon: *The Rules of the Game*

Alfred T. Mahan: *Mahan on Naval Strategy: selections from the writings of Rear Admiral Alfred Thayer Mahan* (Classics of Sea Power series)

Julian S. Corbett: *Some Principles of Maritime Strategy* (Classics of Sea Power series)

Geoffrey Till: *Seapower Theory & Practice*

James Cable: *The Political Influence of Naval Force in History*

OTHER PUBLICATIONS

Stewart Fraser: *US Maritime Strategy: issues and implications* (Centre for Defence and International Security Studies)

NOTES

1   Sir John Knox Laughton, ed., *The Barham Papers* (London: Navy Records Society, 1911; Lord Barham's instructions to Lord Nelson, letter dated 5 September 1805), XXXIX

2   Sir Eugene Millington-Drake, *The Drama of the Graf Spee and the Battle of the Plate* (London: Peter Davies, 1964), pp 165, 172, 222

3   Admiral of the Fleet Sir Philip Vian, *Action This Day: a war memoir* (London: Frederick Muller Ltd, 1960), p84

4   Vian, *Action This Day: a war memoir*, p57

5   Robert B. Vice Admiral Carney, *'Logistical Planning for War'*, Naval War College Review, October (1948)

6   John Gooch, *'Maritime Command: Mahan and Corbett'*, in *Seapower and Strategy*, ed. by Colin S. Gray and Roger W. Barnett (London: Tri-Service Press, 1989), pp. 27-46

7   Paul M. Kennedy, *'British and American Strategies, 1898- 1920', in Maritime Strategy and the Balance of Power: Britain and American in the Twentieth Century* (Oxford: Macmillan in association with St Antony's College, 1989), pp.165-88

8   John B. Hattendorf, *Mahan on Naval Strategy: selections from the writings of Rear Admiral Alfred Thayer Mahan*, Classics of Sea Power edn (Annapolis: Naval Institute Press, 1991)

9   Donald M. Schurman, *The Education of a Navy: the development of British naval strategic thought 1867-1914* (London: Cassell, 1965), p17, p19, p171, p174

10 Julian S. Corbett, *Some Principles of Maritime Strategy*, Classics of Sea Power edn, with an introduction and notes by Eric J Grove (Annapolis: Naval Institute Press, 1911), pp 15-16

11 Gooch, *Maritime Command: Mahan and Corbett*

12 Peter Paret, *Makers of Modern Strategy: from Machiavelli to the nuclear age* (Princeton: Princeton University Press, 1986)

13 Michael I. Handel, *Masters of War: classical strategic thought*, Second Revised Edition edn (Portland, OR: Cass, 1992)

14 R. Grenfell, *Sea Power by T124* (New York: Doubleday, Doran, 1941)

15 H. Richmond, *Sea Power in the Modern World* (London: G Bell & Sons, 1934)

16 B. B. Scholfield, *British Sea Power* (London: Batsford, 1967)

17 Peter Gretton, *Maritime Strategy: a study of British defence problems* (London: Cassell, 1965)

18 Stephen W. Roskill, *The Strategy of Sea Power: its development and application* (London: Collins, 1962)

19 S. O. Makarov, *Discussions of Questions in Naval Tactics*, Classics of Sea Power edn (Annapolis: Naval Institute Press, 1990; with an introduction by Robert B Bathhurst)

20 Raoul Castex, *Strategic Theories*, Classics of Sea Power edn (Annapolis: Naval Institute Press, 1994; selections translated by and with an introduction by Eugenia C Kiesling)

21 Wolfgang Wegener, *The Naval Strategy of the World War*, Classics of Sea Power edn (Annapolis: Naval Institute Press, 1989; with an introduction by Holger H Herwig)

22 Vice Admiral Philip H. Colomb, *Naval Warfare*, Classics of Sea Power edn (Annapolis: Naval Institute Press, 1891; introduced by Barry M Gough)

23 Charles E. Calwell, *Military Operations and Maritime Preponderance*, Classics of Sea Power edn (Annapolis: Naval Institute Press, 1905; edited and introduced by Colin Gray)

24 Rear Admiral Raja Menon, *Maritime Strategy and Continental Wars* (London: Frank Cass, 1998)

25 Norman Friedman, *The US Maritime Strategy* (London: Jane's, 1988)

26 Stewart Fraser, *US Maritime Strategy: issues and implications*, Bailrigg Paper, 25 (Lancaster: Centre for Defence and International Security Studies, 1997)

27 James Cable, *Gunboat diplomacy 1919-1991, political applications of limited naval force* (Basingstoke: Macmillan, 1994)

28 Geoffrey Till, ed., *The Future of British Sea Power* (Annapolis: Naval Institute Press, 1984)

29 James Cable, *Britain's Naval Future* (Annapolis: Naval Institute Press, 1983)

30 Rear Admiral J. R. Hill, *Maritime Strategy for Medium Powers* (London: Croom Helm, 1986)

31 Colin S. Gray, and Roger W. Barnett, eds, *Seapower and Strategy* (Annapolis, Md: United States Naval Institute, 1989)

32 John B. Hattendorf, and Robert S. Jordan, eds, *Maritime Strategy and the Balance of Power: Britain and America in the twentieth century* (Oxford: St Antony's/Macmillan, 1989; foreword by Robert O'Niell)

33 Keith Neilson, and Elizabeth J. Errington, eds, *Navies and Global Defense: theories and strategy* (Westport, Conn: Praeger, 1995)

34 Geoffrey Till, *Seapower Theory & Practice* (Ilford: Frank Cass, 1994)

35 Colin S. Gray, *The Leverage of Sea Power* (New York: The Free Press, 1992)

36 David A. Rosenberg, 'American Naval Strategy in the Era of the Third World War: an inquiry into the structure and process of general war at Sea, 1945-90', *Naval Power in the Twentieth Century*, ed. by Nicholas A. M. Rodger (London: Macmillan, 1996), pp. 242-54. A longer version of this essay also appeared in James Goldrick, and John B. Hattendorf, eds, *Mahan is Not Enough: the proceedings of a*

conference on the works of Sir Julian Corbett and Admiral Sir Herbert Richmond (Newport RI: Naval War College Press, 1993)

37 Admiral Sir Peter Abbott, 'The Maritime Component of British and Allied Military Strategy', *Royal United Services Institute*, December (1996), pp 6-11

38 Eric Grove, and Peter Hore, eds, *Dimensions of Sea Power: strategic choice in the modern world* (Hull: Hull University Press, 1998), pp 3-25

39 Brigadier Rob Fry, 'End of the Continental Century', *Royal United Services Institute*, (1998),

40 David French, *The British Way in Warfare 1688-2000* (London: Unwin Hyman, 1990)

41 Admiral Sir Jock Slater, 'The Maritime Contribution to Joint Operations', *Royal United Services Institute Journal*, (1998),

42 James Cable, *The Political Influence of Naval Force in History* (London: Macmillan Press Ltd, 1998)

43 Andrew Gordon, *The Rules of the Game: Jutland and British Naval Command* (London: John Murray, 1996)

44 Roger Hill, *Destroyer Captain* (Periscope Publishing, 2004)

ABBREVIATIONS

ACNS	Assistant Chief of the Naval Staff
ACSC	Advanced Command and Staff Course
ACT	Area Capability Training
AEW	Airborne Early Warning
AI	Air Interdiction
ALSS	Advanced Logistics Support Site
AAW	Anti-Air Warfare
ASaCS	Airborne Surveillance and Control System
ASW	Anti-Submarine Warfare
ASuW	Anti-Surface Warfare
ATF	Amphibious Task Force
ATG	Amphibious Task Group
AWACS	Airborne Warning and Control System
BDD	British Defence Doctrine
BRNC	Britannia Royal Naval College
C2W	Command and Control Warfare
C4I	Command, Control, Communications, Computers and Information
CAG	Carrier Air Group
CAS	Close Air Support
CDL	Chief of Defence Logistics
CDS	Chief of the Defence Staff
CESM	Communications Electronic Warfare Support Measures
CIMIC	Civil-Military Co-operation

CJO	Chief of Joint Operations
COA	Course of Action
CTCRM	Commando Training Centre Royal Marines
CTT	Command Team Training
CVS	Aircraft Carrier, ASW
DD	Destroyer
EA	Environmental Assessment
EEZ	Exclusive Economic Zone
EFZ	Extended Fisheries Zone
EXTACs	Experimental Tactics (NATO)
EU	European Union
EW	Electronic Warfare
FAC	Fast Attack Craft
F/A2	Sea Harrier
FF	Frigate
FIAC	Fast Inshore Attack Craft
FLS	Forward Logistics Site
FMRO	Forward Maintenance and Repair Organization
FRS	Forward Repair Ship
GR7	Ground Attack Harrier
HMS	Her (formerly 'His') Majesty's Ship
HNS	Host Nation Support
ICSC(M)	Initial Command and Staff Course (Maritime)
IMINT	Imagery Intelligence
ISTAR	Intelligence, Surveillance, Target Acquisition and Reconnaissance

JCA	Joint Combat Aircraft
JDCC	Joint Doctrine and Concepts Centre
JFH	Joint Force Harrier (Joint RN and RAF Harrier Aircraft Force)
JMC	Joint Maritime Course
JFACC	Joint Force Air Component Commander
JOA	Joint Operations Area
JRRF	Joint Rapid Reaction Force
JSCSC	Joint Services Command and Staff College
JTFC	Joint Task Force Commander
JTFHQ	Joint Task Force Headquarters
LCAC	Landing Craft Air Cushion
LPD	Landing Platform Dock
LPH	Landing Platform Helicopter
LSD(A)	Landing Ship Dock (Auxiliary)
LSL	Landing Ship Logistics
MACA	Military Assistance to Civil Authorities
MACC	Military Assistance to the Civil Community
MACP	Military Aid to the Civil Power
MAGD	Military Assistance to Government Departments
MCC	Maritime Component Commander
MCJO	Maritime Contribution to Joint Operations
MCM	Mine Countermeasures
MCT	Maritime Counter Terrorism
MJLC	Multinational Joint Logistics Centre
MM	Mine Countermeasures Vessel

MMM	Multinational Maritime Manuals
MMO	Multinational Maritime Operations Manual
MNLC	Multinational Logistics Commander
MOU	Memorandum of Understanding
MTO	Maritime Trade Operations
NATO	North Atlantic Treaty Organization
NCAGS	Naval Co-operation and Guidance for Shipping
NEO	Non-Combatant Evacuation Operation
NGO	Non-Governmental Organization
OJT	On-Job Training
OPCOM	Operational Command
OPCON	Operational Control
OPS	Operational Performance Statement
OR	Operational Requirement
OST	Operational Sea Training
OSCE	Organization for Security and Co-operation in Europe
PGM	Precision Guided Munitions
PJHQ	Permanent Joint Headquarters
PJT	Pre-Joining Training
PSO	Peace Support Operation
RAS	Replenishment at Sea
RC	Regional Commander (NATO)
REA	Rapid Environmental Assessment
RM	Royal Marines
RMA	Revolution in Military Affairs

RMP	Recognised Maritime Picture
RN	Royal Navy
ROE	Rules of Engagement
SACO	Supreme Allied Commander Operations
SACT	Supreme Allied Commander Transformation
SC	Strategic Commander (NATO)
SDR	Strategic Defence Review
SF	Special Forces
SIGINT	Signals Intelligence
SLOCS	Sea Lines of Communications
SOC	Scheme of Complement
SSBN	Ballistic Missile Carrying Submarine
STOVL	Short Take-off/Vertical Landing
TAG	Tailored Air Group
TLAM	Tomahawk Land Attack Missile
TPS	Training Performance Statement
UK	United Kingdom
UN	United Nations
UNCLOS	United Nations Convention on the Law of the Sea
UNCLOS III	Third UN Conference on the Law of the Sea
UNFICYP	United Nations' Force in Cyprus
UNPROFOR	United Nations' Protection Force
US	United States
USMC	United States Marine Corps
WMD	Weapons of Mass Destruction

GLOSSARY

The Glossary that follows represents the best definitions of those terms included at the time that the book went to press. When the definition is taken from another publication, the source is placed in brackets at the end of the entry. Otherwise, definitions can be quoted as coming from *BR 1806*.

Source Documents

AAP-6(2003)	NATO Glossary of Terms and Definitions
ADP Vol 1	Army Doctrine Publications Volume 1:Operations
AJP-01(B)	Allied Joint Operations Doctrine
AJP-3.1	Allied Joint Maritime Operations
AJP-3.4	Non-Article 5 Crisis Response Operations
AP 3000 3rd Ed	British Air Power Doctrine
ATP-1(D)	Allied Maritime Tactical Instructions and Procedures
ATP-2	Allied NCS Manual
ATP-8(B)	Allied Doctrine for Amphibious Operations
BDD	British Defence Doctrine
BR 3012	Handbook on the Law of Maritime Operations
FM100-5	Field Manual 100-5: Operations (United States Army)
JP 1-02	The DOD Dictionary of Military and Associated Terms
JDP 01	Joint Operations
JSP 398	UK Compendium of National Rules of Engagement
JWP 0-01.1	UK Joint Glossary of Joint and Multinational Terms and Definitions
JWP 3-00	Joint Operations Execution
JWP 3-50	Peace Support Operations
JWP 5-00	Joint Operations Planning

NDP 1	Naval Doctrine Publication 1: Naval Warfare (US Navy)
OED	Concise Oxford English Dictionary
SDE	Statement of Defence Estimates (Annual)
SDR	Strategic Defence Review
STANAG 1166	Standard Ship Designator System

A

Access (Military)
The freedom of action to manoeuvre to achieve control of a designated environment or to bring target sets within range of organic firepower or other military capabilities. (*JWP 0-01.1*)

Accompaniment
A voluntary arrangement in which participating merchant ships may be organized for passage through a specific area of increased risk in company with military assets.

Administration
The management and execution of all military matters not included in tactics, [operations] and strategy. (*AAP-6*)

Administrative Authority
A commander vested with those aspects of command that are concerned with administration. (*JWP 0-01.1*) See also *full command*.

Advance Force
A temporary organization within the amphibious task force which precedes the main body to the objective area. Its function is to participate in preparing the objective for the main assault by conducting such operations as reconnaissance, seizure of supporting positions, minesweeping, preliminary bombardment, underwater demolitions, and air support.

Advance Operation

Operation in advance of a main force. Advance operations include precursor operations and *advance force operations*. (*JWP 0-01.1*)

Advanced Logistic Support Site (ALSS)

The primary transhipment point for *materiel* and personnel destined to and from afloat units. In a NATO operation the ALSS commander reports to the *Multinational Logistic Commander* (MNLC). Daily co-ordination must be conducted with *Forward Logistics Sites (FLS)*. (*JWP 0-01.1*)

Aim (Military)

A single unambiguous military purpose that must be established before a plan can be developed at any level of command for a military operation. (*JWP 0-01.1*)

Air Interdiction (AI)

An air operation conducted to destroy, neutralise or delay the enemy's military potential before it can be brought to bear effectively against friendly forces at such a distance from friendly forces that detailed integration of each air mission with the fire and movement of friendly forces is not required. (*AAP-6*)

Air Operations for Strategic Effect

Air Operations for Strategic Effect are aimed to destroy or disrupt the defined strategic centre of gravity of an opponent. The effect sought by air power could be destructive, non-destructive or a combination of both, against target sets which undermine the opponent's ability, will and means to continue his aggression. Air operations for strategic effect are not limited to bombing or solely the domain of attack aircraft. All combat aircraft and associated weapon systems are capable of action for strategic effect. (*AP3000*)

Air Superiority

That degree of dominance in the air battle of one force over another which permits the conduct of operations by the former and its related land, sea and air forces at a given time and place without prohibitive interference by the opposing force. (*AAP-6*)

Air Supremacy

That degree of air superiority wherein the opposing air force is incapable of effective interference. (*AAP-6*)

Airborne Early Warning and Control

Air surveillance and control provided by airborne early warning aircraft which are equipped with search and height finding radar and communications equipment for controlling weapon systems (*AAP-6*)

Airhead:

A designated area in a hostile or threatened territory which, when seized and held, ensures the continuous air landing of troops and *materiel* and provides the manoeuvre space necessary for projected operations. Normally it is the area seized in the assault phase of an airborne operation.

A designated location in an area of operations used as a base for supply and evacuation by air. (*AAP-6*)

Amphibious Assault

The principal type of amphibious operation which involves establishing a force on a hostile or potentially hostile shore. (*AAP-6*)

Amphibious Demonstration

A type of amphibious operation conducted for the purpose of deceiving the enemy by a show of force, with the expectation of deluding the enemy into a course of action unfavourable to him. (*AAP-6*)

Amphibious Objective Area (AOA)

A geographical area, delineated in the initiating directive, for purposes of *command and control* within which is located the objective(s) to be secured by the amphibious task force. This area must be of sufficient size to ensure accomplishment of the amphibious task force's mission and must provide sufficient area for conducting necessary sea, air and land operations. (*AAP-6*)

Amphibious Operation

A military operation launched from the sea by a naval and landing force embarked in ships or craft, with the principal purpose of projecting the landing force ashore tactically into an environment ranging from permissive to hostile. (*AAP-6*)

Amphibious Raid

A type of amphibious operation involving the swift incursion into or temporary occupation of an objective followed by a planned withdrawal. (*AAP-6*).

Amphibious Ready Group (ARG)

A high readiness amphibious force, based around a commando group with supporting joint assets, operating forward in the area of likely employment.

Amphibious Task Force (ATF)

The task force formed for the purpose of conducting an amphibious operation. The amphibious task force always includes Navy forces and a landing force, with their organic aviation and may include maritime ships and Air Force forces when appropriate. (*ATP-8*)

Amphibious Withdrawal

A type of amphibious operation involving the extraction of forces by sea in naval ships or craft from a hostile or potentially hostile shore. (*AAP-6*)

Anti-Surface Air Operation

An air operation conducted in an air/sea environment against enemy surface forces. (*AAP-6*)

Archipelagic Sea-Lanes Passage

Under the terms of the **1982 UNCLOS** Archipelagic States may designate sea lanes and air routes suitable for continuous and expeditious passage of foreign ships and aircraft, in their normal mode of operation (thus implying submarines may transit dived), through or over its archipelagic waters and the adjacent territorial sea. (*BR 3012*)

Archipelagic State
An independent state consisting entirely of an archipelago of islands.

Archipelagic Waters
Waters over which an *Archipelagic State* claims sovereignty under the **1982 UNCLOS** (*BR 3012*)

Area Forces
Maritime forces declared to NATO at similar levels of readiness to the force categories of Reaction and *Main Defence Forces*, but not allocated to *Multinational NATO Maritime Forces*.

Area of Influence
A geographical area wherein a commander is directly capable of influencing operations, by *manoeuvre* or fire support systems normally under his command and control. (*AAP-6*)

Area of Interest
That area of concern to a commander relative to the objectives of current or planned operations, including his areas of influence, operations and/or responsibility, and areas adjacent thereto. (*AAP-6*)

Armed Suasion
The use of military forces in support of diplomacy to influence the decisions of a government or quasi-governmental authority (such as the leadership of a faction). Suasion can be latent (as in *presence* and general *deterrence*) or active. Active suasion can be supportive (as in *coalition building*) or *coercive* in which case it can seek to *deter* or *compel*.

Armour
Tanks and armoured reconnaissance vehicles.

Assault
See *Amphibious assault*.

Asymmetric Attack
Actions undertaken by state or non-state parties (friendly or adversary), to circumvent or negate an opponent's strengths and capitalise on perceived weaknesses through the exploitation of dissimilar values, strategies, organizations and capabilities. Such actions are capable, by design or default, of achieving disproportionate effects, thereby gaining the instigator an advantage probably not attainable through conventional means. (*JWP 0-01.1*)

Attrition
The reduction of the effectiveness of a force caused by loss of personnel and *materiel*. (*AAP-6*)

Attrition Warfare
A style of warfare characterised by the application of substantial combat power that reduces an enemy's ability to fight through loss of personnel and equipment. Essentially it aims at the physical destruction of the enemy. (*JWP 0-01.1*)

Augmentation Force (AF)
Any force designated by a nation to strengthen its national forces. (*AAP-6*)

B

Balance of Advantage
The qualitative advantage of a force over an opposing force taking into account quantity, quality and categories of capability. (*JWP 0-01.1*) See *exchange ratio*.

Balanced Fleet
A naval force that can be generated and sustained with a full range of capabilities for such independent (unilateral) strategic and operational

action as is envisaged in defence policy and national military strategy. (*JWP 0-01.1*)

Balanced Force

A military force that has all the necessary capabilities to carry out a particular mission without unnecessary redundancy. (*JWP 0-01.1*)

Battle Damage Assessment

The timely and accurate estimate of damage resulting from the application of military force, either lethal or non-lethal, against a pre-determined objective assessment. (*AP 3000*)

Battleforce

A force comprising several *battlegroups*. A battleforce is typically a three star command and equates in NATO Reaction Force parlance to a NATO *Expanded Task Force*.

Battlegroup

A standing naval task group consisting of a carrier, surface combatants, and submarines, operating in mutual support with the task of destroying hostile submarine, surface, and air forces within the group's assigned area of responsibility and striking at targets along hostile shore lines or projecting fire power inland. (*JP 1-02*) (Note that *JWP 0-01.1* has a UK Army definition)

Battlespace

All aspects of air, surface, subsurface, land, space and the electromagnetic spectrum that encompass the area of operations. (*JWP 0-01.1*)

Battlespace Dominance

The degree of control over the dimensions of the *battlespace* that enhances friendly freedom of action and denies the enemy freedom of action. It permits *power projection* and force sustainment to accomplish the full range of potential missions. (*JWP 0-01.1*)

Beachhead

A designated area on a hostile, or potentially hostile, shore which, when seized and held, provides for the continuous landing of troops and *materiel*, and provides *manoeuvring* space required for subsequent projected operations ashore. (*AAP-6*)

Benign Application

The use of armed forces solely for the capabilities not directly associated with combat that they can provide.

Blockade

A legal definition is "An operation intended to disrupt the enemy's economy by preventing ships of all nations from entering or leaving specified coastal areas under the occupation and control of the enemy. Blockade is an act of war and the right to establish it is granted to belligerents under the traditional laws of war. This law requires, *inter alia*, that the blockade must be effective, that it is to be declared by the belligerent so that all interested parties know of its existence and that it is confined to ports or coasts occupied by the enemy". The expression is used more broadly to mean a combat operation carried out to prevent access to, or departure from the coast or waters of a hostile state.

'Blue on Blue' Engagement

(colloquial) Incident involving casualties caused by friendly fire.

Branch (in operational planning)

An option for a particular phase, designed to anticipate opportunities or reverses, providing the commander with the flexibility to retain the initiative. (*JWP 3-00*)

C

Campaign

A set of military operations planned and conducted to achieve a strategic objective within a given time and geographical area, which normally involve maritime, land and air forces. (*AAP-6*)

Carrier Air Group (CAG)

A group of aircraft squadrons placed under a single command for administrative and tactical control of operations from an aircraft carrier. (*AAP-6*)

Carrier Group

Task group or *battlegroup* whose core is a carrier and whose function is principally to deliver carrier capabilities.

Catastrophic Damage

The sudden loss of a substantial collection of resources and capabilities, such as the sinking of a major warship.

Centre of Gravity

Characteristic(s), capability(ies) or locality(ies) from which a nation, an alliance, a military force or other grouping derives its freedom of action, physical strength or will to fight. (*AAP-6*)

Civil War

War conducted largely within the boundaries of a state in which a significant part of the population is associated with opposing sides. One or both sides may have external help. (*JWP 0-01.1*)

Close Air Support (CAS)

Air action against hostile targets which are in close proximity to friendly forces and which require detailed integration of each air mission with the fire and movement of those forces. (*AAP-6*)

Close Blockade

A *blockade* that denies an enemy access to or from his ports. See *distant blockade*.

Close Escort

Escort of shipping where the escorting force is in company with escorted shipping and can provide a measure of direct defence.

Close Operations
Operations conducted at short range, in close contact and in the immediate timescale. (*JWP 0-01.1*)

Coalition Building
Military action in support of diplomacy to further the building of an ad hoc coalition by providing reassurance, evidence of support and, perhaps, the opportunity for military meetings in theatre.

Coercion
The use of force, or the threat of force to persuade an opponent to adopt a certain pattern of behaviour, against his wishes. (*JWP 0-01.1*)

Collateral Damage
Damage to personnel and property adjacent to, but not forming part of, an authorised target. (*JWP 0-01.1*)

Combat
Military combat is a contest in which the parties attempt to achieve mutually incompatible aims through the organized use of *violence* by armed forces.

Combat Air Patrol (CAP):
An aircraft patrol provided over an objective area, over the force protected, over the critical area of a combat zone, or over an air defence area, for the purpose of intercepting and destroying hostile aircraft before they reach their target. (*AAP-6*)

Patrols by fighter aircraft over an objective area, a force to be protected, over the critical area of a combat zone or over an air defence area for the purpose of intercepting and destroying hostile aircraft before they reach their targets. (*AP 3000*)

Combat Enhancement Training (CET)
A period of Continuation Training specifically designed to train a ship, or group of ships, for a specific operational task.

Combat Identification (Combat ID)

The process of combining situational awareness, target identification, specific tactics, training and procedures to increase operational effectiveness of weapons systems and reduce the incidence of casualties caused by friendly fire. (*JWP 0-01.1*)

Combat Power

The total means of destructive and/or disruptive force which a military unit/formation can apply against the opponent at a given time. (*AAP-6*)

Combat Service Support (CSS)

The support provided to combat forces, primarily in the fields of administration and logistics. (*AAP-6*)

Combat Support

Fire support and operational assistance provided to combat elements. (*AAP-6*)

Combat Support Air Operations

Air operations designed to enhance or support the effectiveness of air, surface and sub-surface combat forces. (*AP3000*)

Combined

Adjective used to describe activities, operations and organizations, in which elements of more than one nation participate. (*AAP-6*). (The term 'multinational' is preferred within the UK and Allied joint communities)

Combined Joint Task Force (CJTF)

A multinational, multi-service task force. The CJTF Headquarters Concept provides for deployable multinational multi-service headquarters of variable size formed to command and control CJTFs of NATO and possibly non-NATO nations. A CJTF HQ could also be deployed for EU led operations.

Command

The authority vested in an individual of the armed forces for the direction, co-ordination and control of military forces (*AAP-6*). See *full command*.

Command and Control (C2)

Expression used to mean:

The processes through which a commander exercises *command* (whether *full* or *operational* or *tactical command*) or *operational* or *tactical control* to organize, direct and co-ordinate the activities of the forces allocated to him.

The structures and systems through which these processes are exercised. A command, control, (communications) and information system (C3I) is an integrated system comprising *doctrine*, procedures, organizational structure, personnel, equipment, facilities, and communications, which provides authorities at all levels with timely and adequate data to plan, direct and control their activities. (*AJP-01*).

Command and Control Warfare (C2W)

The integrated use of all military capabilities including operations security (OPSEC), deception, psychological operations (PSYOPS), electronic warfare (EW) and physical destruction, supported by all-source intelligence and Communications and Information Systems (CIS) to deny information to, influence, degrade, or destroy an adversary's C2 capabilities while protecting friendly C2 capabilities against similar actions. (*AAP-6*)

Command of the Sea

The ability to use the sea in its entirety for one's own purposes at any time and to deny its use to an adversary. (*JWP 0-01.1*)

Command Post Exercise (CPX)

An exercise in which the forces are simulated, involving the commander, his staff and communications within and between headquarters. (*AAP-6*)

Commander Allied Joint Force (COMAJF)

In NATO the commander appointed by SACO to mount and sustain an Allied operation and to exercise OPCON of all the forces assigned to the operation.

Commander's Estimate of the Situation

A formal analysis of the situation, mission, enemy and own courses of action conducted in preparation for forming a *commander's intentions* and *concept of operations*.

Commander's Intent

A concise expression of the purpose of a *campaign* or *operation*, the desired results and how operations will progress towards achieving the desired end-state. At the tactical level, the Commander's Intent should be focused on the effect that he wishes to achieve on the enemy. (*JWP 0-01.1*)

Commando

A Royal Marines formation of battalion size with *combat support* and *combat service support*.

Compel

The *coercive* use of armed forces to persuade a government by the threat or isolated use of combat to desist from a course of action. (*JWP 0-01.1*)

Component Commander

The commander of the maritime, ground, air, or other component of a *Joint Task Force* (UK national) or *Combined Joint Task Force* (NATO/EU) and reporting to the *Joint Task Force Commander* or *Combined Joint Task Force Commander* respectively.

Concept of Operations

A clear and concise statement of the line of action chosen by a commander in order to accomplish his mission. (*AAP-6*)

Concerted Multinational Operations (basic co-operation)
Operations in which forces of more than one friendly or allied nation are operating in the same theatre but without formal arrangements to co-ordinate operations or an integrated command structure. They co-operate to the extent that mutual interference may be minimised, information may be exchanged and some logistic support and mutual training offered.

Conditions for Success
The situation and state of affairs that must pertain if a military campaign or operation can be considered successful. The conditions may be *military conditions* which are normally expressed as control of the environment, or may be non-military such as the decision of a hostile government to desist from action. (*JWP 0-01.1*) See *end state*.

Conflict
(Armed) Conflict (usually abbreviated) is a situation in which violence or military force is threatened or used. Generally it is a contest between two opposing sides, each seeking to impose its will on the other; however, intra-state conflict may involve several factions. (*JWP 0-01.1*)

Conflict Prevention
A peace support operation employing complementary diplomatic, civil, and – when necessary – military means, to monitor and identify the causes of conflict, and take timely action to prevent the occurrence, escalation, or resumption of hostilities. (*AAP-6*) See also *peacebuilding*, *peacekeeping*, *peacemaking*, *peace support operation*.

Consolidation
The replenishment of organic *logistic* shipping by freighting vessels.

Constabulary Application
The use of military forces to uphold a national or international law, mandate or regime in a manner in which minimum violence is only used in enforcement as a last resort and after evidence of a breach or intent to defy has been established beyond reasonable doubt. The level and type of

violence that is permitted will frequently be specified in the law, mandate or regime that is being enforced. Also called policing.

Containment:

Military containment: The geographical restriction of the freedom of action of enemy forces.

Crisis containment: Measures to limit the geographical spread of a crisis.

Containment as grand strategy: Measures taken to limit the geographic spread of an ideology or the influence of a power.

Containment by Distraction

Containment achieved by posing so great a threat to an enemy in one area (particularly in home waters or close to critical interests) that enemy forces are retained in defence allowing friendly forces elsewhere to be unmolested.

Contiguous Zone

A belt, usually 12 miles in width, immediately adjacent to the *territorial sea* and extending to a distance not more than 24 miles measured from the baselines from which the breadth of the territorial sea is measured. (*BR 3012*)

Continental Shelf

Comprises an area of the sea bed and the sub-soil adjacent to the coast but beyond the territorial sea in which the coastal state has sovereign rights for the purpose of exploration and exploitation of the natural resources. (*BR 3012*)

Contingency Forces

Forces required to undertake Military Tasks to fulfil UK Defence Roles other than: those forces permanently stationed at home and abroad; and, those additional forces that would be *regenerated* and/or *reconstituted* in the event of general war. (*JWP 0-01.1*)

Control:

That authority exercised by a commander over part of the activities of subordinate organizations, or other organizations not normally under his command, which encompasses the responsibility for implementing orders or directives. All or part of this authority may be transferred or delegated. (*AAP-6*)

The process through which the commander organizes, directs and co-ordinates the activities of the forces allocated to him.

Military control (of the environment) is the condition in which one protagonist has freedom of action to use one or more *warfare environments* (land, sea, air, space, information or electromagnetic spectrum) for his purposes and to deny its use to an opponent. See *sea control; control of the air*.

Authority which may be less than full command exercised by a commander and part of the activities of subordinate or other organizations. (*ATP-1*)

Control of the Air

The three degrees of control of the air are: *favourable air situation*; *air superiority*; and *air supremacy*. (*AP 3000*)

Convoying

The aggregation of shipping to be protected into groups to reduce losses through enemy action, with or without escort protection. The presence of escorting forces may increase losses to attacking enemy forces.

Co-operation, Multinational Operations Under Basic

See *concerted multinational operations*.

Co-ordinated Multinational Operations

Operations in which participating friendly or allied nations share objectives to the extent that formal arrangements can be made to apportion tasks or areas of responsibility and to provide mutual assistance. However there is no integrated command structure.

Counter-Air Operations
Operations to achieve and maintain the required degree of *control of the air*.

Counter-Terrorism
Measures taken to prevent, deter, and respond to terrorism. (*US FM 100-5*)

Crisis
A situation, which may or may not be foreseen, which threatens national security or interests or international peace and stability, and which requires decision and action. (*JWP 0-01.1*)

Crisis Management
The co-ordinated actions taken to defuse crises, prevent their escalation into an armed conflict and contain hostilities if they should result. (*AAP-6*)

Crisis Prevention
Diplomatic, economic and, on occasion, military measures to modify the causes of a potential crisis and prevent its onset. (*JWP 0-01.1*)

Culminating Point
An operation reaches its culminating point when the current operation can just be maintained but not developed to any greater advantage. (*JWP 0-01.1*)

D

Deception
Those measures designed to mislead the enemy by manipulation, distortion, or falsification of evidence to induce him to react in a manner prejudicial to his interests. (*AAP-6*)

Decisive Points
A point from which a hostile or friendly centre of gravity can be threatened. This point may exist in time, space or the information environment. (*AAP-6*)

Deep Operations
Operations conducted against forces or resources not engaged in close operations. They expand the battle area in time and space, help to shape the close battle, make it difficult for the enemy to concentrate combat power without loss, and diminish the coherence and tempo of his operations. (*JWP 0-01.1*)

De-Escalation
A decrease in the level of extent of *violence* during *hostilities*. See *escalation*.

Defence Diplomacy
To provide forces to meet the varied activities undertaken by the MOD to dispel hostility, build and maintain trust and assist in the development of democratically accountable armed forces, thereby making a significant contribution to conflict prevention and resolution. (**SDR White Paper**)

Defence in Depth
The siting of mutually supporting defence positions designed to absorb and progressively weaken attack, prevent initial observations of the whole position by the enemy, and to allow the commander to manoeuvre his reserve. (*AAP-6*)

Defensive Operation
Operation in which forces await for the approach of the enemy before attacking.

Démarche
Formal request or statement of policy or opinion issued through diplomatic channels by a government alliance, coalition or group of nations.

Demobilisation Operations
In the context of *peace support operations*, the controlled withdrawal, demobilisation and rehabilitation of belligerents. They might include cantonment of belligerents' vessels.

Demonstration
An attack or show of force on a front where a decision is not sought, made with the aim of deceiving the enemy. (*AAP-6*)

Deterrence
The convincing of a potential aggressor that the consequences of coercion or armed conflict would outweigh the potential gains. This requires the maintenance of a credible military capability and strategy with the clear political will to act. (*AAP-6*)

Directive:
A military communication in which policy is established or a specific action is ordered.

A plan issued with a view to putting it into effect when so directed, or in the event that a stated contingency arises.

Broadly speaking, any communication which initiates or governs action, conduct, or procedure. (*JWP 0-01.1*)

Disaster Relief
The organized response to alleviate the situation resulting from a catastrophe, the aims of which are to save life and lessen suffering, limit damage and restore essential services to a level that enables local authorities to cope. Disaster relief demands the total integration of the relief effort with the life-support assets and infrastructure available within the stricken area. (*JWP 0-01.1*)

Dislocation
To dislocate is to deny another party the ability to bring his strengths to bear, or to persuade him that his strength is irrelevant. (*JWP 0-01.1*)

Disruption
Use of force to shatter the cohesion of a military formation and prevent it from functioning effectively in combat. (*JWP 0-01.1*)

Distant Blockade
A *blockade* that denies the enemy passage through a sea area through which all ships must pass in order to reach the enemy's territory.

Distant Escort
Escort of shipping where the protective forces are not sufficiently close to provide a measure of direct defence but effect protection by *deterrence* through the threat of reprisals.

Distraction:
Situation in which an enemy is unable to concentrate forces in a time and place of his choosing because of the threat of attack elsewhere. (*JWP 0-01.1*)

Measures taken to offer alternative targets to a weapons control or missile homing system so that a false target is selected. (*ATP-1*)

Doctrine
Fundamental principles by which the military forces guide their actions in support of objectives. It is authoritative but requires judgement in application. (*AAP-6*)

E

Economy of Force Operation
A *distractive* or *defensive* maritime operation using modest resources so as to concentrate force for the main effort. Sometimes called a *holding operation* when associated with an offensive manoeuvre. (*JWP 0-01.1*)

Effect
The cumulative consequence across the security environment of one or more actions (or tasks) taken at any level with any instrument of Government.

Effects Based Operations

Operations designed to influence the will of an adversary, own forces or neutrals through the co-ordinated application of military capability, in order to achieve the desired Strategic objectives.

Elan

Offensive spirit. Ardour.

Electronic Warfare:

Military action to exploit the electromagnetic spectrum encompassing: the search for, interception and identification of electromagnetic emissions, the employment of electromagnetic energy, including directed energy, to reduce or prevent hostile use of the electromagnetic spectrum, and actions to ensure its effective use by friendly forces. (*AAP-6*)

Military action to exploit the electromagnetic spectrum for the purposes of combat. (*ATP-1*)

Embargo

A prohibition on the entry or egress of shipping into a port. Nowadays frequently used for prohibitions of certain categories of cargo such as munitions. (*JWP 0-01.1*)

Embroilment

Military embroilment is the involvement of forces in *conflict* at a level of *violence* that is greater than that for which they are equipped or prepared or that envisaged in their strategic *directive*.

End-State

The political and/or military situation to be attained at the end of an operation, which indicates that the objective has been achieved. (*AAP-6*)

Endurance

See *sustainability*. The time an aircraft can continue flying, or a ground vehicle or ship can continue operating, under specified conditions e.g. without refuelling. (*AAP-6*)

Entitled Personnel

In a Non-Combatant Evacuation Operation, those personnel entitled to evacuation by UK forces. Personnel are categorised in priority order: British nationals; unrepresented EU nationals and EU nationals with prior agreement from HM Representative to be included; and Australian, Canadian, New Zealand and US nationals if UK arranges evacuation before they do or UK agrees to take the lead for the NEO and they wish to be included.

Envelopment/Envelop

An offensive *manoeuvre* in which the main attacking force passes around or over the enemy's principal defensive position to secure objectives to the enemy's rear. (*AAP-6*)

Escalation/de-escalation

A qualitative transformation in the character of a conflict where the scope and intensity increases or decreases, transcending limits implicitly accepted by both sides. (*JWP 0-01.1*) See *vertical escalation, horizontal escalation, qualitative escalation* and *prolongation*.

Escort:

A method of protection of shipping short of the establishment of full *sea control* in which protection is achieved primarily by the *deterrent* presence of protective forces.

Colloquial generic expression for a destroyer or frigate.

Exchange Ratio

The numerical ratio of friendly to enemy forces taking into account quantity, quality and categories of capability. See *balance of advantage*.

Exclusive Economic Zone (EEZ)

The zone of sea around a state over which it has exclusive rights under international law to exploit economic resources. (*JWP 0-01.1*)

Expeditionary Forces

Forces projected from the home base capable of sustained operations at distance from that home base. (*JWP 0-01.1*)

Expeditionary Operations

Military operations which can be initiated at short notice, consisting of forward deployed, or rapidly deployable, self-sustaining forces tailored to achieve a clearly stated objective in a foreign country. (See *maritime expeditionary forces; power projection*)

Exploit

Exploit is the fourth of four operational functions (Shape, Attack, Protect and Exploit). It is to be able to exploit the unfolding situation by any appropriate means available, eg modified plans, new branches or sequels or committal of reserves to capitalise on a favourable situation. (*JWP 3-00*)

Exploitation:

1. Taking full advantage of success in battle and following up initial gains.

2. Taking full advantage of any information that has come to hand for tactical or strategic purposes.

3. An offensive operation that usually follows a successful attack and is designed to disorganize the enemy in depth.

(*JWP 0-01.1*)

Extended Fisheries Zone (EFZ)

A zone declared for fisheries management purposes beyond the limit of the Territorial Sea but within what would be the permissible limits of the *exclusive economic zone* if the state were to declare one. The UK does not as yet have an EEZ but has had an EFZ since 1 January 1977.

F

Favourable Air Situation

An air situation in which the extent of air effort applied by the enemy air forces is insufficient to prejudice success of friendly sea, land or air operations. (*JWP 0-01.1*)

Fighting Instructions, The

Publication subordinate to *BR 1806* containing Royal Navy operational and tactical doctrine.

Find

The employment of Intelligence, Surveillance and Reconnaissance capabilities to locate, identify and assess the intentions of an adversary or protagonist.

Fire Support

The application of fire, co-ordinated with the manoeuvre of forces, to destroy, neutralise or suppress the enemy. (*AAP-6*)

Fix:

In land operations:
Actions taken to prevent the enemy from moving any part of his forces from a specific location or for a specific period of time by holding or surrounding them to prevent their withdrawal for use elsewhere.

A tactical obstacle effect that integrates fire planning and obstacle effort to slow down an attacker within a specified area, normally an engagement area. (*JWP 0-01.1*)

Flag Staff

The staff supporting a flag officer, who may be embarked at sea or based at a shore headquarters.

Fleet in Being
The use of options provided by the continued existence of one's own fleet to constrain the enemy's options in the use of his.

Fog of War
Uncertainty and confusion generated in wartime by a combination of limited, incomplete, inaccurate and contradictory information, deliberate deception and the mayhem and stress caused by combat. From Clausewitz' *On War*.

Force Generation
The process of providing suitably trained and equipped forces, and their means of deployment, recovery and sustainment to meet all current and potential future tasks, within required readiness and preparation times. (*JWP 0-01.1*)

Force Integration Training (FIT)
A period of training designed to integrate a group of individual units so that they can operate more effectively as a Task Group/Force.

Force Packaging
The process by which elements of those forces delivered by Force Generation are combined into a coherent, mission orientated, joint force in order to conduct a specific operation or campaign.

Force Projection
See *maritime force projection*, *maritime power projection*, and *power projection*.

The projection, application and sustainment of joint military capabilities, at global range, to achieve effects in support of joint campaign objectives.

Force Protection
All measures and means to minimise the vulnerability of personnel, facilities, equipment and operations to any threat and in all situations, to

preserve freedom of action and the operational effectiveness of the force. (*JWP 3-00*)

Forward Line of Own Troops (FLOT)
A line which indicates the most forward positions of friendly forces in any kind of military operation at a specific time (*AAP-6*). Primarily used in land operations.

Forward Logistics Site (FLS)
Normally the final land transhipment point for *materiel* and personnel which provides a bridge between an *Advanced Logistic Support Site* (ALSS) and the sea. (*JWP 0-01.1*) It will be linked to the ALSS by intra-theatre airlift. In a NATO operation the FLS commander reports directly to the *Multinational Logistic Commander* (MNLC). Daily co-ordination with the ALSS commander must be conducted.

Forward Presence
Strategic choice to maintain forces deployed at distance from the home base or stationed overseas to demonstrate national resolve, strengthen alliances, dissuade potential adversaries, and enhance the ability to respond quickly to contingencies. (*JWP 0-01.1*)

Fratricide
The accidental death or injury which occurs when friendly forces engage their own forces believing either them, or their location, to be an enemy target.

Freedom of Navigation (FON) Operations
Operations of *naval diplomacy* designed to challenge an attempt to restrict free use of the seas by the passage of combat forces. FON operations may be *symbolic* or *coercive*. (*JWP 0-01.1*)

Friction
The accumulation of chance errors, unexpected difficulties, enemy actions, and confusion in battle. It is the force that resists all action and which

makes the simple difficult and the difficult seemingly impossible. (*JWP 0-01.1*) The expression was used by Clausewitz in *On War*.

Full Command
The military authority and responsibility of a superior officer to issue orders to subordinates. It covers every aspect of military operations and *administration* and exists only within national Services (*AAP-6*). In the UK full command is exercised by the single Service commanders (eg CinCFleet) who report to the United Kingdom Government through the Chief of the Defence Staff. See *administrative authority*.

Functional Organization
Command organization for maritime forces reflecting the functions, missions or tasks of the component elements. See *type organization*.

G

General War
A conflict between major powers in which their large and vital national interests, perhaps even survival, are at stake. (*JWP 0-01.1*)

Goal
An expression of broad meaning embracing *aim*, *mission*, *objective*, and purpose.

Grand Strategic Level
The level of command and planning for armed conflict (*level of war*) at which all national resources (diplomatic, economic, military, political, informational and technological) are applied to achieve national security policy objectives.

Guerre de Course
A campaign consisting of attacks on enemy shipping.

Gunboat Diplomacy
Colloquial expression for *naval diplomacy*.

H

Harmonisation (of ROE)
The process whereby the *rules of engagement* of more than one nation taking part in a *multi-national* operation are compared and altered where possible to achieve similar levels of permission and prohibition through the various national systems.

High Seas
All parts of the sea which are not included in the *territorial seas* or *internal waters* of States. All states have the freedom to navigate or conduct other activities, subject to certain restrictions, on the high seas. Where states have declared other zones beyond the territorial sea (*contiguous zone*, *exclusive economic zone*, *continental shelf*) the traditional high seas freedoms are affected by the rights that coastal states can exercise in such zones.

Holding Area
Area of sea occupied by surface forces with a stationary speed of advance.

Holding Operation
See *economy of force operation*.

Horizontal Escalation
Escalation by extension of combat into new geographic areas or environments. (*JWP 0-01.1*)

Host Nation Support (HNS)
Civil and military assistance rendered in peace, crisis or war by a host nation to NATO and/or other forces and NATO organizations which are located on, operating on/from, or in transit through the host nation's territory. (*AAP-6*).

Hostilities

Period between the onset of regular *combat* between parties and any cease fire or truce.

Humanitarian Assistance

Support provided to humanitarian and development agencies, in an insecure environment, by a deployed force whose primary mission is not the provision of humanitarian aid. Should the deployed force undertake such humanitarian tasks, responsibility should be handed over/returned to the appropriate civilian agency at the earliest opportunity. (*JWP 0-01.1*)

Humanitarian Disaster Relief Operations

Operations where the primary mission of a deployed force is to relieve human suffering. HDR operations are conducted in an entirely benign posture (except for essential force protection) and are normally conducted in support of the co-ordinating humanitarian agency. (*JWP 0-01.1*)

I

Immediate Reaction Forces (IRF)

NATO forces held routinely at the highest readiness. The *Standing Naval Forces* are maritime IRF.

Infiltration

A technique and process in which a force moves as individuals or small groups over, through or around enemy positions without detection. (*AAP-6*)

Information Campaign

Co-ordinated information output of all Government activity to influence decision-makers in support of policy objectives, while protecting one's own decision-makers. (*JWP 0-01.1*)

Information Operations

Co-ordinated actions undertaken to influence an adversary or potential adversary in support of political and military objectives by undermining his will, cohesion and decision making ability, including his information, information based processes and systems while protecting one's own decision-makers and decision making processes. (*JWP 0-01.1*)

Innocent Passage
Defined as navigation through the *territorial sea* of a State for the purpose of either traversing that sea without entering *internal waters*, or of proceeding in either direction between the high seas and internal waters. Vessels have the right to take innocent passage through *territorial seas* without interference by the coastal States concerned.

Insurgency
An organized movement aimed at the overthrow of a constituted government through use of subversion and armed conflict. (*AAP-6*)

Integrated Military Structure (IMS)
See *NATO Integrated Military Structure (NIMS)*.

Integrated Multinational Operation
Operation in which forces of two or more nations operate under a *unified* command structure. Only integrated operations are truly combined. (*JWP 0-01.1*)

Interdiction
Actions to divert, disrupt, or destroy the enemy before he can affect friendly forces. (*JWP 0-01.1*)

Internal Conflict
Situation in which *violence* is threatened or used within a state's borders between competing groups for political reasons beyond levels that might be controlled by levels of civilian policing that are normal for that state. (*JWP 0-01.1*)

Internal Waters
All waters actually within the territory of a State such as harbours, rivers and lakes; together with all other waters to landward of the baseline from

which the State's *territorial sea* is measured. They are an integral part of the territory of the State and in them the laws of the land are supreme.

International Strait

Considered to be a route which is used for international navigation which either connects one part of the *high seas* with another, or passes between one part of the high seas and the *territorial sea* of a State. Where there is no similarly convenient alternative route, the United Kingdom recognises certain rights including unimpeded passage through international straits even where these pass through States' territorial seas.

Interoperability

The ability of Alliance forces and, when appropriate, forces of Partner and other nations to train, exercise and operate effectively together in the execution of assigned missions and tasks. (*AAP-6*)

Intervention

A *campaign* or *operation* with limited objectives, involving the entry of another state where opposition is expected. (*JWP 0-01.1*)

J

Joint

Adjective used to describe activities, operations and organizations in which elements of at least two services participate. (*AAP-6*)

Joint Commander (Jt Comd)

The Joint Commander, appointed by CDS, exercises the highest level of operational command (OPCOM) of forces assigned with specific responsibility for deployment, sustainment and recovery. (*JWP 0-01.1*)

Joint Headquarters (JHQ)

A tri-Service staff organized on functional lines responsible for the planning and exercise of operational command of forces assigned to joint, potentially joint and multinational operations. (*JWP 0-01.1*)

Joint Operations Area (JOA):

A temporary area defined by a NATO strategic or regional commander, in which a designated joint commander plans and executes a specific mission at the operational level of war. Note: it is defined in co-ordination with nations and approved by the North Atlantic Council or the Military Committee as appropriate, in accordance with NATO's Operational planning Architecture. A joint operations area and its defining parameters, such as time, scope of the mission and geographical area, are contingency- or mission-specific and may overlap areas of responsibility. (*AAP-6*)

An area of land, sea and airspace defined by higher authority, in which a designated Joint Task Force Commander plans and conducts military operations to accomplish a specific mission. A Joint Operations Area including its defining parameters, such as time, scope and geographic area, is contingency/mission-specific. (*JWP 0-01.1*)

Joint Sea Basing

Use of the sea as a base within Joint Operations in order to contribute to an optimum force footprint ashore. (*JWP 0-01.1*)

Joint Services Command and Staff College

The UK armed forces Staff College was established in 1997 at Bracknell and moved to a purpose built building at Shrivenham in 2000. It is a combination of the former Joint Service Defence College at Greenwich, the RN Staff College at Greenwich, the Army Staff College at Camberley and the RAF Staff College at Bracknell. All UK armed forces staff training is now conducted on a joint basis at the JSCSC, including the Higher Command and Staff Course for those likely to fill higher joint command and staff posts.

Joint Task Force Commander (JTFC)

The operational commander of a nominated joint force. (*JWP 0-01.1*)

Joint Task Force Headquarters (JTFHQ)

A purely national deployable joint headquarters of variable size commanded at the operational level by a Joint Task Force Commander. (*JWP 0-01.1*)

Joint Theatre Plans

Contingency plans for specific crisis operations in various parts of the world (*JWP 0-01.1*)

L

Land Attack Missile

Submarine, surface ship, or air launched missile capable of engaging land targets.

Landing Force

The task organization of ground and aviation units assigned to an amphibious operation. (*AAP-6*)

Layered Defence

The disposition of protective assets possessing a mixture of anti-submarine, anti-surface and anti-air capabilities in layers of screens and patrol areas about units of high value or crucial waters.

Levels of Warfare (war)

The recognised levels of warfare from which the levels for the planning and command of operations are derived. They are *grand strategic*, *military strategic*, *operational* and *tactical*. (*JWP 0-01.1*)

Leverage (military)

Disproportionate strategic or operational advantage gained by the use of a form of military power to exploit its geographical circumstances.

Lift

The capability to move resources between two points. (*JWP 0-01.1*)

Limited War

War waged towards limited *war aims*, and/or in a limited geographical area and/or employing limits on means and methods of fighting. It is a phrase that came into currency after the Second World War to distinguish limited wars from the type of general war that was experienced in 1939-45. It also came to imply a restriction on means, in particular the non-use of nuclear weapons.

Line of Operation

In a campaign or operation, a line linking decisive points in time and space on the path to the centre of gravity. (*AAP-6*)

Linear Operation

Operation planned to proceed along a physical *line of operation*. (*JWP 0-01.1*)

Lines of Communications (LOC)

All the land, water and air routes that connect an operating military force with one or more bases of operations and along which supplies and reinforcements move (*AAP-6*). See *sea lines of communications (SLOC)*.

Littoral Region

Coastal sea areas and that portion of the land which is susceptible to influence or support from the sea. (*JWP 0-01.1*)

Lodgement Area

Following the invasion of a hostile coast and the establishment of a bridgehead ashore, the operations of invading forces are directed to the seizure of a lodgement area. This is an area which comprises adequate port, airfield and communications facilities and sufficient space for the assembly and maintenance of the total forces destined to take part in the campaign. (*JWP 0-01.1*)

Logistics

The science of planning and carrying out the movement and maintenance of forces. In its most comprehensive sense, those aspects of military operations which deal with:

- design and development, acquisition, storage, transport, distribution, maintenance, evacuation and disposition of materiel;

- transport of personnel;

- acquisition, construction, maintenance, operation and disposition of facilities;

- acquisition or furnishing of services.

- medical and health service support. (*AAP-6*)

M

Main Defence Forces (MDF)

Active and mobilisation capable NATO components which are assigned to the SC/RC as appropriate in order to dissuade coercion, deter attack and defend against aggression.(*JWP 0-01.1*)

Main Effort

A concentration of forces or means, in a particular area, where a commander seeks to bring about a decision. (*JWP 0-01.1*) See *economy of force* and *holding operations*.

Mal-deployment

Force posture that is strategically or operationally disadvantageous in the pertaining circumstances. (*JWP 0-01.1*)

Manoeuvre:

A movement to place ships or aircraft in a position of advantage over the enemy

A tactical exercise carried out at sea, in the air, on the ground or on a map in imitation of war.

The operation of a ship, aircraft or vehicle to cause it to perform a desired movement.

The employment of force on the battlefield through movement in combination with fire, or fire potential, to achieve a position of advantage in respect to the enemy in order to accomplish the mission. (*AAP-6*)

Manoeuvre Warfare
Manoeuvre Warfare is a war-fighting philosophy that seeks to defeat the enemy by shattering his moral and physical cohesion - his ability to fight as an effective, co-ordinated whole - rather than by destroying him physically through incremental attrition. (*JWP 0-01.1*) Capital initial letters are used in this publication to distinguish *Manoeuvre Warfare* from *manoeuvre* above.

Manoeuvrist
A term describing an approach that employs the principles of Manoeuvre Warfare.

Maritime Component Commander
The Maritime Component Commander is an officer subordinate to the Joint Force Commander responsible for maritime operational advice to him and the tactical employment of assigned *maritime forces*. See *component commander*.

Maritime Domain
The series of jurisdictional zones that surrounds the coast of a state. It includes territorial seas and the *Exclusive Economic Zone*.

Maritime Exclusion Zone
Declaration by a state of sea areas, including parts of the *high seas* in which conditions are imposed on the passage of ship and aircraft. (*BR 3012*)

Maritime Expeditionary Force

A self-sustaining forward deployed joint maritime force that demonstrates UK interest with its physical presence and latent power. Operating from international waters, the joint maritime force is free of political and economic encumbrances, and independent of overseas bases or host nation support, which may not be accessible due to domestic or international concerns. (See also *expeditionary operations*)

Maritime Fires

Fire support applied from the sea to the land originating from surface, subsurface and maritime based air platforms together with the supporting C4ISTAR systems necessary to maximise the effectiveness of the capabilities.

Maritime Forces

Forces whose primary purpose is to conduct military operations at and from the sea. The expression includes warships and submarines, *auxiliaries*, chartered shipping, *organic* aircraft, fixed seabed installations, fixed shore installations (such as batteries) for the defence of seaways, shore based maritime aircraft and other shore based aircraft permanently assigned to maritime tasks.

Maritime Force Projection

The projection, application and sustainment of maritime combat capabilities, at global range, to achieve effects in support of joint campaign objectives. Also see *Force Projection*.

Maritime Interdiction Operations

Maritime Interdiction Operations encompass sea-borne enforcement measures to interdict the movement of certain types of designated items into or out of a nation or specific area. These measures may include enforcing economic sanctions via an embargo of a particular country's international trade. (*AJP-3.1*)

Maritime Manoeuvre

Maritime manoeuvre is the ability to use the unique access provided by the sea to apply force or influence at a time or place of political choice.

Maritime Power Projection (MPP)

The threat or use of maritime combat capabilities, at global range, to achieve effects in support of national policy objectives. Also see *power projection*.

Maritime Superiority

The capability of a state to establish *sea control* at will in any area of importance to that state.

Maritime Trade Operations

Incorporates varying degrees of liaison with the merchant shipping community at the strategic, operational and tactical levels during periods of tension, crisis or conflict to provide for the safety of UK economic and Crisis Response Shipping (CRS).

Materiel

The stores and equipment (as opposed to personnel) available or required for an undertaking. (*JWP 0-01.1*)

Merchant Shipping

The complete merchant shipping industry including that of a nation's fishing industry.

Mexeflote

Large, slow-moving, powered pontoon capable of offloading heavy stores from amphibious shipping.

Military Aid to the Civil Power (MACP)

The use of armed forces personnel to aid the civil power in the maintenance of law and order and the enforcement of law within the domestic jurisdiction. It is most often associated with the type of support provided by all three Services to the RUC in Northern Ireland since 1969. However, it extends also to such maritime activities as drug interdiction operations (in support of Customs and Excise) and fishery protection, the UK's longest running and permanent example of MACP, in which the RN provides support to the UK's fisheries ministries to enforce fisheries law in the EFZ (since 1977) and in the inshore fisheries zone (since 1964).

Military Application

Applications of armed force in which *combat* is used or threatened, or in which combat potential is a prerequisite for success.

Military Assistance:

Training, advice, and other forms of assistance rendered by a government through its military services to another government in the process of developing and/or improving the operational performance of its armed forces.

In the context of peace *support operations*, all forms of mandated military assistance rendered to a foreign civil authority including the supervision of a transfer of power, reforming security forces, and developing or supporting civil infrastructure facilities.

Military Assistance to Civil Authorities (MACA)

This is a legal doctrine forming a part of the UK's constitutional and administrative law that regulates the domestic use of armed forces and maintains democratic and civil authority control of them when they are employed within the UK's domestic jurisdiction (including the *maritime domain*). The collective term covers three categories of activity: MACC, MAGD and MACP. See adjacent Glossary entries.

Military Assistance to Government Departments (MAGD)

The use of armed forces personnel to ensure the continued provision of essential services, including during industrial disputes (eg the firemen's strike in 2002-2003). Personnel employed on such duties are invariably unarmed; if protection is required it is either provided by the civil power itself (the police) or, in exceptional circumstances (eg during the Ulster

Workers Council strike in Northern Ireland in 1974) by other armed forces personnel who are deployed in a MACP role.

Military Assistance to the Civil Community (MACC)

The use of unarmed Servicemen to provide assistance to the community. This includes help in natural disasters and emergencies (search and rescue operations, for example). However, it can also be of a more routine nature and, in the *maritime domain*, includes the provision of hydrographic surveying and the provision of explosive ordnance disposal assistance to the fishing community, who still from time to time haul up First and Second World War mines in their nets.

Military Capability (MC)

The overall potential of the Armed Forces to achieve military objectives in support of a political purpose.

Military Condition

A description of the degree of military control in a theatre possessed by protagonists in the *warfare environments* of land, sea, air, space, information and the electromagnetic spectrum. A primary planning task of an *operational commander* during *hostilities* is to define the military conditions that will achieve his given strategic *objectives*.

Military Containment See *containment*

Military Data Gathering (MDG)

Activities in the ocean and coastal waters involving classified and unclassified marine data collection, by military or government owned or chartered vessels, for military purposes. MDG can include the gathering of hydrographic, oceanographic, marine geological, geophysical, chemical, biological and acoustic data. MDG activities are not specifically addressed in UNCLOS and there is no language stating or implying that MDG may be regulated in any manner by coastal States outside their territorial sea or archipelagic waters. It is fully consistent with UNCLOS that such MDG is a high seas freedom.

Military Exclusion Zone (MEZ)

Geographical (usually maritime) area including parts of the *high seas* within which a government states its intention to enforce the exclusion of all military units of a designated nation or nations or other grouping, using force if necessary. See *maritime exclusion zone* and *total exclusion zone (TEZ)*

Military Strategic Level (of conflict)

The level of command and planning for armed conflict (*level of war*) at which military resources are applied to achieve policy objectives. (*JWP 0-01.1*)

Military Strategy

That component of national or multinational strategy, presenting the manner in which military power should be developed and applied to achieve national objectives or those of a group of nations. (*AAP-6*)

Military Use of Force

See *military (or combat governed) application of force*.

Mission:

A clear, concise statement of the task of the command and its purpose.

One or more aircraft ordered to accomplish one particular task. (*AAP-6*)

Mission Command

A style of command that seeks to convey understanding to subordinates about the intentions of the higher commander and their place within his plan, enabling them to carry out missions with the maximum freedom of action and appropriate resources. (*JWP 0-01.1*)

Mission Orders

A style of orders to subordinate commanders that specify what is to be achieved without constraining the subordinate as to how it is to be achieved.

Mobility

A quality or capability of military forces which permits them to move from place to place while retaining the ability to fulfil their primary mission. (*AAP-6*)

Multinational Logistic Commander (MNLC)

Assigned by the Strategic Commander (SC) for a NATO operation. The MNLC and staff plan, co-ordinate and control, based on NATO Military Authorities' and national prearranged agreement, all maritime *logistic* shore support for *Multinational NATO Maritime Forces (MNMF)*. Additionally he will assume responsibility for all shuttle ships not under the control of the MNMF commander. The MNLC will report to the NATO Commander having *operational control (OPCON)* of the MNMF.

Multinational Maritime Forces (MMF)

Multinational NATO *Reaction Forces* consisting of *Standing Naval Forces*, *NATO Task Groups*, *NATO Task Forces* and NATO *Expanded Task Forces*.

N

NATO Expanded Task Force (NETF)

A force consisting of the elements of NATO *Task Forces* with multiple carriers, amphibious ships/landing forces and an enhanced complement of multi-mission capable escorts and submarines. It is a fully battle-capable force with a significant *maritime power projection* capability.

NATO Integrated Military Structure (NIMS)

The Integrated Military Structure of NATO comprises the NATO Military Command Structure (including the Defence Planning Committee, Military Committee, Strategic Commanders (SCs) and subordinate commands), the associated command boundaries, the Integrated Military Staffs at NATO Headquarters and those of subordinate commands, the Defence Planning System, the NATO Force Structure and NATO Infrastructure Programme.

NATO Task Force (NTF)

A force consisting of the elements of a NATO *Task Group (NTG)* with amphibious ships/landing forces and a carrier, or both, to provide *control of the air* and limited *maritime power projection*.

NATO Task Group (NTG)

A *task group* of one or more cruisers, and destroyers and frigates with submarines, maritime patrol aircraft and mine countermeasures forces as required.

Naval Co-operation and Guidance for Shipping (NCAGS)

The provision of NATO military co-operation, guidance, advice, assistance and supervision to merchant shipping to enhance the safety of participating merchant ships and to support military operations. (*ATP-2 Vol 1*)

Naval Diplomacy

The use of naval force in support of diplomacy to support, persuade, *deter* or *compel*.

Naval Fire Support (NFS)

In naval operations, fire support [to land operations] provided from warships. (*AAP-6*).

Naval Forces

Seaborne military forces including warships, submarines, amphibious forces, *organic* aircraft and *auxiliaries*.

Naval Service(s)

The *Naval Service* is the Royal Navy, Royal Marines, Queen Alexandra's Royal Naval Nursing Service, their respective Reserves, the *Royal Fleet Auxiliary*, the Royal Maritime Auxiliary Services and members of the Civil Service under the direct management of the Navy Board. The United Kingdom *Naval Services* are the Naval Service and the Merchant Navy.

Naval Staff

The staff serving in the Ministry of Defence and supporting the activities of the Navy Board. The core of the Naval Staff is in the Naval Staff Directorate.

Navy Board

The executive committee of the Admiralty Board. The Navy Board is chaired by the First Sea Lord, in contrast to the full Admiralty Board, which is chaired by the Secretary of State for Defence.

No Fly Zone

Zone of airspace established by international mandate (or conceivably unilaterally as a military or total exclusion zone) in which the flying of specified types of aircraft is prohibited. (*JWP 0-01.1*)

Non-Combatant Evacuation Operation (NEO)

An operation conducted to relocate designated non-combatants threatened in a foreign country to a place of safety. (*AAP-6*)

O

Objective

The physical object of the action taken, e.g. a definite tactical feature, the seizure and/or holding of which is essential to the commander's plan. (*AAP-6*) See *aim* and *mission*.

Offensive Operations

Operations in which forces seek out the enemy in order to attack him. (*JWP 0-01.1*)

Operation

A military action or the carrying out of a strategic, tactical, service, training, or administrative military mission; the process of carrying on combat, including movement, supply, attack, defence and manoeuvres needed to gain the objectives of any battle or campaign. (*AAP-6*)

Operational Art

The skilful employment of military forces to attain strategic and/or operational objectives through the design, organization, integration and conduct of theatre strategies, campaigns, major operations and battles. (*NATO*) It is the essence of admiral-ship and general-ship.

Operational Capability (OC)

The potential of the Armed Forces to achieve success in relation to a specific operation.

Operational Command (OPCOM)

The authority granted to a commander to assign *missions* or tasks to subordinate commanders, to deploy units, to reassign forces and to retain or delegate *operational* and/or *tactical control* as may be deemed necessary. It does not include responsibility for *administration*. (*AAP-6*). This is usually exercised by a national Single Service or *joint* commander of Flag or equivalent rank (e.g. CinCFleet) and is the highest degree of command authority that nations will delegate to a NATO commander.

Operational Commander

A commander exercising command at the *operational level*.

Operational Control (OPCON)

The authority delegated to a commander to direct forces assigned so that the commander may accomplish specific *missions* or tasks which are usually limited by function, time or location; to deploy units concerned, and to retain or assign tactical control of those units. It does not include authority to assign separate employment of components of the units concerned. Neither does it of itself include *administrative* or *logistic* control. (*AAP-6*)

Operational Level of War

The level of conflict at which *campaigns* and major operations are planned, conducted, and sustained to accomplish strategic objectives within theatres or areas of operation. (*AAP-6*)

Operational Manoeuvre From The Sea (OMFTS)

A USMC concept which places emphasis on the rapid projection of combat power ashore at the right time and in the right place to accomplish an operational objective. OMFTS includes the sub-concepts of Over The Horizon (OTH) operations and Ship-To-Objective-Manoeuvre (STOM).

Operational Pause

A periodic pause in operations while initiative is retained in other ways. (*JWP 0-01.1*) Operational pauses may be required because a force has temporarily reached the end of its *sustainability*; because forces are exhausted; because of terrain or weather; because the character of the *campaign* has changed; (for political reasons); or for a combination of these factors.

Operational Requirement

An established need justifying the timely allocation of resources to achieve a capability to accomplish approved military objectives, operations, missions, or actions. (*AAP-6*)

Operational Sea Training (OST)

Training of individual naval units and groups of *maritime forces* in their operational roles and tasks under the supervision of a sea training authority and with the assistance of specialist training staff and facilities. See *work up*.

Operations Other Than War (OOTW)

Those military operations which are conducted in situations of conflict other than war. Such operations, in which military activities are likely to be firmly subordinated to the political throughout, will be designed to prevent conflict, restore peace by resolving or terminating conflict before escalation to war, or assist with the rebuilding of peace after conflict or war. (*JWP 0-01.1*)

Operations Security (OPSEC)

The process which gives a military operation or exercise appropriate security, using passive or active means, to deny the enemy knowledge of dispositions, capabilities and intentions of friendly forces. (*AAP-6*)

Organic

In a naval context used to mean capabilities and resources that are borne within a *naval force* or formation. Often used of aircraft, *logistics*, weapons and sensors.

P

Partnership for Peace (PfP)

This initiative provides for non-NATO European nations who are members of the Organization for Security and Co-operation in Europe to become individual partners of the Alliance. Each Partner agrees a specific programme with NATO Headquarters to meet its own needs and requirements. NATO will consult with a Partner who perceives a direct threat to its territorial integrity, political independence or security. Partners may participate in political and military bodies in NATO with respect to Partnership activities. They may take part in planning, military exercises and in creating an ability to operate with NATO forces in such fields as *peacekeeping*, search and rescue, humanitarian operations, and others as may be agreed.

Peace Building

A peace support operation employing complementary diplomatic, civil and – when necessary – military means, to address the underlying causes of conflict and the longer-term needs of the people. It requires a commitment to a long-term process and may run concurrently with other types of peace support operations. (*AAP-6*) See also *conflict prevention*, *peacekeeping*, *peacemaking*, *peace support operation*.

Peace Enforcement

A peace support operation conducted to maintain a cease-fire or a peace agreement where the level of consent and compliance is uncertain and the threat of disruption is high. A Peace Support Force must be capable of applying credible coercive force and must apply the provisions of the peace agreement impartially. (*AJP-3.4*) See also *conflict prevention, peace building, peacekeeping, peacemaking, peace support operation.*

Peacekeeping

A peace support operation following an agreement or ceasefire that has established a permissive environment where the level of consent and compliance is high, and the threat of disruption is low. The use of force by peacekeepers is normally limited to self-defence. (*AAP-6*) See also *conflict prevention, peace building, peace enforcement, peacemaking, peace support operation.*

Peacemaking

A peace support operation, conducted after the initiation of a conflict to secure a ceasefire or peaceful settlement, that involves primarily diplomatic action supported, when necessary, by direct or indirect use of military assets. (*AAP-6*) See also *conflict prevention, peace building, peace enforcement, peacekeeping, peace support operation.*

Peace Support Force (PSF)

A military force assigned to a peace support operation. (*AJP-3.4*)

Peace Support Operation (PSO)

An operation that impartially makes use of diplomatic, civil and military means, normally in pursuit of United Nations Charter purposes and principles, to restore or maintain peace. Such operations may include conflict prevention, peacemaking, peace enforcement, peacekeeping, peace building and/or humanitarian operations. (*AAP-6*) See also *conflict prevention, peace building, peace enforcement, peacekeeping, peacemaking.*

Permanent Joint Headquarters

This is the HQ of the Chief of Joint Operations (CJO) located at Northwood in North London. All UK joint operations are commanded through the HQ, with the in-theatre commander reporting to the Joint Commander at

PJHQ. For most operations the designated Joint Commander will be the 3 Star CJO himself. However, the option is retained of appointing one of the 4 Star single Service CinCs as the Joint Commander if the scale and nature of the operations being commanded warrant a more senior officer in the chain of command.

Phase

A phase is a discrete and identifiable activity along a Military *Line of Operation* in time and/or space that allows for the reorganization and redirection of forces as part of the superior commander's plan. (*JWP 0-01.1*)

Piracy

As defined in **1982 UNCLOS**, piracy is an act that can only be committed on the *high seas* and for which universal jurisdiction applies (that is to say, any state can apprehend a pirate vessel, regardless of its flag state). As defined, piracy consists of the following:

(a) Any illegal acts of violence, detention or any act of depredation, committed for private ends by the crew or passengers of a private ship or private aircraft, and directed:

on the *high seas* against another ship or aircraft, or against persons or property on board such ship or aircraft;

against any ship, aircraft, persons or property in a place outside the jurisdiction of any State.

(b) Any act of voluntary participation in the operation of a ship or of an aircraft with knowledge of facts making it a pirate ship or aircraft.

(c) Any act of inciting or of intentionally facilitating an act described in a. and b. above.

Such acts of piracy committed by a warship, government ship or government aircraft whose crew has mutinied and taken control of the ship or aircraft, are treated in the same way as acts committed by a private ship.

Poise
An attribute of a *maritime force* which permits it to remain in international waters for long periods while retaining the ability to become engaged in events ashore or withdrawn without risk of *embroilment*.

Policing See *constabulary applications*

Power Projection
For the purposes of this publication, as distinct from the meaning of the Military Task of the same name:

The threat or use of joint military capabilities and other instruments of national power, at global range, to achieve strategic effects in support of national policy objectives.

Pre-Emption
To pre-empt the enemy is to seize an opportunity, often fleeting, before he does, in order to deny him an advantageous course of action. (*JWP 0-01.1*)

Precursor Operation
An *advance operation* to eliminate enemy sea denial forces such as conventional submarines, fast attack craft and mines from the path of the main force, a *holding area* or *amphibious objective area* (AOA).

Presence
The exercise of *naval diplomacy* in a general way involving deployments, port visits, exercising and routine operating in areas of interest to declare interest, reassure friends and allies and to *deter*.

Preventative Deployment
Deployment of forces to avert a conflict. (*JWP 0-01.1*)

Principles of War

The Principles of War are guides to action and fundamental tenets forming a basis for appreciating a situation and planning, but their relevance, applicability and relative importance change with circumstances. (*JWP 0-01.1*)

Proactive

Action that seeks to pre-empt and control rather than respond to events by seizing and maintaining the initiative. The antithesis of "reactive".

Prolongation

The deliberate extension of the length of a *conflict* as a means of outlasting or wearing down an enemy, or to provide an opportunity for new allies or reinforcements to be brought to bear. It can be considered as a form of *escalation*. (*JWP 0-01.1*)

Psychological Operations (PSYOPS)

Planned psychological activities designed to influence attitudes and behaviour affecting the achievement of political and military objectives. (*AAP-6*)

Q

Qualitative escalation

Escalation between categories of warfare, for instance from conventional warfare to chemical and then to nuclear warfare.

Quarantine

Expression used loosely to mean a restriction on the egress of certain types of cargo. Also used to mean embargo enforcement.

R

Raid see *Amphibious raid*

Rapid Environmental Assessment

The direction, collection, processing and dissemination in a shortened timescale of relevant information relating to the physical environment of a battlespace and the development of products and databases to suit the tempo of the operation for use by warfare commanders and in weapons and command support systems.

Rapid Reaction Forces (RRF)

NATO *Reaction Forces* at longer *readiness* than *Immediate Reaction Forces (IRF)* and available to respond to a crisis which exceeds the capacity for IRF to *deter* or counter. (*JWP 0-01.1*)

Reach

The ability to operate for extended periods at considerable distance from shore support. (*JWP 0-01.1*)

Reaction Forces (RF)

Highly mobile and capable multinational land, air and maritime forces allocated to major NATO commands and available at short notice, in order to provide an early military response to a crisis and demonstrate NATO's cohesion and resolve and, if required, facilitate the timely build-up of forces in the crisis area. They are composed of smaller *Immediate Reaction Forces*, and more capable *Rapid Reaction Forces*, both with maritime, ground and air components. (**NATO**)

Reactive

The state that exists when a force is responsive to enemy activity. The antithesis of proactive.

Readiness

The time within which a unit or formation can be made ready to perform unit-type tasks. This time is amplified or measured by indicators of its current personnel, *materiel* and training state. The time does not include transit time. (*JWP 0-01.1*) Ships and their *organic* air units will have the required *combat* load and other *logistic materiel* embarked or appropriately positioned. A Royal Marine formation will have the required weapons and equipment, as well as basic loads of supply, collocated or appropriately positioned.

Rear Operations
Operations which establish and maintain our own forces in order to generate the freedom of action to allow for the conduct of close and deep operations. (*JWP 0-01.1*)

Recognised Environmental Picture (REP)
The total set of shared Environmental Information on a particular operation, or Joint Operations Area (JOA), available through a secure information environment on CIS networks to support Situational Awareness and decision-making by commanders, and facilitate information sharing with allies and partners

Recognised Maritime Picture (RMP)
The fullest achievable agreed level of identification and tracking of all surface and sub-surface contacts in the area of interest. The RMP is normally associated with the Recognised Air Picture (RAP) of the same area.

Reconnaissance
A mission undertaken to obtain, by visual observation or other detection methods, information about the activities and resources of an enemy or potential enemy, or to secure data about meteorological, hydrographical or geographic characteristics of a particular area.(*AAP-6*) See *surveillance*.

Reconstitution
A strategic term that covers the expansion of force structures and infrastructure beyond existing levels, including the raising of force levels and the expansion of industrial capacity to support the procurement of equipment and stocks. Reconstitution will have to be initiated early in the planning phase in order for it to be timely. (*JWP 0-01.1*) See *regeneration*.

Regeneration

The timely activation, in full or in part, of existing force structures and infrastructure, including the restoration of manning, equipment and stocks to designated levels. (*AAP-6*) See *reconstitution*.

Ro-Ro shipping

Roll on-Roll off shipping into and from which vehicles can be driven from and to a wharf or jetty.

Roulement

The rotation of personnel or units in the front line with those in reserve in order to maintain the fighting effectiveness of the forces engaged in an operation. (*JWP 0-01.1*)

Royal Fleet Auxiliary (RFA)

The Royal Fleet Auxiliary (RFA) is a civilian manned flotilla owned and operated by the Ministry of Defence to provide logistic support for the armed services but primarily the Royal Navy.

Rules of Engagement (ROE)

Directions for operational commands that set out the circumstances and limitations under which armed force may be applied by UK forces to achieve military objectives for the furtherance of UK government policy. ROE are thus issued as a set of parameters to inform commanders of the limits of constraint imposed or of freedom permitted when carrying out their assigned tasks. They are designed to ensure that any application of force is appropriately controlled. (*JSP 398*)

S

Sanction (United Nations)

A penalty imposed on a state with the intention of influencing that state to comply with a Security Council Resolution or otherwise to abide by international law.

Screening

System of defence of a force or area using protective units deploying sensors and weapon systems in sectors or patrol areas around the force. See *layered defence*.

Sea Communications

See *sea lines of communications (SLOC)*.

Sea Control

The condition that exists when one has freedom of action to use an area of sea for one's own purposes for a period of time and, if necessary, deny its use to an opponent. Sea control includes the airspace above the surface and the water volume and seabed below. (*JWP 0-01.1*)

Sea Denial

The condition short of full *sea control* that exists when an opponent is prevented from using an area of sea for his purposes. (*JWP 0-01.1*)

Sealift

The movement of resources between points by carriage in shipping.

Sea Lines of Communications (SLOC)

The sea routes that connect an operating military force with one or more bases of operations and along which supplies and reinforcements move. The expression is sometimes used more broadly in a strategic sense to include commercial shipping routes.

Sequel *(in operational planning)*

An option for the next phase. One of the sequels of the current phase may be the next pre-planned phase. However, to ensure that a phased campaign can proceed in the face of setbacks, or in the event of unexpected success (for example the collapse of an adversary at the tactical level), several options or sequels should be planned. (*JWP 3-00*)

Sequencing
The arrangement of activities within a *campaign* in the order most likely to achieve the elimination of the enemy's *centre of gravity.* (*JWP 0-01.1*)

Shakedown (colloquial)
Period of basic sea or harbour training for naval units after a period without training or operation experience, or for a naval force on first assembling to build interoperability. Shakedown may be part of or precede *operational sea training* or it may be informal.

Shaping
Creating the conditions for mission success.

Ship-To-Objective-Manoeuvre (STOM)
Projection from maritime sea based platforms of joint assets by surface or air assault direct to objectives.

Simultaneity
Element of campaign and operational design that seeks to disrupt the decision-making process of the enemy commander by confronting him with a number of problems simultaneously. (*JWP 0-01.1*)

Spectrum of Conflict
The full range of levels of *violence* from stable peace up to and including *general war.* (*JWP 0-01.1*) Often displayed graphically relating military tasks and types of operation to levels of violence, and sometimes also to probability of occurrence.

Standing Naval Forces (SNF)
NATO's maritime multinational *Immediate Reaction Forces.* They are the Standing Naval Force Atlantic (STANAVFORLANT), Standing Naval Force Mediterranean (STANAVFORMED), Naval Mine Countermeasures Force North (MCMFORNORTH) and Naval Mine Countermeasures Force Mediterranean (MCMFORMED). The first two are principally frigate and destroyer formations. The others are mine countermeasures forces.

Statement on the Defence Estimates (SDE)

Annual statement presented to Parliament by the Secretary of State for Defence that may include the public presentation of Defence Policy. Also known as the Defence White Paper.

Straits Transit Passage

This is a right of passage through international straits used for navigation between different areas of *high seas*. It exists when a strait is narrower than 24 nautical miles wide and when the coastal states on both sides of the strait have territorial waters extending out to the maximum permitted limit of 12 nautical miles. The resultant lack of a high seas corridor through the straits would have restricted rights of passage to those allowed for in territorial sea (innocent passage). However, awareness of this difficulty led to the idea of straits transit passage being enshrined in *1982 UNCLOS*. In effect, it provides the right of unimpeded passage through a strait, a right that cannot be suspended.

Strategic Defence Review (SDR)

The comprehensive defence policy review conducted by the Government following the General Election of 1997.

Strategic Level

See *grand strategic* and *military strategic levels*.

Strategic Nuclear Deterrence

Deterrence of aggression effected by the existence of long range nuclear weapons capable of holding at risk objects of value in the homeland of any possible aggressor. (*JWP 0-01.1*)

Strike

An attack which is intended to inflict damage on, seize, or destroy an objective. (*AAP-6*)

Suasion See *armed suasion*.

Sub-Strategic Nuclear Deterrent Capability
The capability to deliver more limited nuclear attacks than that maintained for *strategic nuclear deterrence* to provide nuclear deterrence in circumstances in which the threat of strategic nuclear attack may not be credible. (*JWP 0-01.1*)

Supported Commander:
A commander having primary responsibility for all aspects of a task assigned by a higher authority. (*JWP 0-01.1*)

A commander having primary responsibility for all aspects of a task assigned by a higher NATO military authority and who receives forces or other support from one or more supporting commanders. (*AAP-6*)

Supporting Commander
A commander who provides a supported commander with forces or other support and/or who develops a supporting plan. (*AAP-6*)

Supreme Commander (SC)
The highest level of NATO military command beneath the Military Committee. The two SCs are the Supreme Allied Commander Operations (SACO), and the Supreme Allied Commander Transformation (SACT).

Surveillance
The systematic observation of the aerospace, surface and sub-surface areas, places, persons or things by visual, aural, electronic, photographic or other means. (*AAP-6*)

Survivability
The ability of a ship to continue fighting when it has suffered damage.

Sustainability
The ability of a force to maintain the necessary level of combat power for the duration required to achieve its objectives (*AAP-6*). See *endurance*.

Symbolic Use of Force

A form of *naval diplomacy* in which naval forces can be used purely to signal a message to a specific government while not in themselves posing any threat to an opponent or providing significant military assistance to a friend.

Synchronisation

The focusing of resources and activities to produce maximum combat power at the decisive time. (*JWP 0-01.1*) *Synchronisation* differs from *simultaneity* as the purpose is to achieve decisive coincidence of the effects of activities rather than the activities themselves.

Systemic Disruption

Reduction by the selective use or threat of *combat* of the cohesion of an enemy forces total combat system to the extent that it is unable to deliver combat to achieve the military objectives required of it. See *disruption*.

T

Tactical Command (TACOM)

The authority delegated to a commander to assign tasks to forces under his command for the accomplishment of the mission assigned by higher authority. (*AAP-6*)

Tactical Control (TACON)

The detailed and, usually, local direction and control of movements or manoeuvres necessary to accomplish *missions* or tasks assigned. (*AAP-6*)

Tactical Level of war

The tactical level of war at which battles and engagements are planned and executed to accomplish military objectives assigned to tactical formations and units. (*AAP-6*)

Task Element (TE)

The fourth and lowest level in a *task organization*.

Task Force (TF)

A temporary grouping of units, under one commander, formed for the purpose of carrying out a specific operation or mission. (*AAP-6*) TF is the highest level in a *functional* or *task organization*. See *battleforce*.

Task Group (TG)

A grouping of units under one commander subordinate to a *task force* commander, formed for the purpose of carrying out a specific function or functions. The second highest level in a *task organization*. See *battlegroup*.

Task Organization

Functional command *organization* in which the component units and formations are organized according to task into *task forces*, *task groups*, *task units* and *task elements*.

Task Unit (TU)

The third level in a *task organization*.

Tempo

The rate or rhythm of military activity relative to the enemy, within tactical engagements and battles and between major operations. It incorporates the capacity of the force to transition from one operation of war to another. (*JWP 0-01.1*)

Territorial Sea

The territorial sea of a state consists of a belt of water adjacent to the coast of the state and extending up to a maximum distance of 12 nautical miles to the seaward of the baselines drawn in accordance with the accepted principles of international law. It forms part of the sovereign territory of the state and is under that state's control and jurisdiction. (*BR 3012*)

Theatre of operations

A geographical area defined by the military-strategic authority which includes and surrounds the area delegated to the operational commander within which he will conduct operations - known as the *joint operations area*. (*JWP 0-01.1*)

Total Exclusion Zone (TEZ)
Maritime geographical area including parts of the *high seas* within which a government states its intention to enforce the exclusion of all ships and aircraft, both military and civilian, of a designated nation or nations or other grouping, using force if necessary. See *maritime exclusion zone* and *military exclusion zone (MEZ)*.

Total War
General war waged towards unlimited objectives. (*JWP 0-01.1*)

Turning Movement
A variation of the envelopment in which the attacking force passes around or over the enemy's principal defensive positions to secure objectives deep in the enemy's rear to force the enemy to abandon his position or divert major forces to meet the threat. (*AAP-6*)

Type Organization
Command organization of *naval forces* by type or class of unit normally used for *administrative* purposes. See *functional organization*.

U

Unified
Forces under the command or control of a single commander. A command that includes forces from different Services and/or nations. An imprecise expression variously meaning joint, combined, and integrated.

V

Versatility
The ability to change fighting posture quickly without recourse to outside resources.

Vertical escalation

An increase in intensity of *combat* during *hostilities*. It is sometimes understood to include *qualitative escalation*. (*JWP 0-01.1*)

Violence

Conduct involving the use of great physical force. In the military context violence may result in injury and damage to or destruction of resources.

W

War

The most extreme manifestation of armed conflict, characterised by intense, extensive and sustained combat, usually between states. (**JWP 0-01.1**). The expression is normally associated with combat at high levels of intensity but criteria of intensity would exclude some *civil* and guerrilla wars. Whether or not a state of war exists is very much in the perception of the parties involved. One party may believe that it is at war, for instance a group of *insurgents*, while the other party, in this case a government, may consider that it faces a problem of peace disorder. To Thomas Hobbes (Leviathan) the relationship between combat and war is that of a shower to bad weather. *Hostilities* is a more precise expression for any period between the onset of regular combat between parties and any cease-fire or truce. See *general war*, *limited war*, *civil war*, and *operations other than war* (**OOTW**).

War Aim

The grand strategic or political aim of a government or faction on outbreak of war and during its conduct and termination phases. *War aims* are loosely used to mean grand strategic *objectives* generally that are being pursued during hostilities.

Warfare Environment

The six warfare environments of the joint battlespace are surface, subsurface, air (including space), land and information environments and the electromagnetic spectrum.

Withdrawal

See *amphibious withdrawal*.

Work-Up

Colloquial expression for *operational sea training*. It is also used for a period of informal sea training.

INDEX

Abbott, Admiral Sir Peter 220
Abbreviations 229–33
Access **28–9**, 235
    amphibious operations 158
    future operations 203, 205
    intelligence gathering 60
    international law 21
    joint operations 30, 36
    leverage and 32
    manoeuvre and 48, 49
    maritime power projection and 45, 46
    naval diplomacy 76
    Normandy landings 33
    peace support operations 79
    see also Blockades; Mine countermeasures; Sea control
Accompaniment 73, **150**, 235
Adaptability 30, 206
Adderbury Talks 65
Aden 88, 156
Administration **235**
Administrative authority **235**
ADP Land Ops 6
Advance forces **155–6**, 186, 235
Advance operations **155–6**, 163, 236
    see also Mine countermeasures; Sea control; Shaping
Advanced Command and Staff Course (ACSC) 4
Advanced Logistic Support Sites (ALSSs) 100, 236
Afloat support 98, 157, 187, 189
    see also Joint sea basing; Replenishment at sea (RAS)
Agility 36, 140, 203, 204, 205, 206, 208
    see also Mobility
Aim (military) 9, 132, **132–3**, 236
    see also Strategic aims; War aims
Air Component Commander 162, 197

Air defence 78, 153, 162, 187, 196
Air interdiction (AI) 163, 196, **236**
Air operations
    anti-surface 78, **162**, 187, 238
    co-ordination 124, 162
    for strategic effect **78**, 236
    Gulf War 146–7
    weather effects 25
    see also Aircraft carriers; Combined Air Operations Centres (CAOCs); Organic aircraft
Air superiority 42, **236–7**
Air supremacy 42, **237**
Airborne early warning (AEW) aircraft 153, **187**, 237
Airborne Surveillance and Control System (ASaCS) helicopters 181
Aircraft 151, 153, 154, 181, 187, 198
    see also Helicopters; Organic aircraft
Aircraft carriers 84, 146–7, 181–3, 189, 195–8
    see also Carrier Air Groups (CAGs); Carrier Groups
Aircraft movements 142
Airheads 98, 159, **237**
Airspace 42, 60
Alamein, El 100–1
Allied Joint Logistics Doctrine 96
Amphibious assaults 48, **159**, 160–1, 237
Amphibious demonstrations 158, **159**, 160, 237
Amphibious forces 45, 51, 181, **183–5**, 186
Amphibious landings 25, 140, 155–6
Amphibious objective areas (AOAs) 161, **237–8**
Amphibious operations 78, **158–62**, 238
    clearing sea areas 152
    command and control 126, 157–8

force protection 155

logistics 78, 95

mobility 183, 184

shaping operations 36, 155, 158, 161

surveillance 156

Amphibious raids 158, **159**, 160, 238

Amphibious Ready Group (ARG) **238**

Amphibious shipping 183–4, 189

Amphibious Task Forces (ATFs) **158**, 161, 238

chartered shipping 189

joint and multinational operations 30

mine countermeasures 44

reconstitution 160

Amphibious withdrawals 158, **160**, 161, 164, 238

Antarctic 187

Anti-air warfare (AAW) 146–7, **153**, 185

Anti-piracy operations 67, 150

see also Piracy

Anti-submarine helicopters 154, 181

Anti-submarine warfare (ASW) 3, 60, **154**, 155, 183, 185, 187

Anti-surface air operations 78, **162**, 187, 238

Anti-surface warfare (ASuW) **154**, 155, 183

Antwerp 126

Approaches

clearing 152, 186

see also Mine countermeasures

Archipelagic sea lanes passage **21**, 238–9

see also Rights of passage

Archipelagic states **239**

Archipelagic waters 20–1, **239**

Area Capability Training (ACT) 192

Area forces **239**

Area operations **152**

Area sea control operations **69**, 72, **151**

Area surveillance 78

Areas of influence 195, **239**

Areas of interest 29, 50, **239**

Armed conflict see Conflict

Armed suasion **239**

Armour 184, **239**

Assaults see Amphibious assaults

Assistance see Humanitarian Disaster Relief Operations (HDRO); Military Assistance

Asymmetric attack **240**

Asymmetric warfare

force protection 70, 93, 94, 156, 196

future concepts 202

littoral operations 27

maritime trade operations 73

Atlantic, Battle of the 53

Attrition 26, 134, **240**

Attrition warfare 47, 48, **54–5**, 240

Augmentation Forces (AFs) **240**

Balance of advantage 25, 54, **141–2**, 150, 240

Balanced Fleets 180, **240–1**

Balanced Forces **30**, 66, 189, 241

Ballistic missile submarines (SSBNs) 3, **181**

Baltic States 66

Barham, Lord 211, 212, 213

Barnet, Roger 219

Barrier operations 49, 55, 72, 78, 152

Bateman, Sam 220

Battle damage assessment 10, 196, **241**

Battle Groups 12

Battleforces **241**

Battlegroups **241**

Battlespace dominance **43**, 45, 152, 241

Battlespace **26**, 241

advance operations 155–6

amphibious operations 159, 161

C4I systems' role 116

digitising 208

future concepts 202, 203, 206

sea denial 43

shaping and exploitation 33, 35, 116, 135–6, 140, 159

urban environments as 28

see also Sea control

Beachheads 33, 140, **158**, 242

Benign applications **58**, 88, 167, 242

see also Defence diplomacy; Humanitarian Disaster Relief Operations (HDRO); Military Assistance to the Civil Community (MACC); Naval diplomacy; Peace support operations

Biological weapons *see* Nuclear, biological and chemical (NBC) defence; Weapons of mass destruction

Bismarck 214

Blackwood, Captain 212

Blockades 44, 55, 71, 77, **151–2**, 242

'Blue on Blue' Engagement **242**

see also Fratricide

Bosnia 83

Branches **146**, 242

Breemer, Jan 219

Britain's Naval Future 219

Britannia Royal Naval College (BRNC) 4

British Air Power Doctrine 6

British Antarctic Survey 187

British Defence Doctrine (BDD) ii, iv, v 2, 6

fighting power 28

joint approach 3, 171

levels of operations 6–8, 171

Mission Command 110

nature of doctrine 5

principles of war 8–14

British Military Advisory and Training Teams (BMATTs) 64

Cable, Sir James 219, 221, 223

Calder, Vice-Admiral Sir Robert 211, 212

Calwell, Charles E. 218

Campaigns **242**

planning 73, 95, 97, 112, 116, 131–64

proactive and reactive choices 52–5

see also Expeditionary campaigns; Falklands Campaign; Information campaigns; Joint campaigns; NATO, campaigns

Cantonment supervision 80

Carney, Vice Admiral Robert B. 113

Carrier Air Groups (CAGs) **182**, 190, 243

Carrier Groups 152, 158, 162–3, **181–2**, 243

Carriers *see* Aircraft carriers

Castex, Raoul 218

Casualty evacuation 80, 100, 189, 194

see also Hospital ships; Non-combatant Evacuation Operations (NEOs)

Catastrophic damage 36, **243**

Central America 85, 86

Centre of gravity 47, **133–4**, 243

Changing Face of Maritime Power, The 222

Chartered shipping *see* Merchant shipping

Chatham, Lord 126

Chemical weapons *see* Nuclear, biological and chemical (NBC) defence; Weapons of mass destruction

Chief of Defence Logistics (CDL) 94

Chief of Joint Operations (CJO) 107, 132

Chief of the Defence Staff (CDS) 107, 131–2, 167

Choke points 20, 23, 27, 152, 156, 185, 196

see also International straits; Straits transit passage

Churchill, Sir Winston S. 76

Civil authorities **62–3**, 67, 142

Civil wars 243

see also Aden; Internal conflict; Spanish Civil War

Civil-Military Co-operation (CIMIC) 119, 142

Clausewitz, Karl von 217

Climate data collection 60

Close air support (CAS) 84, 181, 196, **243**

Close blockades 55, **151–2**, 243

Close escort **150**, 243

Close operations 54, **244**

Co-operation 13, 120–5, 145
  see also Civil-Military Co-operation (CIMIC); Interoperability; Naval Co-operation and Guidance for Shipping (NCAGS)

Co-ordinated multinational operations **250**

Co-ordination
  air operations 124, 162
  anti-submarine warfare (ASW) 154
  joint operations 158
  logistics 94
  multinational operations 122, 124, 145, 149
  peace support operations (PSOs) 81

Coalition building **75**, 244

Coalition operations see Multinational operations

Coercion ii, 35, 68, **76**, 244
  conditions for success 133
  freedom of navigation operations 72
  land attack missiles 163
  Maritime Power Projection (MPP) and 45
  naval diplomacy 45, 57, 75, 76
  nuclear powered submarines 183
  poise and 32
  see also Leverage; Peace enforcement

Collateral damage 36, 221, **244**

Collective performance 191–3

Collective training 204, 207

Collingwood, Vice-Admiral 211, 212

Colomb brothers 216

Colomb, Philip 218

Combat 50, 51, 57, 58, 88, **244**

Combat air patrols (CAPs) **244**

Combat Enhancement Training (CET) **143**, 193, 244

Combat identification (Combat ID) **124**, 245

Combat operations against the land 78

Combat power **139**, 245
  amphibious assaults 159
  amphibious withdrawals 164
  collective performance 191
  D-day 160
  force generation 148
  force projection 158
  force protection 70, 139, 151
  future concepts 202, 203, 204, 206
  Gallipoli 140
  joint and multinational operations 30
  see also Sustainability

Combat Service Support (CSS) 84, 184, **245**

Combat stress 178–9

Combat support 78, 184, **196**, 245

Combat support air operations 78, 162, **245**

Combined **245**

Combined Air Operations Centres (CAOCs) 197
  see also Air operations

Combined Joint Task Force (CJTF) **119**, 245

Combined Joint Task Force (CJTF) Commanders 182

Command 8, **105**, 107, 172, 246
  styles of 110, 112, 174, 222
  training courses 4
  see also Decentralised command; Framework nation command; Integrated command; Mission Command; NATO, command; Operational command (OPCOM);

Parallel command; Tactical Command (TACOM)

Command and control (C2) **105–28**, 246

  aircraft carrier capabilities 182

  amphibious operations 157–8, 164

  area sea control operations 151

  concept of operations and 136, 139

  European Union (EU) forces 119, 181

  interoperability 149

  joint operations 107–8, 113, 197

  Landing Platforms Dock (LPDs) facilities 184

  logistic support 95

  maritime force projection operations 157–8

  maritime patrol aircraft capabilities 187

  maritime pollution incidents 86

  multinational operations 119–26, 149, 181

  Non-combatant Evacuation Operations (NEOs) 158

  peace support operations (PSOs) 81

  planning for 145, 149

  unity of effort 145

Command and control (C2) systems 22

Command and Control Warfare (C2W) **118**, 246

Command, Control, Communications, Computers and Intelligence (C4I) systems **114–18**

Command of the sea 35, **41**, 42, 246

  see also Maritime Power Projection (MPP); Sea control

Command Post Exercises (CPXs) **246**

Command Team Training (CTT) 192

Commander Allied Joint Force (COMAJF) **247**

Commander in Chief Fleet 168, 169

Commanders see Component Commanders (CCs); Joint Task Force Commanders (JTFCs); Multinational Maritime Force Commanders; National Contingent Commanders (NCCs); Operational commanders; Regional Commanders; Strategic Commanders; Subordinate commanders

Commander's Estimate 124–5, 133, **135**, 247

Commander's intent **145**, 247

3 Commando Brigade, Royal Marines 85, 183

  see also Landing Forces

Commando Training Centre, Royal Marines (CTCRM) 4

Commandos 4, 183, **247**

Commercial shipping see Merchant shipping; Protection of shipping

Communications 28, 78, 107, **109–10**, 112–13, 197, 203–4

  see also Command, Control, Communications, Computers and Intelligence (C4I) systems; Electronic warfare; Lines of communications (LOC)

Communications Electronic Warfare Support Measures (CESM) 196

Compel 44, 76, **247**

Component commanders (CCs) **107–8**, 109, 247

  see also Air Component Commanders; Land Component Commanders; Maritime Component Commanders (MCCs); National Maritime Component Commanders

Computer Network Operations 118–19

Concentration of force 12

Concept of operations 125, 132, **135–46**, 247

  see also Future concepts

Conceptual component, fighting power 169–72, 180

Concerted Multinational Operations **248**

Concluding operations 125

Conditions for success 51, **132–3**, 148, 164, 248

  see also End-states; Shaping

Conflict 68, 82, **248**

  see also Internal conflict; Spectrum of conflict

Conflict prevention **82**, 248

Conjunct Operations 37

Consolidation 46, 94, 97, 99, 139–40, **248**

Consolidation shipping 31, 47, 157

Constabulary applications v, **58**, 88, 167, 248–9

Constabulary operations 21–2, 48, 63, 68, 132, 187

  see also Anti-piracy operations; Counter-contraband operations; Counter-insurgency operations; Drug trafficking and interdiction; Embargoes; Illegal immigration; Quarantine; Sanctions enforcement

Containment 43, 44, 55, **71**, 152, 249

  see also Blockade

Containment by distraction **55**, 249

Contiguous zones **21**, 249

Continental shelves 18, 20, **21**, 62, 63, 249

Contingency forces **249**

Contingency plans 158, 191

Contingent overseas operations 68–78, 205

Control **105**, 162, 250

  see also Command and control

Control of the air **250**

  see also Air superiority; Air supremacy; Favourable air situation

Convoy assembly and dispersal areas, clearing 152

Convoying **52–4**, 70, 73, 149–50, 156, 250

Corbett, Sir Julian S. 2, 37–8, 41, 216–17, 218, 223

Core Maritime Roles (CMRs) 206–7

Counter-air operations 78, **162**, 196, 251

Counter-contraband operations 67

  see also Illegal trade

Counter-insurgency operations 67

  see also Insurgency

Counter-terrorism iii, 62, **63**, 187, 201, 202, 251

  see also Terrorism

Cover **44–5**

Crises **147–8**, 251

Crisis management **45**, 251

  chartered shipping 99

  force deployment 145

  force generation 148

  intelligence requirements 60

  marine pollution control 86–7

  Maritime Trade Operations 73

  see also Naval diplomacy; Non-combatant Evacuation Operations (NEOs)

Crisis prevention 50, **77**, 251

  see also Diplomacy

Cryptology 107, 117

Culminating point **134**, 251

Culmination 97

Custance 218

Cyprus 64, 83

D-day iii, 33–4, 160–1

Dardanelles 140–1

Data *see* Command, Control, Communications, Computers and Intelligence (C4I) systems; Information; Intelligence

De-escalation 114, **252**

  see also Escalation

Decentralised command 112, 136, 145

Deception **118**, 251

  amphibious demonstrations 159

  anti-submarine warfare 154

  battlespace shaping 140

C4I systems protection 117

electronic warfare 196

Falklands Campaign 11–12

force protection 70, 139

manoeuvre from the sea and 51

St Nazaire raid 160

see also Surprise

Decision-making 107, 110, 118, 136, 145

Decision superiority 205

Decisive points 47, **134**, 251

Deconfliction 73, 151

Deep operations 203, **252**

Defence capabilities 172

Defence Council 107

Defence Diplomacy **64–5**, 75, 219, 252

Defence in depth **55**, 153, 252

Defence Strategic Guidance 202

Defensive actions 26, 27, 52

Defensive operations 50, **68**, 252

Delegation 106, 112, 176, 179

Démarche **252**

Demobilisation operations **252**

Demonstrations **45**, 50, 60, 253

Antarctic 187

freedom of navigation 72

Gulf War 48

presence 75–6, 150

see also Amphibious demonstrations; Deception

Deployment *see* Force deployment; Preventative deployment; Redeployment; Theatre entry

Design for battle *see* Concept of operations

Destroyer Captain 222

Destroyers 185, 189

Deterrence ii, **59–60**, 68, 253

maritime manoeuvre 50

Maritime Power Projection (MPP) 45

naval diplomacy 45, 75

nuclear powered attack submarines (SSNs) 183

peace support operations 82

poise 32

presence 76, 150

sea control 41

see also Accompaniment; Close escort; Distant escort; Strategic nuclear deterrence

Devolved decision-making *see* Decentralised command

Dimensions of Sea Power 220–1

Diplomacy 29, 32, 57

see also Defence Diplomacy; Naval diplomacy; Peacemaking

Diplomatic instruments of national power 75, 204

Directives 124, 125, 131–2, **253**

see also Rules of Engagement (ROE)

Disaster relief **253**

see also Humanitarian Disaster Relief Operations (HDRO)

Discipline 173, 177, 178

Dislocation 140, **253**

Displaying 107, 115

Disruption ii, 139, **253**

battlespace shaping 140

C4I systems' role 116

logistic support 97

manoeuvre from the sea and 33, 51

manoeuvrist warfare 109–10

raiding and 50

simultaneity and 145

Distant blockades 55, **152**, 254

Distant escort **150**, 254

Distraction 54, **55**, 254

anti-submarine warfare 154

battlespace shaping and 140

force protection 70

manoeuvre from the sea and 33

Dockyard Ports 64

Doctrine 2, **169–71**, 213–15, 216, 218, 254

collective performance and 191
communications and 110
dogma and 5, 70, 213, 222
equipment and 5
fighting power and 28
future concepts 205, 207
hierarchy of 5–6
nature of 4, 5
planning and 135
see also Allied Joint Logistics
   Doctrine; British Defence
   Doctrine (BDD); Joint doctrine;
   Maritime doctrine; Military
   doctrine; NATO, doctrine; Single
   service doctrine; Tactical doctrine
Drug trafficking and interdiction 20,
   21–2, 63, 67, 148
Duffy, Michael 219

Eastern Europe 64, 66
Economic dimension, maritime strategic
   environment 18–20
Economic instruments of national power
   204
Economic sanctions see Sanctions (UN)
Economy, logistic support 96
Economy of effort 12, 176
Economy of force operations 139, 145,
   254
Education 4
   see also Training
Education of a Navy, The 216
Effect **254**
   decisive points 134
   equipment 5, 138
   force projection capability and 35
   initiative and 3
   joint operations 101
   manoeuvre warfare 48, 49
   mission command 111
   see also Strategic effect
Effects based operations (EBO) **203–4**,
   205, 206, 255

Élan 54, **255**
Electronic warfare (EW) 118, **196–7**, 255
   air defence 153
   battlespace shaping and dominance
      43, 142
   command and control 107
   multinational maritime forces 124
   see also Intelligence; Surveillance
Embargoes 18, 73, **77**, 80, 84, 148,
   151, 255
   see also Sanctions enforcement
Embroilment **35**, 255
End-states 47, 125, 131–2, **133**, 148,
   255
   see also Aim (military); Conditions for
      success; Termination
Ends, effects based operations (EBO)
   203, 204
Endurance 30, 206, **255**
   see also Sustainability
Entitled personnel **87**, 256
   see also Non-combatant Evacuation
      Operations (NEOs)
Envelopment **33**, 256
Equipment 5, 22–3, 25, 169, **180–90**,
   204, 207
   see also Materiel
Escalation 8, 50, 82, 114, **256**
   see also De-escalation
Escort **150**, 256
   convoys 53, 150
   force protection 156, 157
   in Gulf War 48, 147, 157
   Maritime Trade Operations (MTOs)
      73
Ethos 173
European Union (EU) forces and
   operations 23, 81, 119, 181
Evacuation see Casualty evacuation;
   Force extraction; Non-combatant
   Evacuation Operations (NEOs);
   Withdrawal
Exchange ratios **142**, 256
Exclusion Zones 71

Exclusive economic zones (EEZs) **18–19**, 21, 256
Expeditionary campaigns 42
Expeditionary capability 45, 204, 205, 206
Expeditionary forces 33, 257, **271**
Expeditionary operations **62**, 257
Exploit **257**
Exploitation 137–8, **141**, 257
    amphibious operations 159
    battlespaces 33, 35, 116, 136
    concept of operations and 136, 141
    flexibility and 97
    information systems 117, 119
    leverage and 32
    limited warning time 27
    manoeuvre and 51
    operational tempo and 145
    power projection and 45
    proactive and reactive options 54
    space 119
    weather limitations 25
    see also Recognised Environmental Picture (REP)
Extended Fisheries Zones (EFZs) 19, **62**, 63, 257

F-35 Joint Combat Aircraft 198
Falklands Campaign 8–14, 23, 25, 45, 74, 134
Fatigue 178–9
Favourable air situation **42**, 258
Favourable balance of advantage *see* Balance of advantage
Fighting Instructions, The vi, 1, 6, 7, 131, **214**, 258
Find 159, **258**
Fire support 78, **196**, 258
    advance bombardments 163
    controllers 156
    frigates and destroyers 185
    Gulf War 147

littoral operations 28
    Normandy landings 33
    see also Maritime Fires
Fisheries protection 62, 63, 187
Fishery Protection Squadron 187
Fishing industry 18–19, 21–2
Five Powers Defence Arrangements (FPDA) 64
Fix 33, 147, 159, **258**
Flag Staff 4, **258**
Fleets in being **43–4**, 54, 259
Flexibility
    C4I systems 118
    concept of operations 126, 141
    disaster relief operations 85
    future concepts 206
    logistic support 97
    manpower 180
    principle of war 13
    Trident submarines 60
    see also Versatility
Flexible global reach 206
Flying operations *see* Air operations
Fog of War **259**
Footprint optimisation 32, 94
Force deployment 145, **149–50**, 197, 203
    see also Lift; Preventative deployment; Redeployment
Force Development and Definition 205
Force extraction 50, 160
    see also Withdrawal
Force generation **148–9**, 259
Force Integration Training (FIT) 143, 145, **193**, 259
Force packaging 29, 32, 172, **189–90**, 259
Force projection **157–64**, 189–90, 259
    capability 35
    defence capability 172
    future concepts 206, 208
    manoeuvre warfare 46–7, 49

mine countermeasures vessels (MMs) 186

proactive and reactive choices 52

sea control and 150

see also Maritime force projection; Power projection

Force protection 68, 70, **152–4**, 196, 259–60

  amphibious operations 155, 164

  asymmetric warfare 70, 93, 94, 156, 196

  convoying and choke points 156

  defence capability 172

  Falklands Campaign 10

  future concepts 203, 208

  joint forces 78, 196

  littoral regions 28, 196

  logistics 93, 94, 95

  manoeuvre from the sea 51

  maritime force projection 163

  mine countermeasures vessels (MMs) 186

  planning for 139, 145, 149

  sea control and 42

  survey vessels 187

  withdrawals 50, 164

  see also Cover; Sea lines of communications

Foresight

  logistic support 95, 96

  see also Planning

Forward from the Sea 220

Forward line of own troops (FLOT) **46**, 260

Forward Logistics Sites (FLSs) **100**, 189, 260

Forward Maintenance and Repair Organization (FMRO) 189

Forward operating bases 98

Forward presence 48, **76**, 260

  see also Presence

Forward repair ships (FRSs) 189

Framework nation command 121, 122

France/Russia/UK/US (FRUKUS) talks 65, 66

Fraser, Stewart 218, 223

Fratricide 124, **151**, 260

Freedom of Navigation (FON) Operations 41, **72**, 260

  see also Rights of passage; Territorial seas

French, David 221

Friction **260**

Friedman, Norman 218

Friendly fire incidents *see* Fratricide

Frigates 154, 185, 189

From the Sea 220

Fry, Brigadier Rob 221

Full command **261**

Functional organization 108, **261**

Fundamentals of British Maritime Doctrine, The 2

Future concepts 169–70, 171–2, 201–9

Future Maritime Operational Concept (FMOC) v, 205, **206–7**, 208

Future Navy (FN) 201, 203, **205–6**, 207, 208

Future Navy Process (FNP) **204–7**, 208

Future of British Sea Power, The 219

Gallipoli 140–1

General war **7–8**, 214, 261

Georgia 66

Glossary 234–97

Goals **261**

Goldrick, James 220

Gooch, John 217

Gordon, Dr Andrew 222, 223

Gough, Barry 219

Graf Spee 111, 213

Grand-strategic level 6, **261**

  doctrine 1–2, 171

  effects based operations 203

  NATO command 132

Gray, Colin 36, 219, 220, 223

Grenfell, R. 218

Gretton, Peter 218

Grove, Eric J. 216, 223

Guerre de course **43**, 261

Gulf War (1991) 48, 55, 146–7, 156–7, 160

   see also Iraq

Gunboat Diplomacy 219

Gunboat diplomacy 262

   see also Naval diplomacy

Handbook on the Law of Maritime Operations 21

Handel, George 217

Harmonisation, Rules of Engagement **124**, 262

Harwood, Commodore 111, 213

Hattendorf, John B. 216, 218, 223

Helicopters

   aircraft carriers 181, 183

   amphibious operations 183, 184–5

   anti-submarine warfare 154, 181

   anti-surface warfare 154

   area and barrier operations 152

   chartered shipping 189

   frigates and destroyers 185

   humanitarian assistance and disaster relief 85

   joint operations 198

   multinational operations 124

   peace support operations 80

   RFA vessels 189

   surveillance 154, 181

   see also Joint Helicopter Command; Landing Platforms Helicopter (LPHs)

Heseltine, Michael 219

High intensity operations 8, 29, 167

High Level Operational Concept (HLOC) 202, 203

High seas **21**, 67, 72, 86, 262

Hill, Rear Admiral Richard 219

Hill, Roger 222

HM Customs and Excise 63

Holding areas **155**, 262

Holding operations *see* Economy of force operations

Horizontal escalation **262**

Hospital ships 189

Host nation support (HNS) 49, 93, 98, **158**, 163, 262

Hostilities 22, 46, 71, 132, 167, **263**

   see also Naval diplomacy; War

Hughes, Wayne 218

Humanitarian assistance **263**

Humanitarian Disaster Relief Operations (HDRO) 58, **84–7**, 88–9, 164, 263

   contingent overseas operations 68

   future concepts 202

   Maritime Power Projection (MPP) and 45

   multinational forces 66

   planning for 142

Hungnam 161

Hydrographic, Meteorological and Oceanographic (HM) capability 25, 60, 63–4, 186–7, 190

Ice Patrol Ship 187

Identification Zones 71

Illegal immigration 20, 67

Illegal trade 20

   see also Counter-contraband operations; Drug trafficking and interdiction

Immediate Reaction Forces (IRF) **263**

Infiltration **263**

Influence of Sea Power upon History, The 215

Information 70, 172, 197

   see also Intelligence; Military Data Gathering (MDG)

Information campaign **76**, 263

Information exchange 124

Information operations 107, **118–19**, 140, 203, 204, 263–4
  see also Deception; Electronic warfare (EW); Operational security; Psychological operations (PSYOPS)
Information superiority 119
Initial Command and Staff Course (Maritime) (ICSC(M)) 4
Initiative 3, 5
Innocent passage **21**, 264
  see also Rights of passage
Instruments of national power, effects based operations (EBO) 204
Insurgency **88**, 264
  see also Counter-insurgency operations
Integrated command 122
Integrated Military Structure (IMS) **276**
Integrated multinational operations **119**, 264
Integration see Interoperability
Intelligence
  amphibious operations 78
  command and control 107, 112
  concept of operations and 136–7
  crisis identification 147–8
  joint operations 197
  peace support operations (PSOs) 80
  see also Command, Control, Communications, Computers and Intelligence (C4I) systems; Electronic warfare (EW); Information
Intelligence gathering 50, 80, 136–7, 148, 183
  see also Reconnaissance; Surveillance
Interdiction 71, **196–7**, 264, 271
  area and barrier operations 152
  battlespace shaping 140
  containment operations 152
  drug trafficking 21–2, 63, 67, 148
  manoeuvre warfare 196–7

surface and sub-surface land attack missiles 163
  see also Air interdiction (AI); Drug trafficking and interdiction
Internal conflict **264**
  see also Civil wars
Internal waters **21**, 142, 264–5
International law see Law
International Military Staff, NATO 132
International Staff, NATO 132
International straits 20, 21, **72**, 265
  see also Choke points; Straits transit passage
Interoperability **265**
  air operations 162
  C4I systems 116, 118
  command and control 149
  FRUKUS talks 65
  joint operations 132
  logistic support 96
  multinational operations 23, 25–6, 120–1, 123, 124, 149, 180–1
  training for 192
  Versatile Maritime Force (VMF) concept 205
Intervention 68, **197**, 265
  access for 29
  Iraq (2003) 75
  maritime power projection forces 45
  peace support operations 82
  sustainment 163
Iraq ii, v, 75, 85, 89, 157
  see also Gulf War (1991)
Iterative planning 132, 146

Joint **265**
Joint air defence plan 153
Joint approach **2–3**, 265–6
Joint campaign 46, 72, 78, 94, 100, 107–8, 133–4, 147–64
Joint Commander (Jt Comd) **107**, 132, 207, 265

Joint Contingency Plans 158

Joint doctrine 94, 171

Joint Doctrine and Concepts Centre iv, 202

Joint Force Air Component Commander (JFACC) 162

Joint Force Harrier 163, 181, 198

Joint Headquarters (JHQ) **265**

Joint Helicopter Command 163, 183

Joint Maritime Courses (JMCs) 192

Joint operations iii, 2–3, 78, 195–9

  access 28–9, 36

  battlespace dominance 43

  C4I 116

  co-ordination 158

  command and control (C2) 107–8, 113, 197

  effect 101

  future concepts 205, 206, 207, 208, 209

  Gallipoli 140–1

  interoperability 132

  logistic support 31, 94, 95, 101

  manoeuvre warfare 46–7, 48–9, 195–9

  maritime forces' attributes 28–34, 36

  maritime manoeuvre 49

  mission command 110–11

  mobility 29

  operational art 133–4

Joint Operations Area (JOA) 78, **108**, 266

Joint Operations Execution (JWP 3-00) 171

Joint Operations (JDP 01) 6, 171

Joint Operations Picture (JOP) 138

Joint Operations Planning (JWP 5-00) 131, 135, 171

Joint Planning Guides 158

Joint Rapid Reaction Force (JRRF) 32

  see also Rapid Reaction Forces (RRF)

Joint sea basing 30, 31, 36, 94, 163, **197–8**, 266

  see also Afloat support

Joint Services Command and Staff College (JSCSC) iv, **4**, 266

Joint staffs 4, 108

Joint Task Force Commander's Estimate 131

Joint Task Force Commander (JTFC) 30, **107**, **108–9**, 131, 197, 266

  Chief of Joint Operations (CJO) and 132

  logistic support 95

  National Contingent Commanders (NCCs) and 120

Joint Task Force Headquarters (JTFHQ) **108–9**, 120, 182, 267

Joint Task Force Headquarters (JTFHQ) (Afloat) 109, 164, 197

Joint Task Force Logistics Component 95

Joint Theatre Plans **267**

Joint Warfare Publications (JWPs) 171

Jomini, Antoine H. 217

Jutland, Battle of 214, 217, 222

Kazakhstan 66

Korean War 47–8, 161

Lambert, Andrew 219

Lambert, Nicholas 219

Land attack missiles 35, 45, 60, 78, **163**, 183, 267

Land Component Commanders 197

Landing Craft Air Cushion (LCAC) 184

Landing Force Movement Assets 184–5

Landing Force 182, **183–4**, 267

  see also Amphibious operations

Landing Platforms Dock (LPDs) 183, 184, 198

Landing Platforms Helicopter (LPHs) 182–3, 184, 189, 196, 198

Landing Ships Dock (Auxiliary) (LSD(A)s) 184

Landing Ships Logistic (LSLs) 184

Language, multinational operations
122, 123

Laughton, Sir John 216

Law 8, 21–2, 88–9, 149
    blockades 77, 151
    constabulary operations 58, 67, 77
    Exclusion and other Zones 71
    forces' domestic activities 62–3
    high seas 86
    maritime domains 62
    sanctions enforcement 77

Layered defence **55**, 72, 139, 153, 154,
157, 267

Leadership 8, 28, 139, **174–6**, 178, 179

Levels of warfare **6–8**, 267
    see also Grand-strategic level;
Military-strategic level;
Operational level; Strategic level;
Tactical level

Leverage (military) **32–3**, 34, 48, 140,
150, 159, 267
    see also Coercion

Leverage of Sea Power, The 36–7, 220

Leyte Gulf 113

Liaison 72, 119, 142, 149

Liaison officers 123

Liddell-Hart, Captain Sir Basil 221

Life at sea 176–9

Lift **32**, 48, 149, 267
    chartered shipping 189
    future concepts 203, 207
    LSLs and LSD(A)s 184
    Normandy landings 34
    see also Sealift

Limited war 217, **268**

Line of Operation **268**

Linear operations 134, **268**

Lines of communications (LOC) 36, **46**,
72, 94, 134, 268
    see also Sea lines of communications
(SLOC)

Lines of Development (LoD) 204–5, 206,
207

Lines of operation 47

Littoral Manoeuvre 206

Littoral regions 17, **27–8**, 268
    air defence 78
    battlespace dominance 43, 45
    force protection 28, 196
    future concepts 206
    information requirements 138
    Maritime Power Projection (MPP) 45
    naval fire support 163
    operations in 3, 22, 37
    risk management 36
    sea control 42
    sea denial 43
    weapons of mass destruction in 143
    see also Amphibious operations;
Territorial seas

Lodgement Area **268**

Logistics **93–102**, 187, 189
    amphibious operations 78
    amphibious withdrawals 164
    C4I systems' role 116
    concept of operations and 139–40
    force generation 149
    humanitarian assistance and disaster
relief 85–6
    joint sea basing 30
    manoeuvre warfare 46–7, 163
    multinational operations 95–6, 125
    peace support operations 80
    planning 94, 95, 97, 116, 139–40,
145
    shore-based aircraft 187
    see also Advanced Logistic Support
Sites (ALSSs); Afloat support;
Forward Logistics Sites (FLSs);
Joint sea basing; Sustainability;
Transport

MacArthur, General 113

Machiavelli, Niccolo 217

Mahan, Rear Admiral Alfred Thayer 2,
41, 215–16, 217, 218, 223

Mahan on Naval Strategy 216

Main Defence Forces (MDF) **269**

Main effort 96, 139, **269**

Makarov, S. O. 218

Makers of Modern Strategy 217

Mal-deployment 77, **269**

Management 176

    see also Crisis management; Micro-management; Risk management

Manoeuvre **47–52**, 112, 150, 163, 195, 269–70, 272

Manoeuvre from the sea 33, 46, 47–8, 51–2, 158

    see also Operational manoeuvre from the sea (OMFTS)

Manoeuvre warfare 3, **46–9**, 270

    command and control 109–10, 112

    future concepts 206, 208

    joint operations 28–34, 141, 195–9

    logistic support 31

    maritime force projection 163

    see also Centre of gravity

Manoeuvrist **270**

Manpower 179–80, 194

    see also Personnel

Mapping and survey services 60, 186–7

Marine pollution control 63, **86–7**

Maritime battlespace *see* Battlespace

Maritime Component Commanders (MCCs) 131, 132, 133, 141, 155, 182, 214, 270

Maritime Contribution to Joint Operations (MCJO) iv–v, 201, 206, 221

Maritime doctrine 1–14

Maritime domains **20–1**, 62, 63, 67, 270

Maritime environment 17–38

Maritime Exclusion Zones **270**

Maritime Expeditionary Forces 33, 257, **271**

Maritime fighting power 28, 167–99, 206

    see also Maritime power; Operational capability (OC)

Maritime Fires **271**

    see also Fire support

Maritime force projection 52, 78, **157–8**, 206, 271

    see also Force projection

Maritime forces 28–34, **271**

Maritime Interdiction Operations 271

    see also Interdiction

Maritime manoeuvre **49–52**, 272

    see also Manoeuvre

Maritime Patrol aircraft (MPA) 151, 154, 187

Maritime power 17–38, 41–55, 57–90, 208

    see also Maritime fighting power

Maritime Power Projection (MPP) 272

    see also Power projection

Maritime strategic environment 17–26

Maritime Strategy and Continental Wars 218

Maritime Strategy and the Balance of Power 219

Maritime Strategy and the Twenty First Century 219–20

Maritime Strategy for Medium Powers 219

Maritime strike 206

Maritime superiority 37, **43**, 54, 272

Maritime trade 18, 71

    see also Protection of shipping

Maritime Trade Operations (MTOs) **72–3**, 74, 272

Maritime Warfare Centre iii, 65, 169, 171

Masters of War 217

Materiel 97, 98, 100, 184, **272**

Means, effects based operations (EBO) 204

Media 10, 178

Media operations 119, 142–3, 203

Menon, Rear Admiral Raja 218, 220

Merchant shipping **18**, 272
 Amphibious Task Forces (ATFs) 189
 blockades and 151
 crisis management 99
 logistic support 98–9, 189
 planning for use of 149–50
 sealift provision 32
 see also Maritime Trade Operations
  (MTOs); Protection of shipping;
  Ro-Ro shipping
Meteorological data collection 60,
 186–7
Mexeflotes **184**, 272
Micro-management 109–10, 112
Military Aid to the Civil Power (MACP)
 62–3, 272–3
Military applications **57**, 68, 88, 167,
 273
 see also Blockades
Military Assistance **62–3**, 76, 273
Military Assistance to Civil Authorities
 (MACA) **62–3**, 67, 273
Military Assistance to Government
 Departments (MAGD) **63**, 273
Military Assistance to the Civil
 Community (MACC) **63**, 274
Military capability (MC) 58, **274**
Military Committee, NATO 132
Military conditions 133, **274**
Military Data Gathering (MDG) **186–7**,
 274
Military dimension, maritime strategic
 environment 22
Military doctrine, definition 5
Military Exclusion Zones (MEZs) **275**
Military instruments of national power,
 effects based operations (EBO)
 204
Military operations, levels of 6–8
Military-strategic aims 131–3
Military-strategic level ii, 6, **275**
 doctrine 1, 2, 4, 5, 171
 future concept 205
 logistics 94

NATO command 132
Military strategy **275**
Military Tasks ii, 58, 202
 see also Contingent overseas
  operations; Defence Diplomacy;
  Standing home commitments;
  Standing overseas commitments;
  Standing strategic tasks
Mine countermeasures (MCM) 48, 60,
 80, 147, **154–5**, 156, 187, 190
Mine countermeasures vessels (MMs)
 63, 66, 154, 155, 186, 189
Mine-laying 42, 152
Minefields 42, 73
 see also Mine countermeasures
Mission Command 26, **110–13**, 275
Mission Orders 111, **145**, 275
Missions 111, **131–2**, 145, 275
 organization for 142
 planning for 124–5, 135
 Rules of Engagement and 114
Mobility ii, **29**, 36, 195, 197, 276
 amphibious operations 183, 184
 legal aspects 21
 littoral operations 28
 manoeuvre from the sea and 51–2
 manoeuvre warfare and 47, 48, 49
 multinational operations 30
 Normandy landings 33
 organic air 182
 peace support operations 79
 poise and 32
 weather conditions and 25
 see also Agility
Molyneux, Thomas More 37
Montgomery of Alamein, Viscount 101
Moral component
 fighting power 172–9
 see also Discipline; Leadership;
  Management; Morale;
  Motivation
Morale 9, 139, 173, 174, 177–8
Motivation 4, 28, 173–4, 193

Multinational Interoperability Council (MIC) 121

Multinational Joint Logistics Centre (MJLC) 96

Multinational Logistic Commanders (MNLCs) **96**, 276

Multinational Maritime Force Commanders 123, 125

Multinational maritime forces (MMF) 30, 120, **122–5**, 181, 276

    see also Multinational operations

Multinational operations

    attributes of maritime forces 29, 30

    C4I systems in 116

    co-ordination 122, 124, 145, 149

    command and control 119–26, 149

    force generation 148

    future concepts 202, 204, 205, 206

    interoperability 23, 25–6, 120–1, 123, 124, 149, 180–1

    logistics 95–6, 125

    planning for 124–5, 149

    Rules of Engagement (ROE) 89, 114, 123, 124

    task organization 142

    training for 192–3

    see also NATO operations

Murray, Williamson 219

Narcotics trade *see* Drug trafficking and interdiction

National Contingent Commanders (NCCs) 120

National Maritime Component Commanders 123

NATO

    campaigns 132

    command 132

    doctrine 5, 6, 96, 123, 171, 214

    exercises 192

    maritime power and 35

    multinational formation building 181

    peace support operations (PSOs) 81

    presence 76

NATO Expanded Task Forces (NETFs) **181**, 276

NATO forces, interoperability 23, 25–6

NATO Integrated Military Structure (NIMS) **276**

NATO operations

    command and control 119

    see also Multinational operations

NATO Task Forces (NTFs) 181, **181**, 277

NATO Task Groups (NTGs) **277**

Naval Co-operation and Guidance for Shipping (NCAGS) 72, **74**, 142, 277

Naval diplomacy 33, 45, 71, **74–7**, 132, 167, 277

    see also Freedom of Navigation (FON) Operations; Presence

Naval Expanded Task Forces (NETFs) 120

Naval Fire Support (NFS) 163, **277**

Naval Fire Support (NFS) controllers 156

Naval forces 3, 36, 97, 120, **277**

    see also Balanced Fleets

Naval Service(s) **277**

Naval Staff 2, **278**

Naval Strategic Plan (NSP) 205, 207

Naval War Manual, The 2

Navies 22

    see also Interoperability; Multinational maritime forces (MMF); Multinational operations

Navies and Global Defense 219

Navy Board 4, **205**, 207, 278

Nelson, Lord 105–6, 211, 212, 213

Network Enabled Capability (NEC) 203, 204

Networked C4ISR 207

New Dimensions 222

New technologies 105, 202

    see also Technology

News media *see* Media operations

Nimitz, Admiral 113

No fly zones **80**, 84, 278

Non-combatant Evacuation Operations (NEOs) 45, 50, 68, **87–8**, 100, 157, 158, 278

see also Entitled personnel

Normandy landings iii, 33–4, 160–1

North Atlantic Council 132

Northern Ireland 63, 67, 187

Nuclear, biological and chemical (NBC) defence 143

see also Weapons of mass destruction

Nuclear deterrence *see* Strategic nuclear deterrence

Nuclear powered attack submarines (SSNs) 154, **183**, 189

Nuclear powered ballistic missile submarines (SSBNs) 3, **59–60**, 181

Nuclear powered submarines 152

Nuclear powers 202

Nuclear weapons 59–60

see also Strategic nuclear deterrence

Objectives **278**

dissemination 143

doctrine and 4, 5

effects based operations 203, 204

information operations 119

multinational operations 122, 125

see also Ends; Political objectives

Oceanographic surveying *see* Hydrographic, Meteorological and Oceanographic (HM) capability

Offensive actions 10, 26, 27, 52, 76

Offensive operations 50, **68**, 278

Offshore installations 62, 63

Offshore resources 20

Oil industry 18, 20, 62

On Job Training (OJT) 192

On War 217

Operational art **133–4**, 279

Operational capability (OC) 45, 138, **167–99**, 279

see also Maritime fighting power

Operational command (OPCOM) **107**, 119, 120, 279

Operational commanders 168, **279**

logistic support 93–4, 95, 97

manoeuvre warfare 46

morale-boosting 178

multinational operations 123, 124

Rules of Engagement 114

Operational control (OPCON) **107**, 119, 279

Operational level 6, **279**

doctrine 1, 2, 4

logistics support 94–5

Operational Logistics Pipeline 100

Operational manoeuvre from the sea (OMFTS) **280**

see also Manoeuvre from the sea

Operational organization 107–8

Operational pauses **97**, 139–40, 280

Operational Performance Statement (OPS) 191

Operational planning 112, 116, 124–5, 131–64

Operational requirements **280**

Operational sea training (OST) 145, **192**, 280

Operational security 118

Operations 4, **131–64**, 278

see also Air operations; Area operations; Concluding operations; Military operations

Operations Other Than War (OOTW) **280**

Operations security (OPSEC) **281**

see also Security

Ordnance disposal 58, 63

Organic **281**

Organic aircraft 45, 80, 84, 152, 162–3, 181–2, 185

Organic logistics 31, 46, 93, 187, 189

Organization for Security and Co-Operation in Europe (OSCE) 81
Outreach activities 64–7
Overseas commitments 64–7
Overseas military forces, assistance to 64
Overseas operations 68–78, 202, 205
Overseas Territories 64, 67, 86

Parallel command 122, 123
Paret, Peter 217
Partnership for Peace (PfP) **123**, 281
Patrol vessels 187
    see also Fisheries protection
Peace building 82, **83**, 281
Peace enforcement 82, **83**, 88, 281–2
Peace Support Forces (PSFs) **282**
Peace Support Operations (JWP 3-50) 82
Peace support operations (PSOs) 45, 65, 66, 68, **79–84**, 282
Peacekeeping 82, **83**, 282
Peacemaking **82–3**, 282
People see Illegal immigration; Personnel
Permanent Joint Headquarters (PJHQ), iv **107**, 132, 282–3
Permanent Joint Operating Bases 64
Personnel 98, 172–9, 204, 207
    see also Casualty evacuation; Entitled personnel; Manpower; Non-combatant Evacuation Operations (NEOs); Roulement
Phases 49–50, 82, 146, 161–2, **283**
Philippine Sea 113
Physical component
    fighting power 179–94
    see also Collective performance; Equipment; Manpower; Readiness; Sustainability
Physical dimension, maritime strategic environment 23–5
Pillars, future concept 207
Piracy 20, 2, 150, 283–4

Planning
    C4I systems' role 116
    campaigns and operations 73, 95, 97, 112, 116, 131–64
    information exchange 124
    logistic aspects 94, 95, 97, 116, 139–40, 145
    missions 124–5, 135
    multinational operations 124–5, 149
    Network Enabled Capability 204
    see also Naval Strategic Plan (NSP); Rules of Engagement (ROE)
Poise **32**, 221, 284
    advance sea control operations 155
    Gulf War 48
    manoeuvre warfare 48, 195
    Maritime Power Projection (MPP) and 45
    naval diplomacy 77
    Non-combatant Evacuation Operations (NEOs) 158
    Normandy landings 34
    see also Amphibious demonstrations
Policing see Constabulary operations
Political dimension, maritime strategic environment 20–1
Political Influence of Naval Force in History, The 221
Political objectives 45, 77, 131, 132, 148
Pollution control 63, 86–7
Polmar, Norman 219
Port facilities 142, 152
    see also Blockades
Power projection 41, **45–6**, 51, 68, 183, 205, 272, 284
Power projection forces 155
Pre-emption 140, **284**
Pre-emptive naval diplomacy 77, 132
Pre-Joining Training (PJT) 191–2
Precautionary naval diplomacy 77, 132
Precursor operations **284**
Preparation 143, 145, 172, 193
    see also Readiness

Presence 35, **75–6**, 284
    conditions for success 132
    Defence Diplomacy 65
    frigates and destroyers 185
    future concepts 205
    maritime manoeuvre 49
    protection of shipping 150
    see also Forward presence
Preventative deployments **77**, 82, 132, 284
Principles of Maritime Strategy 216
Principles of war **8–14**, 169–70, 285
Proactive operations **52–5**, 285
Procurement 94, 98, 180
    see also Equipment; Technology
Prolongation **285**
Protection of maritime forces *see* Force protection
Protection of shipping 72, 149–50, 156
    see also Anti-piracy operations; Maritime Trade Operations (MTOs)
Psychological operations (PSYOPS) 118, **285**
Pugh, Michael 219

Qualitative escalation **285**
Quarantine **77**, 285

Radiological weapons *see* Nuclear, biological and chemical (NBC) defence; Weapons of mass destruction
Raiding 50, 158, 159, 160, **238**
Rapid Environmental Assessment (REA) 25, 138, 156, **187**, 286
Rapid Reaction Forces (RRF) **286**
    see also Joint Rapid Reaction Force (JRRF)
Re-supply operations 73
Reach 30–1, 48, **98–9**, 100, 286
    future concepts 205, 206, 207

Maritime Strategy for Medium Powers 219
Normandy landings 34
nuclear weapons 60
poise and 32
Reaction Forces (RF) **286**
Reactive **286**
Reactive operations 52–5
Readiness 29, 97, 143, **193**, 286–7
    see also Preparation
Rear operations **287**
Reassurance 45
Recognised Environmental Picture (REP) 25, **137–8**, 186–7, 287
Recognised Maritime Picture (RMP) 26, **136–7**, 287
Reconnaissance 84, 107, **156**, 287
Reconnaissance aircraft 181, 187
Reconstitution **160**, 287
Recovery 163–4
Redeployment 163–4
Regeneration **94**, 288
Regional Commanders 119
Reinforcement operations 73
Replenishment at sea (RAS) 98, 157
    see also Afloat support
Resilience 31–2, 34, 48
Responsiveness 206
Richmond, Admiral Sir Herbert 216, 218, 221
Rights of passage 20–1, 142
    see also Freedom of Navigation (FON) Operations
Risk management 36
    see also Shaping
Ro-Ro shipping 32, **189**, 288
Robustness 206
Rodger, Nicholas A. M. 219
Rosenberg, David A. 219, 220
Roskill, Stephen W. 218
Roulement 31, **97**, 143, 163, 288
Royal Artillery 183

Royal Engineers 183

Royal Fleet Auxiliary (RFA) 32, 84, **98**, 187, 189, 288

Rules of Engagement (ROE) **114**, 288
constabulary applications 58
containment operations 152
harmonisation 124, 262
legal restraints 8
multinational operations 89, 114, 123, 124
naval diplomacy 77
planning for 149
see also Directives

Rules of the Game, The 222

Russia/UK/US (RUKUS) talks 65

Safety issues, multinational operations 124

St Nazaire 160

Salvage 63, **86–7**

Sanctions (UN) **77**, 151, 288

Sanctions enforcement 71, 80, 148, 151
see also Embargoes

Scholfield, B. B. 218

Schurman, Donald M. 216

Scientific and technological dimension 22–3

Screening **55**, 156, 289

Sea basing see Joint sea basing

Sea Communications

Sea control 3, **41–2**, 43, 68–9, 289
advance operations 155–6
amphibious withdrawals 164
anti-piracy operations 67
area operations 69, 72, 151
barrier operations 72
blockades 71
Exclusion or Identification Zones 71
fleets in being and 44
Gulf War 146
littoral regions 22
manoeuvre warfare 46

maritime force projection operations 78

Maritime Power Projection (MPP) 45

mine countermeasures vessels (MMs) 186

planning for 150–7

proactive and reactive methods 52, 54, 55

protection of shipping 149–50

sanctions enforcement 77

see also Access; Battlespace dominance; Command of the sea; Sea denial

Sea denial 35, **42–3**, 289
blockades 71, 151
Exclusion or Identification Zones 71
fleets in being 44
littoral operations 27
maritime power applications 68–9
nuclear powered attack submarines (SSNs) 183

Sea lines of communications (SLOC) 46, **156–7**, 289
future concepts 203
logistics support 93, 95
protection 72, 145, 149, 163
see also Lines of communications (LOC)

Sealift **32**, 163, 289
see also Lift

Seapower and Strategy 219

Seapower Theory and Practice 219

Search and rescue 58, 63, 86–7, 124, 187

Secretary of State for Defence 107

Security 10, 117–18, 124, 206, 280
see also Force protection; Operations security (OPSEC); Protection of shipping

Sequels **146**, 289

Sequencing 101, **290**

Shakedown 143, **290**

Shaping 33, **140**, 290

amphibious operations 155, 159, 161

concept of operations and 135

joint operations 30, 36

multinational operations 30

sea control and 151, 155–6

Ship-To-Objective-Manoeuvre (STOM) **290**

Shipping see Merchant shipping; Protection of shipping

Shore support 98

Shore-based aircraft 187

Short take-off and vertical landing (STOVL) fighter aircraft 181

Simplicity **97**

Simultaneity **145–6**, 290

Single service doctrine **171**

Slater, Admiral Sir Jock 221

Smuggling 67

Socio-cultural dimension, maritime strategic environment 25–6

Some Principles of Maritime Strategy 2, 37–8

Sonar performance 25

Sovereignty 20–1, 60

Space systems 26, 119

Spanish Civil War 77

Spectrum of conflict ii, 41, 206, **290**

Speed, Keith 218

Standardisation see Interoperability

Standing home commitments 60, 62–4

Standing Naval Force Atlantic (STANAVFORLANT) 120

Standing Naval Forces (SNF) **120**, 263, 290

Standing overseas commitments 64–7

see also Defence Diplomacy

Standing Strategic Tasks 59–60

Statement on the Defence Estimates (SDE) iii, **291**

Strachan, Sir Richard 126

Straits transit passage **21**, 156, 291

see also Choke points; International straits

Strategic aims 143

see also Aim (military); War aims

Strategic Commanders 119

Strategic Defence Review (SDR) ii, v **201**, 202, 221, 222, 291

see also Defence Diplomacy

Strategic deployability 203

Strategic deterrent 59–60

Strategic directives 131–2

Strategic effect

air operations for **78**, 236

tactical decisions and 109, 110, 207

Strategic intelligence 60, 136–7

Strategic level 6, 94

see also Grand-strategic level; Military-strategic level

Strategic mission 131–2

Strategic nuclear deterrence **59–60**, 181, 183, 291

Strategic Trends 202

Strike 159, 206, 207, 291

Structures, future concepts 204, 207

Suasion **239**

Sub-strategic nuclear deterrent capability **60**, 181, 292

Sub-surface land attack missiles 60, 163

Submarines 22, 42–3, 78, 152, 189

see also Nuclear powered submarines

Subordinate commanders

command and control 109–10, 135, 136, 137, 145

logistic support 95

mission command 110–11, 112

Sumida, Jon 219

Sun Tsu 217

Support 44–5, 78, 162–3, 186, 187

see also Afloat support; Close air support (CAS); Combat Service Support (CSS); Combat Support; Fire support; Host nation support

(HNS); Logistics; Peace support operations (PSOs); Shore support

Supported Commander **292**

Supporting Commander **292**

Supreme Allied Commander Operations (SACO) 119, **132**, 292

Supreme Commander (SC) 119, 132, **292**

Surface land attack missiles 163

Surface to surface missile batteries 43

Surprise 37, 51
   Falklands Campaign 11
   Korean War 48
   littoral operations 27
   manoeuvre from the sea and 51
   maritime manoeuvre 49
   St Nazaire raid 160
   see also Deception

Surveillance **136–7**, 292
   amphibious operations 78, 156
   area and barrier operations 72, 152
   area sea control operations 69, 151
   command and control 107
   concept of operations and 136–7
   crisis identification 147–8
   force protection 70
   helicopters 154, 181
   littoral operations 27
   maritime patrol aircraft (MPAs) 187
   maritime pollution control 86
   protection of shipping 150
   recognised maritime picture 26
   space systems 119
   see also Electronic warfare (EW)

Surveying 60, 62, 63–4, 186–7, 190

Survivability 114, 118, **292**

Sustainability **193–4**, 198, 292
   Falklands Campaign 14
   future concepts 204, 206, 207, 208
   intelligence gathering and 60
   joint and multinational operations 30

management for 176

planning for 145

Versatile Maritime Force (VMF) concept 205
   see also Casualty evacuation; Endurance; Logistics; Manpower; Reach; Roulement

Sustainment 31, 47, 163, 172, 221
   see also Logistics; Reach

Symbolic use of force 72, **76**, 293

Synchronisation 158, **293**

Systemic disruption 110, **139**, 293
   see also Disruption

Tactical Command (TACOM) **293**

Tactical Control (TACON) **293**

Tactical decisions, strategic effect of 109, 110, 207

Tactical doctrine 1, 5, 169, 171, 213

Tactical exploitation of the environment 137–8

Tactical level 6–7, **293**

Tactical organization 107–8

Tailored air groups (TAGs) 182–3, 196

Target acquisition 27, 107

Task Elements (TEs) **108**, 293

Task Forces (TFs) 31, **108,** 294

Task Groups (TGs) 22, 30, **108**, 185, 186, 189–90, 294

Task organization **108**, 120, 128, 142, 294

Task Units (TUs) **108**, 294

Tasking Authority facilities 186, 187

Teamwork 173–4, 178, 191, 192

Technology 22–3, 70
   see also Command, Control, Communications, Computers and Intelligence (C4I) systems; Equipment; New technologies

Tempo **145**, 294
   amphibious raids and 159
   battlespace shaping 140
   future concepts 205, 206

Gulf War   147
helicopters and   184
information processing and   118
logistic support and   95, 97, 139–40
manoeuvre warfare   48
mine clearance   155
planning for   112
Termination   142, 163–4, 203
see also End-states
Territorial seas   17, **20–1**, 60, 62, 63, 67, 294
see also Freedom of Navigation (FON) Operations; Littoral region; Rights of passage
Terrorism   28, 70, 88, 157, 201, 202
see also Counter-terrorism
Theatre entry   138, 149, 157
future concepts   206, 207
joint and multinational operations   30
lift capacity and   32
preparation for   143, 152, 193
Task Groups   197
transport   145
see also Force deployment
Theatre of operations   **295–6**
advance deployment of submarines   152
aircraft carriers in   198
build-up in   50
command and control in   107, 113, 162
force protection in   78
intelligence in   118, 136
joint and multinational operations   88–9, 118
liaison with other agencies   142
logistics   95, 96, 97, 98, 100
peace support operations   80, 81
poise in   32, 77, 158
Versatile Maritime Force (VMF) concept   205

see also Non-combatant Evacuation Operations (NEOs)
3 Commando Brigade, Royal Marines   85, 183
Thucydides   217
Till, Geoffrey   219–20, 223
Total Exclusion Zones (TEZs)   **295**
Total War   **295**
Trade   see Maritime trade
Trafalgar, Battle of   211, 212
Training   4, 28, 143, 145, 191–3, 204
see also British Military Advisory and Training Teams (BMATTs); Collective training; Combat Enhancement Training (CET); Force Integration Training (FIT); Operational Sea Training (OST)
Training Performance Statement (TPS)   191
Transport   18, 80, 85, 93, 145, 149, 184, 207
see also Logistics
Trident D5 missiles   59, 181
Trident submarines   see Nuclear powered submarines
Turning movement   **295**
Type Organization   **295**

UK Joint Commander   132
UK Joint Vision (JV)   202, 203
UK Maritime Security   206
UK/Netherlands Amphibious Force (UKNLAF)   120
Ukraine   66
UN Convention on the Law of the Sea (1982 UNCLOS)   21, 67
Unified forces   295
United Nations   81
see also Sanctions (UN)
Unity of effort   122, 145
Urban environments   28, 202
US Maritime Strategy: issues and implications   218
US Maritime Strategy, The   218

Versatile Maritime Force (VMF) concept
201, 205–6, 207

Versatility **29–30**, 32, 33, 48, 79, 295

see also Flexibility

Vertical escalation **296**

Vessel traffic services 64

Vian, Rear Admiral Sir Philip 214

Violence **7–8**, 63, 159, 179, 296

Walcheren 126

War **7–14**, 169–70, 285, 296

War aims 296

see also Aim (military); Limited war;
Strategic aims

Warfare environments **119**, 296

Ways, effects based operations (EBO)
203–4

Weapons of mass destruction (WMD)
31–2, 78, 94, 202

see also Nuclear, biological and
chemical (NBC) defence

Weather 23, 25

Wegener, Wolfgang 218

Weichold, Vice Admiral 100

Wellington, Duke of 37

Withdrawal 50, 125, 142, 197, 203

see also Amphibious raids;
Amphibious withdrawal; Force
extraction

Woodward, Admiral Sir John (Sandy) 9

Work-up 143, 148, 297

Yugoslavia 84, 85, 89